孫子兵法

Sun Tzu's

THE
ART
OF
WAR

Plus

The Warrior Class
306 Lessons in Strategy

Mastering Sun Tzu's Strategy

This book transforms each stanza of Sun Tzu's classical treatise on strategy into a series of easy-to-understand lessons on competitive decision-making. Open to any page and learn a little bit about the principles of Sun Tzu's system. Read the whole book from beginning to end for a complete course in how to use this strategy in your everyday life. Written by America's leading authority on *The Art of War*, Gary Gagliardi, this volume provides a condensed version of Gary's nine-volume work, *Sun Tzu's Rule Book*, which is the world's most detailed exploration of Sun Tzu's science of strategy.

This book is the third in Gary's *Mastering Sun Tzu Series*. It was recognized by *Foreward Magazine* as one of the three best self-help books in 2005. It contains the complete translation from the first book in the series, *The Art of War Plus The Ancient Chinese Revealed*, which won the Independent Publishers Award as 2003' Best Multicultural Nonfiction work. That book remains the only award-winning translation of Sun Tzu. The second book in the series, *The Art of War Plus Its Amazing Secrets*, explains the hidden cultural and philosophical references in Sun Tzu's stanza's work. It was recognized in 2004 as a Multicultural Highlighted Title by Independent Publishers. See following page for a complete list of Gary's award-winning books.

The Warrior Class:
306 Lessons in Strategy

Self-Help
Foreword Magazine
Book of the Year
2005 - Finalist

This book contains the only award-winning translation of Sun Tzu's *The Art of War*

Award Recognition for *Art of War* Strategy Books
by Gary Gagliardi

The Golden Key to Strategy

Psychology/Self-Help
Ben Franklin
Book Award
2006 - Winner

*The Art of War Plus
The Ancient Chinese Revealed*

Multicultural Nonfiction
Independent Publishers
Book Award
2003 - Winner

*Making Money by Speaking:
The Spokesperson Strategy*

Career
Foreword Magazine
Book of the Year
2007 - Finalist

Strategy for Sales Managers

Business
Independent Publishers
Book Award
2006 - Semi-Finalist

*The Art of War Plus
The Art of Marketing*

Business
Ben Franklin
Book Award
2004 - Finalist

Strategy Against Terror

Philosophy
Foreword Magazine
Book of the Year
2005 - Finalist

*The Ancient Bing-fa:
Martial Arts Strategy*

Sports
Foreword Magazine
Book of the Year
2007 - Finalist

*The Art of War
Plus Its Amazing Secrets*

Multicultural Nonfiction
Independent Publishers
Book Award
2005 - Finalist

The Warrior's Apprentice

Youth Nonfiction
Independent Publishers
Book Award
2006 - Semi-Finalist

SUNTZUS.COM
THE SCIENCE OF STRATEGY INSTITUTE

Memberships

Online training

eBooks

Audio books

Audio seminars

Art of War and Strategy Books By Gary Gagliardi

Sun Tzu's Art of War Rule Book in Nine Volumes

Sun Tzu's The Art of War Plus The Art of Sales: Strategy for the Sales Warrior

9 Formulas for Business Success: the Science of Strategy

The Golden Key to Strategy: Everyday Strategy for Everyone

The Art of War Plus The Chinese Revealed

The Art of War Plus The Art of Management: Straegy for Management Warriors

Art of War for Warrior Marketing: Strategy for Conquering Markets

The Art of War Plus The Art of Politics: Strategy for Campaigns (with Shawn Frost)

Making Money By Speaking: The Spokesperson Strategy

The Warrior Class: 306 Lessons in Strategy

The Art of War for the Business Warrior: Strategy for Entrepreneurs

The Art of War Plus The Warrior's Apprentice: Strategy for Teens

The Art of War Plus Strategy for Sales Managers: Strategy for Sales Groups

The Ancient Bing-fa: Martial Arts Strategy

Strategy Against Terror: Ancient Wisdom for Today's War

The Art of War Plus The Art of Career Building: Strategy for Promotion

Sun Tzu's Art of War Plus Parenting Teens

The Art of War Plus Its Amazing Secrets: The Keys to Ancient Chinese Science

Art of War Plus Art of Love: Strategy for Romance

Sun Tzu's

THE
ART
OF
WAR

Plus

The Warrior Class
306 Lessons in Strategy

by Gary Gagliardi

Sciene of Strategy Institute
Clearbridge Publishing

Published by
Clearbridge Publishing

Third Edition
ISBN (13-digit) 978-1-929194-75-9 (10 digit) 1-929194-75-7
Previously published in paperback as *The Art of War Plus The Warrior Class: 306 Lessons in Modern Competition*.
Copyright 2002, 2003, 2004, 2014 © Gary Gagliardi

Printed in USA.

Publisher's Cataloging-in-Publication Data
Sun-tzu, 6th cent. B.C.
       [Sun-tzu ping fa, English]
       The art of war plus the warrior class 306 lessons in strategy / Sun Tzu; [translated by Gary Gagliardi].
       p. 352 cm. 14

   Library of Congress Catalog Card Number: 99-64137
   Previous ISBNs 1-929194-30-7 (hardcover.) ISBN 1-929194-09-9 (paperback.)
       1. Military art and science - Early works to 1800. 2. Competition. I. Gagliardi, Gary 1951—. II. Title.
U101'.S9513 2003
355'.02 — dc19

Clearbridge Publishing's books may be purchased for business, for any promotion use, or for special sales. Please contact:

Clearbridge Publishing
PO Box 33772, Seattle, WA 98133
Fax: (206)546-9756
www.suntzus.com
garyg@scienceofstrategy.org

Contents

The Warrior Class
306 Lessons in Strategy

Lesson Topics

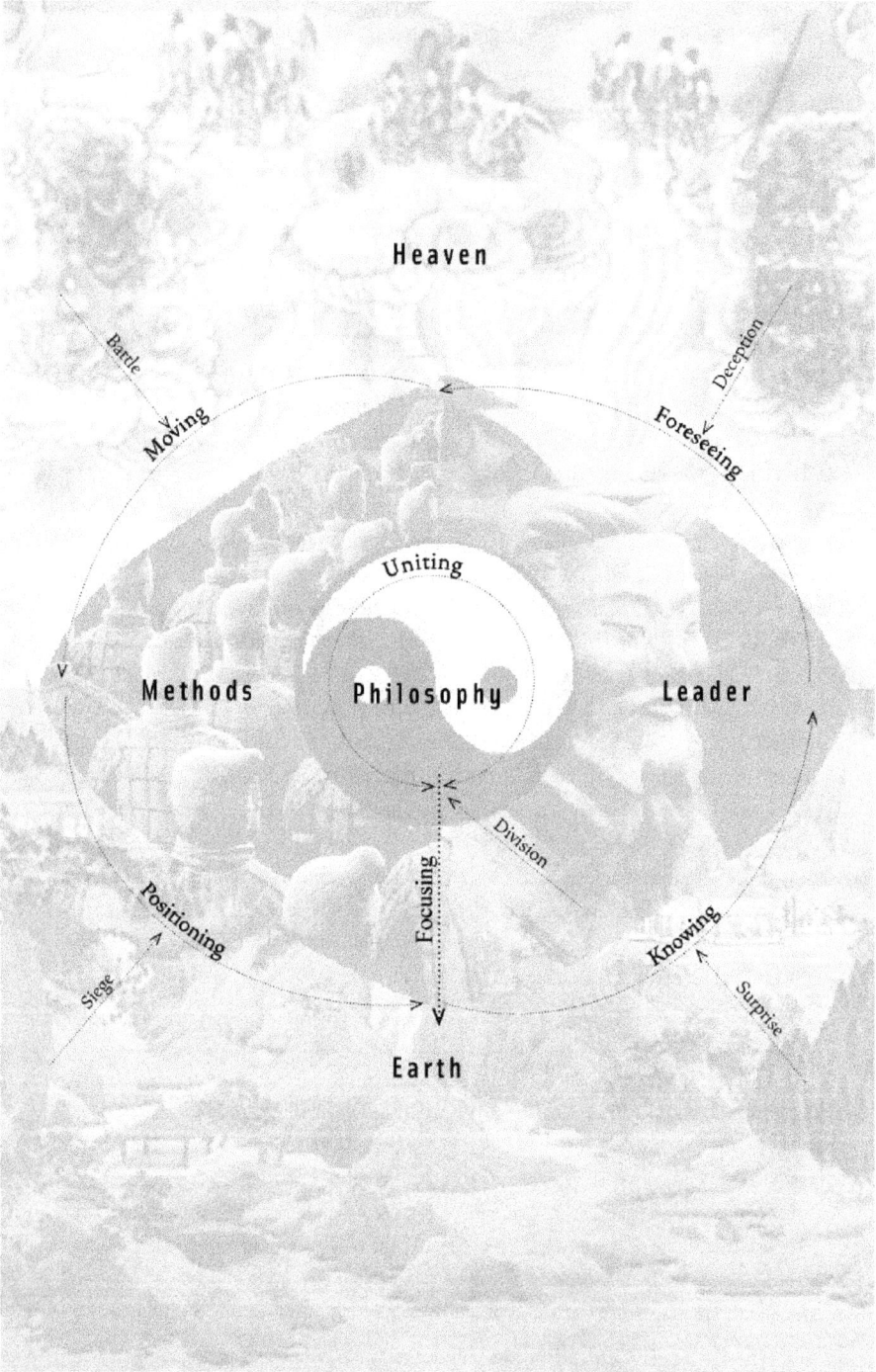

Heaven

Battle

Moving

Methods

Uniting

Philosophy

Leader

Division

Focusing

Positioning

Siege

Knowing

Surprise

Earth

Deception

Foreseeing

Using This Book

To make the complexities of Sun Tzu's strategic system easier to understand, *The Warrior Class* presents *The Art of War* as a unique series of lessons. You can use this book to learn strategy several different ways. You can simply open it randomly, letting fate guide you to a lesson. If you want to address a specific problem, you can use the LESSON TOPICS on the previous pages to find the appropriate lesson. However, if you want a complete course in strategy, you can read the book from beginning to end, building up from the simplest strategic ideas to the most complex.

No matter how you use the book, you may want to first read the following INTRODUCTION. These first twenty-one lessons give you an overview of Sun Tzu's strategic system. In this overview, our lessons present a few selected stanzas of *The Art of War* to illustrate its fundamental precepts. After the INTRODUCTION, the book goes through the stanzas of *The Art of War* one at a time, in the same order as they appear in the original text to preserve the way Sun Tzu logically develops his ideas through the course of his work.

We start each lesson with a simple question about the proper strategy for success. This question stimulates thought or discussion about the nature of competition, progress, and success. We offer four possible answers for each question. These answers represent different schools of thought regarding strategy. Following the question, we present a stanza from *The Art of War*, showing how Sun Tzu answered this particular question. Each stanza and its lines are numbered to follow the Clearbridge standard translation format used in our other books.

After the stanza, we explain its ideas in greater depth. Since many concepts do not translate exactly into English, we often refer to the original Chinese concepts, explaining them in more detail. These lessons sometimes go into greater detail about the various alternative answers to the initial question, explaining why Sun Tzu would not have agreed with these approaches. Other times, we relate the stanza to other parts of Sun Tzu's system and text to provide a larger picture of his approach.

Each lesson is limited to one page. Certainly, much more could be said about each stanza. The goal here is not to exhaust all possible interpretations of the text but to give you a good grasp of its basic concepts.

Introduction: Sun Tzu's Basic Concepts

Sun Tzu developed a complete and sophisticated strategic system. However, he did not write his famous book, *The Art of War*, as a training tool to educate the uninitiated. In ancient China, like ancient Greece, books were not written as how-to manuals. Students learned not from reading, but by listening to and discussing ideas with their master. Books such as Sun Tzu's were designed to preserve knowledge rather than to train novices. Sun Tzu's work in particular was written in several levels of "code," which disguised its secrets from the casual reader. The purpose of this work is to decipher Sun Tzu's strategy so that you can use his ideas effectively in your everyday life.

In this introduction, our first twenty-one lessons give you an overview of Sun Tzu's strategy before we tackle the text itself. Because of its design, the text of *The Art of War* is difficult for any reader—even one who can read the Chinese—to readily understand. The original work is much more than a collection of vague aphorisms, but English readers today have no grasp of the concepts, metaphors, and analogies that Sun Tzu uses in the text. Many of these concepts do not translate well into English, which is why we provide a little of the Chinese itself in our lessons. By outlining Sun Tzu's basic principles, this introduction provides a framework for reading the text itself.

If you have already read the first two books in our MASTERING STRATEGY series, *The Art of War Plus The Ancient Chinese Revealed* and *The Art of War Plus Its Amazing Secrets*, you will have already mastered many of the concepts presented in this introduction. However, you will still enjoy testing yourself against our lesson format to see how well you have internalized Sun Tzu's concepts.

This version of the book is ideal for those of you studying *The Art of War* in study groups, since it was originally developed for our seminars.

Lesson 1: Emotion versus Strategy

What are your natural, instinctual reactions to challenges?

A.   To outwit or outlast your opponents.

B.   To run away from challenges or get into conflicts.

C.   To ask for help because you are being victimized.

D.   To look for someone to blame.

> *Your men must brave their fears.*
>
> THE ART OF WAR 5:4.12
>
> *As leader, you cannot let your anger interfere with the success of your forces.*
>
> THE ART OF WAR 12:4.10
>
> *Unity works because it enables you to win every battle you fight.*
> *Still, this is the foolish goal of a weak leader.*
> *Avoid battle and make the enemy's men surrender.*
> *This is the right goal for a superior leader.*
>
> THE ART OF WAR 3:1.12-15

Answer: B. To run away from challenges or get into conflicts.

Our emotional reactions to threats are called the "fight or flight" reflex. We attack what threatens us or run away from it. Of course, neither of these emotional reactions leads to success. Running away from challenges never gets us anywhere and conflict is too costly.

The great insight of *The Art of War* is that constant conflict always leads to long-term failure. In Sun Tzu's view, the problem with our fight reflex is not just that we might lose. Losing is terrible, but Sun Tzu taught that even if we win a fight we still lose because fighting always costs us something. Even if we destroy our opponent, we are still bloodied and weakened in the process, and, over the long term, eventually destroyed. All victory through conflict is inherently Pyrrhic. This is the central topic of chapter 2, GOING TO WAR.

Sun Tzu saw that human beings had another option. We call that option "strategy." Sun Tzu called it *bing-fa*, martial art or the art of war. Strategy uses the most powerful weapon of all, the human mind, to give us better options than our fight or flight reflex.

Lesson 2: The Framework of Strategy

How do you overcome your natural fight or flight reactions?

A.   By self-control.
B.   By knowledge.
C.   By negotiations.
D.   By power.

> *There are many factors in war.*
> *You may lack knowledge of any one of them.*
> *If so, it is wrong to take a nation into war.*

THE ART OF WAR 11:7.7-9

Answer: B. By knowledge.

We react on impulse or instinct only when we do not know what else to do. If we know what steps we must take to meet a challenge, we focus on the task at hand rather than running away for the problem or getting into useless battles. The better our knowledge, the better our decisions. This is especially true of knowledge about strategy. Strategic knowledge enables us to quickly make the right decisions under a wide variety of circumstances.

As taught by Sun Tzu, strategy is a systematic process. It starts with our knowledge. We analyze our current position in five key areas. We use four steps to improve our position over time, and so on. In the strategic science of *bing-fa*, there is a great deal to know, but once we understand the system, we take control of our situation. Almost every chapter of *The Art of War* ends with a section on the importance of information. The final chapter of the book, USING SPIES, focuses on developing good information sources.

The purpose of learning strategy is developing "the warrior mind." The difference between a warrior and a regular person is that a warrior sees everything as an opportunity while a regular person sees everything as a blessing or a curse. In other words, regular people categorize everything that happens to them as good or bad luck and themselves as pawns in the game. Warriors see themselves as in control of their situation and not at the mercy of others.

Lesson 3: The Goal of Strategy

What is your unchanging goal in every competitive situation?

A.   To defeat your competitors.

B.   To come out ahead of your competitors.

C.   To build up or advance your position.

D.   To keeping fighting no matter what.

> *You have strengths and weaknesses.*
> *These come from your position.*
>
> THE ART OF WAR 5:5.14-15
>
> *Position yourself where you cannot lose.*
>
> THE ART OF WAR 4:3.22

Answer: C. To build up or advance your position.

In strategic situations, most people focus on their opponents. Sun Tzu saw that this was wrong. It is the position that we occupy that is the key to success. Competition is not a zero-sum game. We can win without others losing. Defeating or surpassing our opponents can be useful, but only if it improves our position. Beating opponents does us no good if it leaves us in a worse position than before. The goal is only to improve our position over time.

Our word "position" doesn't quite capture Sun Tzu's concept of *Xing*. *Xing* means both our physical position and our condition. Literally, *xing* means "form," or "shape," and our position describes whether or not we are in good shape. Conflict never leaves us in the best shape, which is why it is avoided. These concepts are covered in chapter 4, POSITIONING, and chapter 6, WEAKNESS AND STRENGTH.

We also must understand that no position is perfect for meeting every challenge, and there is no position that doesn't degrade over time. There is no ultimate victory that ends the strategic struggle. There is no final resting place where everything is perfect. No matter how far we advance, we will always be confronted with new challenges.

Lesson 4: A Unique Position

What must you do initially to eventually advance your position?

A.   Defend your current position.

B.   Compare your current position with your opponents'.

C.   Find your opponents' weaknesses.

D.   Create the appearance of strength.

> *Victory comes from knowing when to attack and when to avoid battle.*
>
> THE ART OF WAR 3:5.2
>
> *Know yourself and know your enemy.*
>
> THE ART OF WAR 3:6.2

Answer: B. Compare your current position with your opponents'.

Opponents' weaknesses are only relevant when they match up against our strengths. We may sometimes want the appearance of strength, but at other times the appearance of weakness is more valuable. We cannot make any assumptions without a careful analysis. This is the point of the first chapter of *The Art of War*, ANALYSIS.

Analysis is not a long, drawn-out process. Situations are dynamic. Analysis is a quick discussion of five key elements that make up our position, ideally with those with an outside perspective. These five elements—philosophy (*tao*), heaven (*tian*), earth (*di*), the leader (*jiang*), and methods (*fa*)—provide the backbone of our strategic approach. All other concepts in Sun Tzu's system relate to these five elements introduced in the first part of his first chapter.

It is important to note here that these elements of our position are only evaluated in relation to the positions of others. There is no such thing as a "good position" in an absolute sense. As the positions of others change, the relative strength of our position changes as well. Inherently, our position erodes because of the passage of time and others working to advance their position against us.

Lesson 5: The Competitive Environment

What are the most important aspects of your environment?

A.   Your place, time, and movement within it.

B.   Your opponents' control over it.

C.   Your access to resources through it.

D.   Your focus on your goals within it.

> *Your momentum must be overwhelming.*
> *Your timing must be exact.*

> THE ART OF WAR 5:3.8-9

> *A hawk suddenly strikes a bird.*
> *Its contact alone kills the prey.*
> *This is timing.*

> THE ART OF WAR 5:3.4-6

Answer: A. Your place, time, and movement within it.

We depend upon our position within the environment. Our position is unique because no two competitors can occupy the same place at the same time. These concepts are introduced in chapter 1, ANALYSIS, and are expanded throughout the book.

Our strategic goal is always to advance our position. As with so many of Sun Tzu's concepts, our environment is defined as two opposite and yet complementary halves, heaven (*tian*) and earth (*di*). Often *tian* is translated as "weather" or "climate," but in Sun Tzu's system it represents uncontrollable change and the power of time. Earth (*di*) is both the ground where we fight and the reward we fight over. Heaven and earth together mark the time and place in which we compete.

Our position changes automatically even if we do nothing because time advances uncontrollably. Our position can either improve or weaken over time, depending on the large trends in the competitive environment.

Lesson 6: The Changing Times

How does timing affect your position?

A.   Your timing and your positioning are the same thing.

B.   Advantages of position only come from timing.

C.   You can choose your position in a contest but not the time.

D.   You can change position only if you wait for the right time.

> *Stop the march when the rain swells the river into rapids.*
> *You may want to ford the river.*
> *Wait until it subsides.*

THE ART OF WAR 9:3.1-3

Answer: D. You can change position only if you wait for the right time.

We use this quote to introduce Sun Tzu's frequent use of metaphor. Water is Sun Tzu's metaphor for change. In his system, water (change) comes from heaven (*tian*) and affects the earth (*di*). Heaven represents the parts of the environment we cannot control. Earth represents what we can control. We must know what we can control and what we cannot. The concepts control (*chi*) and change (*bian*) are central in mastering strategy. Our ability to change is the topic of chapter 8, ADAPTABILITY.

Where are our enemies and allies conceptually in this division between heaven and earth in the environment? To the degree that we can control them, they are part of the earth. To the degree that they are beyond our control, they are part of heaven and we have to adjust to them.

Though we cannot control the changes of heaven or in time, that doesn't mean that we cannot foresee these events. For example, we cannot predict the weather perfectly, but we have a good idea that the summer is going to be warmer than the winter. This ability to see trends in change beyond our control is the basis of good timing. We must predict our opponents' moves.

Lesson 7: Competitive Success

What two elements define you as a competitor in the environment?

A.   Your leadership and your philosophy.

B.   Your philosophy and your vision.

C.   Your vision and your organization.

D.   Your methods and your leadership.

> *A commander provides what his army needs now.*
> *You must be willing to climb high and then kick away your ladder.*
> *You can lead your men deeply into others' territory.*
> *And yet, you can discover the opportunity to win.*
>
> THE ART OF WAR 11:5.12-15

Answer: D. Your methods and your leadership.

A competitor exists at a unique place in time in the environment, but that competitor is defined by decision-making and control. We call the element that makes decisions the leader (*jiang*). The element that controls action is called methods (*fa*). The purpose of *bing-fa* is to supply effective methods for leaders. These ideas are introduced in chapter 1 but developed throughout the book.

Leadership and methods are opposite and yet complementary concepts. Leadership is the realm of ideas. Methods are the realm of action. Leaders make decisions. Methods execute decisions. As leaders, we act alone. Using methods, we interact with others in an organization. Both elements are necessary for success. A good leader without good methods is a dreamer who cannot get anything done. An effective doer without good ideas does a lot of work but without accomplishing anything useful.

Ideas alone don't make us successful. Work alone doesn't make us successful without good ideas. We have to put both together in order to make progress in competition. Our divided nature as competitors creates tension and movement as we switch between our roles of dreamer and doer.

Lesson 8: The Need for a Philosophy

If you are going to be successful, why do you need a philosophy?

A.   To provide unity and focus.

B.   To appeal to higher ideals.

C.   To conceptualize your goals.

D.   To balance your actions.

> *Where you focus, you unite your forces.*
> *When the enemy divides, he creates many small groups.*
>
> THE ART OF WAR 6:4.3-4

Answer: A. To provide unity and focus.

The first four elements—heaven, earth, leadership, and methods—are the outer elements defining our competitive position. Philosophy, or *tao*, is the inner element defining our position. It is the glue that holds our position together. Our philosophy ties us as leaders to our methods. In a larger sense, it holds together the competitive organization. It also focuses us on our unique position in the larger competitive environment, giving relevance to our unique position in time and space.

In Chinese, *tao* literally means "the way," as in the path to a goal. Our philosophy is our motivation. In business, we call this a company mission. In a romantic relationship, we call it love. Sun Tzu taught that strength doesn't come from size. It comes from unity (*quan*) and focus (*zhuan*). A small focused and united force is much more powerful than a divided large force. This is the central lesson of chapter 3, PLANNING AN ATTACK.

As a unifying force, philosophy is not divided into two parts. Instead, it must address the natural divisions within our environment (divided by time and place) and our nature as competitors (divided between leadership and methods).

Lesson 9: Advancing a Position

How do you advance your position?

A.   Create openings that allow you to move.

B.   Move into openings that you can defend.

C.   Move so quickly that the enemy is behind you.

D.   Keep the enemy in front of you and push him back.

> *Be skilled in attacking.*
> *Give the enemy no idea of where to defend.*
> *Be skillful in your defense.*
> *Give the enemy no idea of where to attack.*

THE ART OF WAR 6:2.9-12

Answer: B. Move into openings that you can defend.

We must defend our current position, but we must always look for openings to advance into. The four steps in advancing our position are knowing (*zhi*), foreseeing (*jian*), moving (*hang*), and positioning (*xing*). These Chinese concepts work both as verbs and nouns, so we also refer to *zhi* as knowledge, *jian* as vision, *hang* as movement or action, and *xing* as positioning. Together these four steps define how we make progress. We start by studying our situation to gain knowledge. Knowledge allows us to see an opportunity to advance. We then execute our advance. Our new position rewards us if we can defend it.

We refer to these four steps in terms of skills. We cannot gain knowledge unless we are skilled in listening. We cannot see an opening unless we are skilled in predicting the future. We cannot use an advantage unless we are skilled in execution. We cannot get the rewards of movement unless we are skilled in defending positions. Skills can be developed over time. These four skills together make up the great skill of *bing-fa*, the art of war.

Lesson 10: The Source of Knowledge

Where does your knowledge come from?

A.   Your opponents.

B.   The earth.

C.   Your allies.

D.   Your methods.

> *Each battleground has its own rules.*
> *As a commander, you must know where to go.*
> *You must examine each position closely.*
>
> THE ART OF WAR 10:1.50-52

Answer: B. The earth.

The relevant strategic knowledge (*zhi*) is knowledge of the earth (*di*), that is, knowledge about what we can change. Technically, strategic knowledge, or *zhi*, has a narrower definition than the way we normally use the word "knowledge." Heaven (*tian*) puts a limit on what we can know for certain.

For example, if we see dark clouds on the horizon, we might predict rain, but since we cannot control whether or not it rains, Sun Tzu would not describe this as knowledge. He would call it foreseeing (*jian*). The difference is important because it clearly divides what is absolutely knowable from what is not. Strategy means making the best possible decisions despite this uncertainty.

Strategy requires learning everything about our environment that we can affect. When we get a new job, we learn our duties, but we also want to learn more. We want to learn about our boss, our co-workers, our company's products, our company's competitors, and so on. These are all things we can have an effect on over time.

Knowledge is such an important topic that it is the central focus of both the book's first chapter, ANALYSIS, and its last chapter, USING SPIES.

Lesson 11: The Source of Opportunity

Where do your opportunities come from?

A.   Your enemies create them.

B.   You create them.

C.   Your allies create them.

D.   All of the above.

> *You alone can deny victory to the enemy.*
> *Only your enemy can allow you to win.*

THE ART OF WAR 4:1.4-5

Answer: A. Your enemies create them.

We call the strategic skill of spotting opportunities *jian*, which means "seeing" or "vision." Until we see an opportunity to advance, we simply defend our current position. Opportunity (*li*) is never certain because it involves the future, which is under the control (*chi*) of heaven (*tian*). *Jian* requires knowledge (*zhi*), but the real talent is recognizing the potential fit between others' weaknesses and our strengths. Because we don't create the needs of others, we cannot create our opportunities. Others create them for us.

More deeply, the source of opportunities is Sun Tzu's idea of temporary openings. We express this idea in English when we talk about "windows of opportunity," but in classical strategy it is a much more sophisticated concept.

Strategy teaches that everything in the environment has both weaknesses and strengths, the topic of chapter 6. The concept is called *xu sat*, emptiness and fullness. The emptiness, or needs, of others is an opening or opportunity for us. Vision, or *jian*, is our ability to recognize those opportunities when they match our strengths or abundance.

Lesson 12: Acting on Vision

When you see an opportunity, how do you take advantage of it?

A. By developing a plan.
B. By attacking your opponents.
C. By changing your position.
D. All of the above.

> *Some may see how to win.*
> *However, they cannot position their forces where they must.*
> *This demonstrates limited ability.*
>
> THE ART OF WAR 4:3.1-3

Answer: C. By changing your position.

Strategic action is movement. We cannot control the creation of opportunities, but we can control how we are situated to take advantage of those opportunities. Opportunities never come to us directly. We must adjust our position to take advantage of them. The Chinese concept is *hang*, which means to march, to move, and to act.

In action, we rely on our methods (*fa*). Some people can adjust their methods to take advantage of opportunities. Others cannot. The challenges of moving to a new position are addressed in chapter 9, ARMED MARCH.

People naturally resist change. They want to do what they have always done. Though we are more comfortable repeating proven techniques, strategy requires that we change and improve. To establish momentum (*shi*), we need to combine both standard (*jang*) and innovative (*qi*) methods. The four steps in advancing a position—knowledge, vision, movement, and position—can also be thought of as a cycle of innovation. This is the central topic of chapter 5, MOMENTUM.

Lesson 13: Positioning

How do you define victory and success?

A.   By winning a new position.

B.   By eliminating opponents.

C.   By ending challenges.

D.   By getting rewarded.

> *Make victory in war pay for itself.*
> *Avoid expensive, long campaigns.*
> *The military commander's knowledge is the key.*
>
> THE ART OF WAR 2:5.1-3

Answer: D. By getting rewarded.

The entire point of positioning is to reap a reward. A movement is not successful unless it pays for itself. In Sun Tzu's system, the term for reward is treasure (*bao*). In chapter 2, GOING TO WAR, which discusses the costs of war, Sun Tzu first explains that success is making victory pay, but this is a theme throughout the text.

Rewards come from controlling the ground or earth (*di*). In Sun Tzu's era, treasure was food, metal, or other natural resources, which either grew or were taken out of the earth. Though the nature of the ground has changed, it is still the source of all rewards in competition. A business fighting for market share is fighting for the reward of winning a certain group of customers. A suitor fighting for love is looking for the rewards of a relationship. A politician winning over voters is looking for the rewards of popular support.

It is possible to win a position and not be rewarded for it. Businesses win markets that are never profitable. A suitor might win love but never have a satisfying relationship. A politician can win an election and still lack real power. So the goal isn't simply winning a position but winning a position that rewards us.

Lesson 14: Attacks and Battles

What is the difference between an attack, a battle, and conflict?

A.   Only conflict is inherently destructive.

B.   Only battle is inherently costly.

C.   Only attack is inherently aggressive.

D.   There is no difference.

You must avoid disasters from armed conflict.

THE ART OF WAR 7:1.5

Answer: A. Only conflict is inherently destructive.

In English, conflict, battle, and attack can be used interchangeably. However, Sun Tzu expresses these ideas as three distinct, though related, concepts critical to his strategic theory.

The concept of attack is *gong*. It means movement (*hang*) into a new area. It doesn't necessarily—but can—mean meeting the enemy in battle or conflict with an opposing force. Attacks are the topic of chapter 3, PLANNING AN ATTACK.

The concept of battle is *zhan*, which means meeting challenges or opponents but not necessarily conflict with them. We meet opponents when we have an advantage—when our opponents will back down, surrender, or come to an advantageous agreement.

The final concept is *zheng*, conflict. This is the destructive meeting of forces. Typically, we avoid conflict, but it is not always avoidable. This is the topic of chapter 7, ARMED CONFLICT.

So we have an array of ideas becoming progressively more costly. Movement (*hang*) is the most general. Movement into new areas is attack (*gong*). Attacks that involve confrontation are battles (*zhan*). Battles that involve conflict are *zheng*.

Lesson 15: Moving through Opposition

When do you always attack?

A.   When you have an opportunity to kill your enemy's general.

B.   When you have backed their men into a corner.

C.   When you need to take their resources.

D.   When you have more strength than you need to win.

> *Defend when you have insufficient strength to win.*
> *Attack when you have more strength than you need to win.*
>
> THE ART OF WAR 4:2.5-6

Answer: D. When you have more strength than you need to win.

The nature of competition is that others want to stop our progress. The Chinese word for attack, *gong*, literally means "strike," and, like the English word "strike," it has many different meanings. Most generally, it means going into a new area in the same way that the English phrase describes a young person "striking out on his own."

Sun Tzu identifies five forms of striking opponents who oppose our progress. The purpose of these attacks is not to destroy our opponents but to stop them from preventing our progress. Four of these strikes or attacks— deception (*gui*), battle (*zhan*), innovation (*qi jang*), and siege (*gong cheng*)— are aimed specifically at the skills that allow an opponent to be effective in opposing us. The final form of attack, division (*fen*), is aimed at the underlying philosophy that unites and focuses our opponent's efforts.

Each of these attacks is very specific. *Gui* is deception in the sense of bluffing, spoiling an opponent's foresight. *Zhan*, as battle, does not mean conflict but meeting an opponent. Its purpose is to disrupt anothers' movement into areas that can block our movement. Battle is used with innovation (*qi jang*), which undermines an opponent's knowledge. *Gong cheng* (literally "strike cities") lays siege to an opponent's position with the purpose of winning that position from them. *Fen*, the final form of attack, divides opponents' unity and focus by aiming at their ability to organize.

Lesson 16: Economic Warfare

What defines the risk in advancing your position?
A. Spending too much money.
B. Picking the wrong opponents.
C. Moving too soon.
D. All of the above.

> *If you exhaust your wealth, you then quickly hollow out your military.*
> THE ART OF WAR 2:3.5

Answer: A. Spending too much money.

Certainly, picking the wrong opponents and moving too soon are bad ideas, but in classical strategy risk is an economic concept. Sun Tzu defines three dimensions to risk in movement: distance (*yuan*), time (*jiu*), and size (*wan*). Short, quick, and small movements are inherently less risky than long, slow, and large movements because they are less costly. This is the focus of chapter 2.

Not all our moves are going to be successful and reap a reward. Movements of any kind—attacks, battles, or conflict—always have a cost, but rewards are never certain. Only a percentage of our guesses about the future are going to be correct. By limiting our investments, we are limiting our risk.

Strategy is not a plan. It is a process. We continually make small incremental improvements in our position with the goal of reaping rewards. Each position is a temporary stepping-stone to greater success. No single step is certain of reward. The process increases the certainty of success over time, but we must keep each step along the way affordable. We must never risk more than we can afford to lose, and we must always keep our investments as small as possible.

Lesson 17: The Need for Speed

Why is speed important in strategy?

A.   To beat the competition to the battlefield.

B.   To shorten the cycle between investment and reward.

C.   To avoid more powerful opponents.

D.   All of the above.

> *Mastering speed is the essence of war.*
>
> THE ART OF WAR 11:2.16

Answer: D. All of the above.

Strategy teaches us to advance our position. Since strategy is about movement, speed is always a critical component in our strategic calculations. When we see an opportunity, we want to be the first to take advantage of it. This need is based on the fact that both emptiness and fullness are temporary states. The longer we delay, the more likely it is that our window of opportunity will close and others will beat us.

In Sun Tzu's system, time (*jiu*) and speed are related to size (*wan*). Smaller forces can move more quickly than larger ones. The fewer resources and responsibilities we have, the more quickly we can move. Sun Tzu directly attributes speed to having less baggage to carry. Time (*jiu*) is also related to the final aspect of cost, distance (*yuan*), in that longer distances take more time to travel. In a sense, speed reduces distance.

These three dimensions of cost reduce speed to an economic issue. Time is a component of cost. Our goal is to minimize our investments. The quicker our cycle time, the faster we get a return on our investment. That return is not certain, but the less time we invest, the more certain each cycle is to produce a net gain.

Lesson 18: Looking before We Leap

What must you know for certain before you pursue an opportunity?

A.   What its costs will be.

B.   What its rewards will be.

C.   What its potential will be.

D.   None of the above.

> *Make no assumptions about all the dangers in using military force.*
> *Then you won't make assumptions about the benefits of using arms either.*
>
> THE ART OF WAR 2:2.1-2

Answer: D. None of the above.

We cannot know for certain what the costs, rewards, or potential will be before we act. We can only know our planned actions. We therefore temper speed with analysis. For example, we know that short, quick, small moves are less expensive than long, slow, big ones. We can also know the characteristics of certain opportunities. This is the topic of chapter 10, FIELD POSITION.

Sun Tzu offers us three dimensions for evaluating opportunities. These dimensions are distance (*yuan*), obstacles (*xian*), and danger (*ee*). They are bound by their extremes. In distance, our positions can be spread out (*yuan*) or constricted (*ai*). In obstacles, our positions can be unobstructed (*tong*) or barricaded (*xian*). In dangers, our positions can be supporting (*zhii*) or entangling (*gua*).

None of these characteristics are good or bad in themselves. They do determine the defensive and offensive potential of any given position. Spread-out and unobstructed positions are more difficult to defend, while barricaded and constricted positions are easier to defend. Supporting and entangling positions are more difficult to move out of, which, in Sun Tzu's view, makes them dangerous.

Lesson 19: Changing Conditions

As you advance your position, how does your situation change?

A.   It gets easier to advance over time.

B.   It gets more difficult to advance over time.

C.   You must act consistently to make progress.

D.   You must react to your situation to make progress.

> *You must adapt to the different terrain.*
> *You must adapt to find an advantage.*
>
> THE ART OF WAR 11:5.23-24

Answer: D. You must react to your situation to make progress.

In chapter 11, TYPES OF TERRAIN, Sun Tzu describes nine strategic situations. Each situation requires the appropriate reaction. We must correctly diagnose our situation to act. Then we must know the appropriate prescription or reaction and use it. We must adapt to our situation, but there is a limit to our adaptation. If we fight when the situation calls on us to keep moving, we will fail.

These nine situations can also describe the stages of a competitive campaign. (Think of a campaign as a series of moves, *hang*, with a longer-term goal.) The first four situations tend to occur early in a campaign. These beginning stages are generally less challenging. The next two occur mostly in the middle of a campaign and are more challenging. The last three situations tend to occur toward the end and get very serious. However, as Sun Tzu says, there is no firm rule. Any of these situations can occur at any time.

Our standing orders are always to react appropriately to whichever of these nine situations we find ourselves in. We can advance our position in any of them, but the methods (*fa*) that we must use change.

Lesson 20: Using Leverage

Other than your mind, what is your most dangerous weapon?

A.   Your allies.

B.   The environment.

C.   Your opponent's flaws.

D.   None of the above.

> *Every army must know how to deal with the five attacks by fire.*
> *Use many men to guard against them.*
>
> **THE ART OF WAR 12:2.17-18**

Answer: B. The environment.

Fire is Sun Tzu's metaphor for using the environment as a weapon. The competitive environment is bigger and more powerful than we are. Our environment contains a number of forces that can be used for or against us. The media, the government, and the legal system are all good examples. When conditions are right, we can leverage those forces against our opponents. When conditions are right, those forces can be leveraged against us.

In *The Art of War*, the use of weapons in general and of environmental weapons specifically is addressed in chapter 11, ATTACKING WITH FIRE. Environmental attacks are different than regular attacks because the opportunity to use them doesn't arise only from the weakness of our opponents. It arises from the environment.

To defend against environmental attacks, we must control our reactions. The environment is indifferent to our fate. In a strategic sense, environmental social forces such as the media or government have nothing to gain from destroying us. They operate on a different battlefield entirely. We cannot therefore react to these attacks in the same way that we do to attacks by our opponents. If we don't overreact, we can almost always survive these attacks.

Lesson 21: Acquiring Information

What is the most important source of information?

A.   Calculations.

B.   People.

C.   Experience.

D.   History.

> *You can only get it from other people.*
> *You must always know the enemy's situation.*
>
> THE ART OF WAR 13:1.26-27

Answer: B. People.

Information is the most critical component of strategy. Strategy replaces the costly use of force with the effective use of information. Sun Tzu is specific about what makes up information and the types of information we need. All information comes from people. That is the topic of the last chapter in the book, USING SPIES.

In the end, all information comes from people. This means that our information is never perfect. People are flawed and our knowledge is flawed. Just because information is written in a book (like this one) or broadcast on television doesn't give it any greater authority. It still comes from people, and people are often wrong. The best information comes directly from those we know because then we can evaluate the source.

We also want information directly from people because of the problem with time. Information gets outdated. How do we get information about the future? We can only gain it by learning about other people's intentions. History, experience, and even our calculations are based on the past. To know what could happen in the future, we have to know what people are planning. This special information is the most valuable of all.

Chapter 1

計

Analysis

Sun Tzu's system of strategy is methodical. The title of the first chapter of *The Art of War* is often translated as "Planning," but today we think of planning as putting together a list of tasks. For Sun Tzu, the process does not begin with a to-do list but rather with an objective analysis of our strategic position. This analysis must take place before we undertake any action. We must know where we are before we can decide how we need to move.

In performing this analysis, we start with the basics. What roles does strategy play in life? Why is strategy important? We then analyze the components that make up a strategic position. How do these components determine a successful strategy? What are the characteristics of these components? How do they affect our chances of success?

We judge more than our own situation with this type of analysis. We can judge the quality of our competitors by whether or not they perform this type of analysis. How well do we think they understand their strategic situation?

Given the critical value of information, what information do we want our competitors to have? How do we want to control our competitors' perceptions of the situation? What do we want our competitors to know about the competitive universe?

Sun Tzu's chapter on analysis provides the keys to identifying winning situations. Our goal here is to understand our situations so we can predict where we can win and where we cannot.

Lesson 22: The Role of Strategy

What role does competition play in life?

A.   It is one of the most basic, natural skills in life.

B.   It is a necessary but unpleasant part of life.

C.   Competition creates most of the problems in life.

D.   The ability to compete is the most important skill in life.

> *This is war.*
> *It is the most important skill in the nation.*
> *It is the basis of life and death.*
> *It is the philosophy of survival or destruction.*
> *You must know it well.*

THE ART OF WAR 1:1.1-5

Answer: D. The ability to compete is the most important skill in life.

Sun Tzu begins by putting the importance of strategy into perspective. Competition is natural. We are all the products of evolutionary competition, but skill in competition—that is, an understanding of strategy—is not inborn. Competition creates problems, but only in the sense that if we don't understand strategy, life is unnecessarily difficult. We earn our livelihood, love, and everything else through strategy.

When we say that skill in strategy is important in our lives, we are saying specifically that strategy is a *skill*. It isn't inborn any more than the knowledge of mathematics is inborn. We must learn strategic skills. We develop these skills by working at them. Some people are more comfortable competing than others are, but to become successful at any level of competition we all have to work.

Competition brings out the best in us. It enriches the world in which we live. It replaces less effective methods with more effective methods. The business world competes for our buying dollar. In doing so, business competitors constantly improve our buying choices and decrease product costs. Competition eliminates poorly run businesses and nations and leaves only the best in each category.

Lesson 23: The Factors of Success

How many factors determine your strategic success in competition?

A.   There is only one primary idea you need to master.

B.   There are five factors that determine success.

C.   There are hundreds of different factors that determine success.

D.   Every situation is different in terms of what factors determine success.

> *Your skill comes from five factors.*
> *Study these factors when you plan war.*
> *You must insist on knowing your situation.*
> > *1. Discuss philosophy.*
> > *2. Discuss the climate.*
> > *3. Discuss the ground.*
> > *4. Discuss leadership.*
> > *5. Discuss military methods.*
>
> THE ART OF WAR 1:1.6-13

Answer: B. There are five factors that determine success.

When we develop a competitive strategy, we don't have to individually analyze hundreds of issues. All relevant issues are connected to five key factors. People often fail to do the proper strategic analysis because they think that a comprehensive analysis is too complex. Successful analysis depends on only a handful of relevant factors.

These five factors are the framework components of our strategic position. In modern competition, we can think of them as our strategic mission, the trends of the time, the battlegrounds on which we compete, our strategic skills as leaders, and the processes we use. These five factors determine the eventual outcome of any competition. Planning—or, more precisely, analysis—depends on our evaluation of these five factors.

Sun Tzu's system of strategic thinking is built up as a framework around these five factors. We will see them echoed again and again throughout the text. All the other aspects of strategic thinking are in some way directly connected to them.

Lesson 24: The Philosophy of Strategy

Which of the following is the best competitive strategy?

A. You must always fight no matter what the costs.

B. You must always keep sight of your original goal.

C. You must always consider the needs of others.

D. You must always use any means to succeed.

> *It starts with your military philosophy.*
> *Command your people in a way that gives them a higher shared purpose.*
> *You can lead them to death.*
> *You can lead them to life.*
> *They must never fear danger or dishonesty.*

THE ART OF WAR 1:1.14-18

Answer: C. You must always consider the needs of others.

This answer surprises many competitors. They expect the most successful military strategy of all time to be bloodthirsty. In reality, it is just the opposite. Sun Tzu's teaching is complex, but at its heart it is a philosophy that puts people first. We cannot afford battles that cost more than they are worth. Our goals should and must change. Some means can never lead to real success.

Sun Tzu realized that in any human endeavor we find success through our interactions with others. Only other people can make us successful. They support us only if we satisfy their needs. This means that we must have a higher purpose that we share with them. We all want our lives to mean something. In business, politics, or religion, we must help people see the value and purpose in working together toward a shared goal.

At Clearbridge, for example, our mission is to bring the wisdom of *The Art of War* to the modern business world. By helping everyone become better competitors, we can make the world more productive and enrich everyone's lives. We sell books to do this, but the books are just the start. We have already added on-line training and video and audio seminars. In the future, we plan to extend this training in every way that we can.

Lesson 25: Competitive Trends

What is the most important thing about managing the current trends?

A.   You must prevent adverse trends.

B.   There is no such thing as a bad time to compete.

C.   You have to ignore trends and create your momentum.

D.   You have to be aware of the trends and adjust to them.

> *Next, you have the climate.*
> *It can be sunny or overcast.*
> *It can be hot or cold.*
> *It includes the timing of the seasons.*

THE ART OF WAR 1:1.19-22

Answer: D. You have to be aware of the trends and adjust to them.

In Sun Tzu's teaching, "climate" describes any condition that naturally changes over time but that we cannot control directly. The core meaning of the Chinese character that we translate as "climate" is "heaven," in the sense of higher forces or even the weather. Another good interpretation of this stanza would be a warning that we are at the mercy of higher forces. These forces can be obvious or hidden. Trends can be positive or negative. Most importantly, they will change. Extremes will regress toward the mean.

The strategic key here is to be aware of the trends and the fact that they *always* change. Sometimes we can use these trends. Other times we must seek shelter from them. We cannot fight them. We can only adjust to them. Hubris is a fatal flaw.

The biggest mistake is assuming that the current climate will stay the same. Think back over any stretch of time. What trend has continued uninterrupted for any length of time? The most important thing about the seasons is that they change. What is hot grows cold eventually. We know only one thing about the future: it will be different than today. What succeeds in the long term is continuously adjusting to changing trends.

Lesson 26: The Battleground

How does the battleground affect your chances of success?

A.   A good competitor can be successful on any ground.

B.   The larger the area of competition, the more successful you can be.

C.   You cannot always choose the ground for competition.

D.   Success requires choosing the ground for competition.

> *Next is the terrain.*
> *It can be distant or near.*
> *It can be difficult or easy.*
> *It can be open or narrow.*
> *It also determines your life or death.*

THE ART OF WAR 1:1.23-27

Answer: D. Success requires choosing the ground for competition.

Here, Master Sun is talking literally about the land, the physical battle-field, but he is also talking more generally about any competitive arena in which we choose to compete. We can compete for jobs, in business, for love, in politics, and in a hundred other areas. The point Sun Tzu makes here is that different competitive arenas have different characteristics, which determine their value. Though we may have to compete in areas where we don't have an advantage, most of this book is dedicated to picking the right competitive arena and knowing how to use that arena to find success.

As we will learn in the next chapter, the terrain is also a source of resources and sustenance. The economic productivity of the ground is what makes it a prize worth fighting over.

These battlegrounds are more than physical. In business, the battle-ground is the marketplace that we choose to serve. Like geographical terrain, the market is a place. In the smallest sense, it is the mind of a customer. In a larger sense, it is the marketplace as a whole. Using Sun Tzu's system, we learn to think of different markets as having different shapes and obstacles.

There are many types of competitive terrain: the physical space on retailers' shelves, time given a story in the media, even the cyberspace of the World Wide Web. Each has its own characteristics and dimensions, but they all can be analyzed by Sun Tzu's methods. These elements of the terrain are the source of different advantages and disadvantages.

Lesson 27: Leadership Qualities

What characteristics does strategic leadership require?

A.   You must be quick, forceful, persuasive, forthright, and flexible.

B.   You must be loyal, thrifty, brave, clean, and reverent.

C.   You must be unswerving, dedicated, single-minded, focused, and commanding.

D.   You must be smart, honest, caring, brave, and disciplined.

> *Next is the commander.*
> *He must be smart, trustworthy, caring, brave, and strict.*
>
> THE ART OF WAR 1:1.28-29

Answer: D. You must be smart, honest, caring, brave, and disciplined.

First, leaders must be intelligent. We must appreciate the value of knowledge. If leaders aren't knowledgeable, we cannot successfully compete. In the larger system, intelligence is required to know the ground.

Next, we must be honest. If we are not honest, people will never trust us and we cannot succeed long term. In the larger system, honesty is required to create successful methods.

Next, we must be caring. We must care about people and their feelings. If we are insensitive to others' needs, people will not support us. We must care about and win people over to succeed. Caring is tied to the key factor of philosophy. Leaders must care about their mission to unite the organization.

Next, we must be brave. If we aren't courageous, we will never take the risks necessary to be successful. Bravery is necessary to weather the adversities of climate. We must be able to fail repeatedly and keep going. Even someone well versed in Sun Tzu's methods may fail, but he or she knows to keep going.

Finally, we must be disciplined and strict. We must be willing to do the unpleasant parts of the job as well as the fun parts. We must honor our agreements scrupulously. People must be able to depend on us. If we are not reliable, no one will support us for long.

We learn later in the book that one of the ways that we can defeat an organization is to exploit the weaknesses of its leaders.

Lesson 28: Your Competitive Methods

What is important about the processes by which you achieve success?

A.   You must consistently use the same processes to get the same results.

B.   You must let the situation determine the right methods to use.

C.   You must let your management philosophy dictate your processes.

D.   You should look for shortcuts to speed cycle time.

> *Finally, you have your military methods.*
> *They shape your organization.*
> *They come from your management philosophy.*
> *You must master their use.*

THE ART OF WAR 1:1.30-33

Answer: C. You must let your management philosophy dictate your processes.

As we learn, we learn more efficient and effective methods. Later in the book, Sun Tzu elaborates on the importance of innovation in methods. Though there are a huge variety of potentially good methods, strategic thinking requires that our methods must be consistent with our philosophy—that is, the vision or mission that draws people together. Remember what Sun Tzu said about giving people a "shared higher purpose"? Once we define that purpose, we have to be true to it. Strategy requires that we think over the long term. We cannot define methods, management systems, or business procedures that are inconsistent with our basic philosophy.

When we are building an organization, our philosophy determines the organization's structure. We cannot preach empowerment and create a rigid hierarchical organization. It won't work.

A large part of Sun Tzu's text discusses how to identify the most effective methods to be successful. To use these lessons, we first have to define our mission. We must first know where we are going in order to choose the right methods to get there. We will be confronted with many opportunities to "improve" our methods, but unless they are consistent with our philosophy, we have to let them go.

Lesson 29: The Role of the Five Factors

How important are the five factors in determining your success?

A.   You will be successful if you pay attention to all of them.

B.   You will be successful if you understand some of them.

C.   You will be successful if you master any one of them.

D.   You will be successful when you learn which to ignore.

> *All five of these factors are critical.*
> *As a commander, you must pay attention to them.*
> *Understanding them brings victory.*
> *Ignoring them means defeat.*
>
> THE ART OF WAR 1:1.34-37

Answer: A. You will be successful if you pay attention to all of them.

All five factors are critical to building a successful strategy. We must select the right mission. We must foresee and leverage the trends of the time. We must pick the right battleground or arena for competition. We must have the right leadership qualities. We must use effective methods, consistent with our mission.

If we forget any of these elements, we cannot consistently surpass our opponents. If we do not consistently defeat the competition, we cannot succeed over the long term. Any one of these factors can become a stumbling block preventing our success. A weak philosophy, poorly judged trends, the wrong battleground, poor character, or inconsistent methods lead to failure.

Strategy doesn't mean simply having a plan. It means having a plan that accounts in a realistic way for all the basic factors that can affect the outcome of the strategic situation.

Nor can these factors be considered in isolation. The interactions among the different factors are more important than the factors in isolation. The leader must suit his or her methods. The methods must suit the ground. The philosophy must suit the trends of the time.

Lesson 30: The Purpose of Strategic Analysis

What is the purpose of analysis as it is defined by Sun Tzu?

A.   It is a process which leads you to ask the right questions.

B.   It is a process by which you determine the right actions.

C.   It is a process by which you identify the wrong actions.

D.   It is a process by which you assure your success.

> *You must learn through planning.*
> *You must question the situation.*

THE ART OF WAR 1:2.1-2

Answer: A. It is a process which leads you to ask the right questions.

We tend to think of analysis as something that explains the situation and leads to a planning phase, during which we create a list of to-do items. This is not the process that Sun Tzu describes. He defines our initial analysis as asking questions that force us to confront what we need to learn. His strategic method has many more steps. This is only the first step, the start of the process of shaping a strategy. Analysis of the five factors shows us what we need to learn to understand the big picture.

The core of strategy is replacing costly effort with good decisions based on good information. Why do most people fail? Because they assume that they understand their strategic position and what needs to be done. Sun Tzu has no faith in these assumptions. We cannot afford the mistakes that naturally flow from making assumptions. No matter what we think we know, the first step is questioning our knowledge.

Sun Tzu's methods are based on understanding our specific situation. All situations are unique—though they can fall into the general categories described in chapter 11. Time and place, two of the key factors in competition, are always unique. No two situations develop at the same place and time. All situations also change. They will grow better or worse over time.

Time and place affect our analysis of all the other factors in a competitive challenge. We have to discover how our unique situation works within the context of our philosophy, leadership, and particular methods. This situation is dynamic. We must continually question our situation from year to year, month to month, and day to day.

Lesson 31: The Key Questions

When you question your situation, where do you look for relevant information?

A. You question what differs from past situations.

B. You question how you compare with the competition.

C. You question what is new and unfamiliar.

D. You question your philosophy, leadership, and methods.

> *You must ask:*
> *Which government has the right philosophy?*
> *Which commander has the skill?*
> *Which season and place has the advantage?*
> *Which method of command works?*
> *Which group of forces has the strength?*
> *Which officers and men have the training?*
> *Which rewards and punishments make sense?*
> *This tells when you will win and when you will lose.*
>
> THE ART OF WAR 1:2.3-11

Answer: B. You question how you compare with the competition.

Sun Tzu's method focuses only on relative values. His analysis is comparative analysis. "Good" and "bad" are always relative concepts in strategy. We are only well trained in comparison to someone who is less well trained. We are strong only if our competitors are weaker than we are. We must question our relative ability in each key area *by comparing ourselves to potential competitors or opponents.* In some areas, we may be stronger. In some areas, our competitors may have an advantage.

Comparing our abilities with those of the competition puts our abilities into perspective. We can improve anything, but resources are always limited. We don't have to be perfect. We only have to be better than the competition, and we don't have to be superior in every area, but we must know where we stand.

In the economic marketplace or the marketplace of ideas, people can only choose between real alternatives. We may need to improve in the areas where our competitors are stronger than we are. Comparing ourselves to our competitors tells us where we can focus our limited resources.

Lesson 32: Predicting Success

How can you foresee which people will be successful and which will not?

A.   You cannot foresee the success or failure of others.

B.   People who strive to do their best will succeed.

C.   People who know the right people will succeed.

D.   People who analyze their relative strengths will succeed.

> *Some commanders perform this analysis.*
> *If you use these commanders, you will win.*
> *Keep them.*
> *Some commanders ignore this analysis.*
> *If you use these commanders, you will lose.*
> *Get rid of them.*

THE ART OF WAR 1:2.12-17

Answer: D. People who analyze their relative strengths will succeed.

Sun Tzu teaches that people who ask the right questions and objectively analyze their relative strengths are always successful over time. The heart of Sun Tzu's teaching is making the right decisions. Analyzing our situation is the key to making the correct choices quickly. Matching our strengths against our opponents' weaknesses is the key to making strategic progress.

If we fail to ask the right questions and obtain objective answers, our decisions are emotional. In general, we tend to be overly optimistic at the beginning of every opportunity and overly negative when success doesn't come easily. We must avoid making these emotional decisions ourselves and associating with people who make them.

Predicting the future is the heart of strategy. Peter Drucker, the dean of business advice, says that there are two ways to predict the future. First, we foresee unavoidable changes over time, such as the aging of the populace. Second, we act to build something we want in the future. Sun Tzu describes the first as vision, insight into heaven (*tian*), and the later as control of the ground (*di*), building a position. I can predict with certainty that, if I survive, I will be one year older a year from now. I can also predict with certainty that there will be a paragraph after this one because I intend to write it.

Lesson 33: The Key to Communication

What is the most important communication skill that a competitor must master?

A. Intimidation.

B. Persuasion.

C. Self-promotion.

D. Listening.

> *Plan an advantage by listening.*
> *Adjust to the situation.*
> *Get assistance from the outside.*
> *Influence events.*
> *Then planning can find opportunities and give you control.*
>
> THE ART OF WAR 1:3.1-5

Answer: D. Listening.

Listening is the heart of getting good information. Analysis is important simply because it forces us to listen to others. In other words, it forces us to pay attention. Without this active listening, we don't really know our true situation. Without this active listening, we can never use the power of other people to help us.

Another key idea here is getting assistance from the outside, that is, getting an outside perspective. The other benefits of analysis flow from developing a broader viewpoint about what the key conditions are. If we listen to people with different ideas and different viewpoints, we are more likely to identify missed opportunities that can allow us to become more successful. We can identify the areas in which we can easily beat the competition. We can use our limited resources to win the contest.

Very few people, especially aggressive people, are good listeners. Aggressive behavior encourages self-promotion, persuasion, and confident action. It doesn't necessarily encourage listening. All people say that they want feedback, but few really pay attention to it, take time to evaluate it, and act on it. Solid information is either difficult to solicit or difficult to filter out from the noise. One of the best ways to listen is to get to know our competitors and talk to them, but surprisingly few people take the time to do this.

Lesson 34: The Best Form of Competition

How would you define the best possible form of competitive attack?

A.   Helping people work together.

B.   Bluffing the opponent.

C.   Overcoming the opponent.

D.   Discovering opportunity.

> *Warfare is one thing.*
> *It is a philosophy of deception.*

THE ART OF WAR 1:4.1-2

Answer: B. Bluffing the opponent.

Without studying the text of Sun Tzu's work, especially in the original Chinese, this type of statement is easily misinterpreted. Sun Tzu says earlier that the right philosophy is giving people a higher shared purpose, and he describes honesty as a necessary characteristic of leaders. Now he seems to be saying that we must deceive people. Earlier, he was talking about our general philosophy toward others. Now he is talking about our communication strategy toward our opposition.

This statement is closely connected to what Master Sun has said about listening. We should listen. We should also expect that our competition is listening to us. Since our competitors are listening, we don't want them to know our strengths, our weaknesses, and our plans. We must realize that everything we say or do communicates something to our opponents. We must mislead our opponents as often as possible to be successful.

The Art of War is unique in history because it assumes a dynamic competitive environment. We adjust to our competition, but we must expect that our competition will adjust to us. The dynamic nature of the contest makes secrecy critically important. This dynamic nature of reality is the foundation of all game theory and chaos theory.

In the dynamic battle, information is the key to success. In strategic situations, we must never let our opponents know what we are thinking. Our words and actions must always misdirect them as to our true abilities and intentions. Whenever we know something important, we don't want them to know that we know.

Lesson 35: Your Public Image

How do you portray yourself in a situation in which the competition can hear you?

A.   You give out as little information as possible.

B.   You want to always appear active and ready.

C.   You portray your situation as the opposite of what it is.

D.   You want to always appear assured and confident.

> *When you are ready, you try to appear incapacitated.*
> *When active, you pretend inactivity.*
> *When you are close to the enemy, you appear distant.*
> *When far away, pretend you are near.*
>
> THE ART OF WAR 1:4.3-6

Answer: C. You portray your situation as the opposite of what it is.

The goal is always to mislead our competitors. We don't want to keep them ignorant because ignorance stimulates their curiosity. We want them to have information. We just want that information to lead them into exactly the wrong decisions.

Many people, in promoting their strategy, tend to tell their opponents everything they are doing. This immediately enables others to start working against their strategy secretly. If nothing else, we should learn to keep our strategy a secret.

However, when it comes to controlling people's perceptions, *spinning* is a better strategy than secrecy. By spinning, we mean describing the situation as the opposite of what it really is, while at the same time staying consistent with the facts. If people want to know your plans, secrecy can frustrate them and make them suspicious. Deception, when well done, addresses their curiosity but in a way that misleads them.

The process of deception starts when we learn to control our emotions. Emotionally, we want people to know who we are. This leads to self-promotion, but our potential investors, partners, and customers don't care who we are. They only care about what we can do for them. Only our competitors want to know who we are so that they can use our condition against us.

Lesson 36: Situational Response

How does your condition determine your action?

A.   You must not let your condition predict your actions.

B.   You should stick to your plan despite your condition.

C.   You should follow your instincts in reacting to your condition.

D.   You must react predictably in responding to conditions.

> *You can have an advantage and still entice an opponent.*
> *You can be disorganized and still be decisive.*
> *You can be ready and still be preparing.*
> *You can be strong and still avoid battle.*
> *You can be angry and still stop yourself.*
> *You can humble yourself and still be confident.*
> *You can be relaxed and still be working.*
> *You can be close to an ally and still part ways.*
> *You can attack a place without planning to do so.*
> *You can leave a place without giving away your plan.*
>
> THE ART OF WAR 1:4.7-16

Answer: A. You must not let your condition predict your actions.

We adjust to our conditions, but we must never become predictable, letting our actions expose our condition. Once we become predictable, people will learn how to outmaneuver us. To be successful at bluffing our opponents, they should not be able to look at our actions and determine our true situation. In chapter 9, Sun Tzu goes into a great deal of detail about how we can determine our opponents' true condition by looking at how they behave. We must avoid being this predictable.

There is a positive advantage in behaving contrary to our true conditions. Sun Tzu teaches that we cannot create the openings that lead to our success. Only our opponents can do that. By misleading them, we encourage them to make those mistakes that create an opening for us.

Strategy is like a game of poker. Competitors should never know what to expect from us. We predict their behavior, but we want to remain inscrutable. Our past behavior sets up future expectations. If we fold a series of weak hands, we set up a credible bluff when conditions are right. If we are caught bluffing several times, we can set up a big win with a strong hand.

Lesson 37: The Nurture of Opportunity

How do you create situations in which you can win the strategic battle?

A.   You conserve your strength for a well-planned attack.

B.   You develop a plan that leads step by step to victory.

C.   You wait to find the right situation by misleading opponents.

D.   You lay traps for your opponents and wait for them to fall.

> *You will find a place where you can win.*
> *You cannot first signal your intentions.*
>
> THE ART OF WAR 1:4.17-18

Answer: C. You wait to find the right situation by misleading opponents.

Waiting for an opening created by our opponents is a central theme in Sun Tzu's work. We will hear it repeated often. We cannot create an opportunity. We do not control our competitive environment. We control only our position within it. We are constantly looking for an opportunity to advance, but that opportunity must be provided by others who leave us an opening. The skill of positioning is putting ourselves in the right place at the right time to take advantage of this opening.

We can, however, confuse others about our intentions and abilities so that they don't know what to expect. Opponents will make mistakes and give us an opportunity, but only if we mislead them about our true condition. We have to be patient. Eventually, we will discover an opening that will allow us to move forward.

Strategy is the act and art of discovery. Sun Tzu doesn't believe that we can plan success like writing a to-do list. The art is recognizing a winning situation when we see it. As the chapters of *The Art of War* unfold, Sun Tzu trains us how to recognize a winning situation when it finally arrives. We don't wait inactively. We must act to keep repositioning ourselves to take advantage of the smallest opportunities as they occur.

The word for this approach is opportunistic. The winners in life won't be those who have the best business plans. The winners will be those who are able to see and take advantage of opportunities as they arise and keep adjusting to new opportunities. Bluffing plays a key role in this continual advance because it prevents others from knowing which way we plan to move.

Lesson 38: Identifying True Opportunities

How do you identify an opportunity where you are certain to succeed?

A.   You have the resources and the knowledge to win.

B.   Your opponent is thoroughly confused about the situation.

C.   You have a mathematical understanding of the situation.

D.   Your opponent is at a disadvantage in several key areas.

> *Manage to avoid battle until your organization can count on certain victory.*
> *You must calculate many advantages.*
> *Before you go to battle, you may believe that you can foresee defeat.*
> *You can count few advantages.*
> *Many advantages add up to victory.*
> *Few advantages add up to defeat.*
> *How can you know your advantages without analyzing them?*
> *We can see where we are by means of our observations.*
> *We can foresee our victory or defeat by planning.*

THE ART OF WAR 1:5.1-9

Answer: C. You have a mathematical understanding of the situation.

Sun Tzu's work in the original Chinese is a book of equations. It describes the science of strategy as a systematic, organized process. This doesn't translate well into English and any such translation wouldn't be broadly read, but this stanza cuts to the core of strategy: calculation.

Sun Tzu sees strategic analysis as an ongoing mathematical process of analysis. As many factors as possible should be reduced to numbers. We first analyze our current position. We then analyze the cost of making a move by calculating our strengths, our opponents' weaknesses, and the benefits of our new position. Eventually, we recognize a situation in which the cost of moving to a new position is far outweighed by the benefits of that position. At that point, we commit ourselves to meeting the challenge of moving to that position.

This analysis doesn't take place at some arbitrary starting point in a campaign. We have to continually analyze our shifting situation to recognize our changing opportunities. The five key factors are the framework for understanding our relative strengths and weaknesses. To spot the right moves, we must be totally objective in this analysis.

Chapter 2

作戰

Going to War

After introducing the key elements of strategy, Sun Tzu focuses on the economics of competition. He does not define victory as simply winning battles. Success is making victory pay. Moving to a new position has certain costs. The value of that position must outweigh those costs. This economic focus is one of the reasons that Sun Tzu's strategy works so well in today's business world, but even when the costs are not economic there are always costs in resources, time, and emotion. This chapter provides a great outline for understanding the consequences of strategic decisions and how those decisions are made in light of the costs. The chapter offers a basic analysis of the costs, risks, and benefits of going to war.

We must understand the dynamics of strategic situations. Can we control the scope of competition? Can we reduce its risks? If so, how?

For Sun Tzu, the first step is understanding the costs of action. How do we minimize our costs? Can we prevent costs from escalating?

In planning a strategy, the outcome is never certain. How should we respond to the possibility of failure? How can we balance the potential risks and the potential rewards?

We must understand the definition of success. When we enter into war, what are we trying to win? What is the reward our new position offers?

These are all questions that Sun Tzu deals with in this chapter. Strategy in the real world is more than a game. We are always risking something, if only our time and effort. We must decide before acting what our risks are and whether or not we are willing to undertake them. It is possible to "win" battles and even wars without gaining any reward worth the sacrifice. Foolish competitive battles can leave everyone a loser. Sun Tzu's system is not a method for punishing enemies or winning bragging rights. Its only goal is winning a prize at a cost that makes it worthwhile.

Lesson 39: The Foundation of Strategy

When first creating a strategy, what is the most important issue you should consider?

A.   Your goals.

B.   The costs of your strategy.

C.   How to secure an advantage.

D.   How to undermine your opponents.

> *Everything depends on your use of military philosophy.*
> *Moving the army requires thousands of vehicles.*
> *These vehicles must be loaded thousands of times.*
> *The army must carry a huge supply of arms.*
> *You need ten thousand acres of grain.*
> *This results in internal and external shortages.*
>
> THE ART OF WAR 2:1.1-6

Answer: B. The costs of your strategy.

If we are going to compete, we first have to analyze what our actions are going to cost us. Strategy means focusing on improving our position rather than looking for battles to fight. To improve our position, we must move. Moving to a new position is always expensive. Sun Tzu doesn't believe that long-term success comes easily or, more precisely, that we can plan on it coming easily. We look for the path of least resistance, but every step on the path to success has a cost. Those costs add up over time.

Sun Tzu teaches a systematic process designed to work over time. Despite what we hear about get-rich-quick schemes, virtually no one achieves success without investing time, effort, and usually money. Success takes persistence. It is safer to overestimate our costs than underestimate them. People who expect to reach their goals easily never succeed over the long term.

Everyone's resources are limited. We must choose our priorities. The effort that we put into one area is necessarily taken from some other opportunity. We cannot do everything. We have to decide what opportunities we are willing to sacrifice for the success of others. We have to make choices. The purpose of mastering strategy is to enable us to make the best possible choices in a complex, confused world.

Lesson 40: Setting Limits

How can you set limits on what you are willing to invest to be successful?

A.   You limit your investment by focusing on certain problems.

B.   You limit your investment by focusing on certain opponents.

C.   You limit your investment by ignoring certain opportunities.

D.   You cannot limit your investment.

> *Any army consumes resources like an invader.*
> *It uses up glue and paint for wood.*
> *It requires armor for its vehicles.*
> *People complain about the waste of a vast amount of metal.*
> *It will set you back when you raise tens of thousands of troops.*

THE ART OF WAR 2:1.7-11

Answer: D. You cannot limit your investment.

When we start toward any strategic goal, that campaign expands over time. Costs escalate naturally. Movement into new territory plunders resources from other areas. We are generally too myopic in our strategic thinking, and our attempt to control costs by limiting our thinking just aggravates our problems. The contestants always escalate the contest. They may complain about the costs, but they also continually raise the stakes. We cannot make competition inexpensive. The only way that we can recoup our investment is to win a prize worth more than our investment.

As Sun Tzu says, some costs are cosmetic. Others are defensive. Everyone complains about one type of cost or another, but the real problem is just the number of things that we must attend to.

People are endlessly inventive. As competitors, we are always looking for new forms of advantage. People steal each other's ideas and use them as the springboard for their own inventions. None of us knows what any of these ideas are worth until their value is proven in the marketplace. We cannot guarantee our success. Under competition, only the winners survive.

Once we are locked into a contest, we cannot accurately predict or plan the costs of competition. Instead, we must start with a built-in cost-effective approach. Whatever actions are necessary should always be initially evaluated in terms of their cost effectiveness.

Lesson 41: Assuring Success

Since competition is expensive, what is the best strategy to assure success?

A.   Create the largest army.

B.   Slowly add to your strength as you can afford it.

C.   Move quickly and avoid direct confrontations.

D.   Prepare for a long, expensive campaign.

> *Using a large army makes war very expensive to win.*
> *Long delays create a dull army and sharp defeats.*
> *Attacking enemy cities drains your forces.*
> *Long campaigns that exhaust the nation's resources are wrong.*

THE ART OF WAR 2:1.12-15

Answer: C. Move quickly and avoid direct confrontations.

The size of the effort, the time it takes, and the amount of conflict it generates all add to our costs. Competition is more than fighting the good fight. We have to win something worth the fight in the end. We can all throw money at a problem until it goes away, but in doing so we create more problems. If we spend more than we can ever win, we truly cannot win. Most of the investors who poured money into the Internet market during the dot-com boom never saw a return on their investment. They were simply not weighing their costs against the likely gains.

If we hope to succeed, we have to keep our costs to a minimum. We cannot control what our competitors do, but we must control our own actions. We can keep our investment small by planning small attacks, that is, small movements into new areas. We can avoid direct attacks against entrenched positions by going into areas where others leave openings. We can avoid long, drawn-out confrontations.

In this stanza, Sun Tzu is telling us what doesn't work. The high cost of competition comes from making costly decisions. Risking a large investment does *not* assure our success. It makes success less likely. This is hard advice to follow. The natural reaction is to think that, in any contest, a bigger budget is always better. This is seldom the case. The bigger the cost, the harder it is to justify. Similarly, the longer it takes for a competitive thrust to generate a return on our investment, the more uncertain and dangerous that project is.

Lesson 42: Losing the Initiative

How can you recover your position once you have lost the initiative in competition?

A.   You cannot recover the initiative in a situation once it is lost.

B.   You only have to be smarter than your competition.

C.   You must to be willing to invest everything you have.

D.   You must be patient in looking for an advantage.

> *Manage a dull army.*
> *You will suffer sharp defeats.*
> *Drain your forces.*
> *Your money will be used up.*
> *Your rivals multiply as your army collapses and they will begin against you.*
> *It doesn't matter how smart you are.*
> *You cannot get ahead by taking losses!*

THE ART OF WAR 2:1.16-22

Answer: A. You cannot recover the initiative in a situation once it is lost.

The natural tendency is to think that we are smarter, better, or somehow more worthy than our opponents. The reality is that we aren't. Success comes from taking the initiative to make progress. Once we have lost the initiative and start fighting defensive battles, we have already lost that campaign. We have no chance of long-term success without winning back the initiative. This is not to say that we cannot recover from setbacks. However, we cannot succeed if we pick the wrong battles and fail to move forward.

We never know how much competition is coming. We tend to underestimate our opposition. We tend to overestimate our abilities. Unfortunately, people stampede in a crowd to take advantage of new opportunities. This type of contest makes everyone weaker instead of stronger. If we show weakness, we encourage those who are arrayed against us.

We can easily make the mistake of thinking that we are going to succeed because we are somehow smarter and better than all our opponents. However, if we are really smart, we avoid meeting broad competitive situations. We thereby avoid losing the initiative. We must avoid falling behind because we cannot recover. We must seize the initiative. We must use it to discourage the competition from coming after us.

Lesson 43: Minimizing Risks

How can you minimize the risks of competition?

A.   You can avoid direct competition.

B.   You can choose contests that are decided quickly.

C.   You can limit your goals.

D.   You can carefully pick your opponents.

> *You hear of people going to war too quickly.*
> *Still, you won't see a skilled war that lasts a long time.*
>
> THE ART OF WAR 2:1.23-24

Answer: B. You can choose contests that are decided quickly.

Sun Tzu doesn't demand that we be hasty in identifying an opportunity, but he wants us to act quickly after we do find an opportunity. He says later in lesson 234 that mastering speed is the essence of successful warfare. Speed is necessary for two reasons. First, it reduces the costs of competition. Second, it assures that we get to the battlefield before our opponents do.

What happens when a competitive contest drags on? The costs mount. Any eventual payback grows more distant and uncertain. Good strategy insists that we get to some payoff, no matter how small, as quickly as possible. This turns a costly situation into a productive one.

Failure is always possible, but the chances of failure go up the longer a competitive move takes. It is easier to recover from a quick failure than a long, drawn-out one. Competition is dangerous and uncertain. Good strategy suggests that small, quick contests resulting in small losses are preferable to large, expensive "successes" that cannot pay back their investment.

As we will see in later chapters, strategy requires inventiveness and new ideas. We can never know if our new idea will work, if our new concept will catch on. Will we fire the imagination of the fickle public? We must quickly test our concept in the market to see if it works. Small, quick investments can either prove or disprove our concepts. If our initial small attempt doesn't work, we can quickly regroup and try another approach. Once an idea quickly proves on a small scale that it can make money, we can start building on it. Every war is a test of an idea. If it is successful, a good idea can generate the additional resources we need to build it up.

Lesson 44: Competitive Self-Interest

Can a competition ever be at odds with the best interests of all contestants?

A.   Competition can cost more than it ever returns.

B.   Competition can hurt your opportunities for cooperation.

C.   The competition can be lost.

D.   Competition is always in the best interests of contestants.

> *You can fight a war for a long time or you can make your nation strong.*
> *You cannot do both.*
>
> THE ART OF WAR 2:1.25-26

Answer: A. Competition can cost more than it ever returns.

We cannot ever afford to lose sight of the purpose of strategy. We compete for gain. The contest is not the prize. We compete to win wealth, power, or recognition. Whatever our goal, we can never lose sight of it.

The longer a battle goes on, the more likely we are to make this mistake of forgetting our original goals. Persistence is important in success, but not persistence when there is nothing that we can really win. Contests that drag on and on can make everyone involved in them into losers. Competition is costly. If the costs of competition outstrip the possible gains, we should never compete. No one should.

In all competition, there is a psychological trap hidden within the competitive situations. When we get embroiled in a contest, we can easily forget our original goals. At some point in a long contest, we forget that we are fighting for gain and begin fighting simply to win. This is a terrifying prospect. Sun Tzu knew that this tendency is highly destructive. Many wars have proven destructive to every nation involved.

Here Sun Tzu offers a simple test for the worthiness of any contest. Will we be stronger afterward if we win? Will we be in a better position? Or will the battle itself be so drawn-out, costly, and destructive that by the time we win we will be in a weaker position? If the battle is economic, we cannot spend more money during its course than we can ever win back. If we are only fighting for recognition, we certainly do not want to make ourselves look bad in the process of trying to win. The longer any contest drags on, the more likely it is to create nothing but losers.

Lesson 45: Risks and Rewards

How do the risks of competition affect the rewards?

A.   You must minimize the risks to maximize the rewards.

B.   You must avoid the risks to assure the rewards.

C.   You must embrace the risks to discover the rewards.

D.   You must understand the risks to understand the rewards.

> *Make no assumptions about all the dangers in using military force.*
> *Then you won't make assumptions about the benefits of using arms either.*
> ### THE ART OF WAR 2:2.1-2

Answer: C. You must embrace the risks to discover the rewards.

After all his warnings, Sun Tzu puts the dangers of competition into perspective. Competition is risky. We must appreciate exactly how risky it is. Nevertheless, competition is also the source of all success. If we don't embrace competition and its risks, we will never know how successful we can be. How should we react to this dilemma?

We must always be aware that failure is a possibility, but we cannot let this knowledge paralyze us. Instead, we must commit ourselves to small, quick, decisive actions, remembering that speed is the essence of warfare.

We can never completely protect ourselves against failure. We must carefully evaluate our chances, but every move requires that we take risks. We cannot let this paralyze us into inaction. The future is never certain, but the uncertainty of the future has an upside. The contest may turn out to be more rewarding than we can possibly foresee. The variables that make success uncertain also make great success possible *if* we take the chance.

We must prepare for unforeseen levels of success just like we prepare for failure. Both are possible. If we are ready for one, we must be equally ready for the other. The strategy of "going to war" is not about winning. It is about making winning pay. The problem is that neither the costs nor the payoffs are predictable. We must never pretend that they are. Our fear and greed must balance themselves out in the equation. Our greed keeps us from becoming paralyzed by fear. Our fear keeps us from acting foolishly out of greed. Both of these forms of uncertainty are necessary to make strategy work over the long term.

Lesson 46: Controlling Risk

How do you control the risks of competition?

A.   You must always be willing to obtain more resources.

B.   You must have more resources than you think you need.

C.   You must stop worrying about profit and loss.

D.   You must keep costs low and make the contest pay.

> *You want to make good use of war.*
> *Do not raise troops repeatedly.*
> *Do not carry too many supplies.*
> *Choose to be useful to your nation.*
> *Feed off the enemy.*
> *Make your army carry only the provisions it needs.*

THE ART OF WAR 2:2.3-8

Answer: D. You must keep costs low and make the contest pay.

Sun Tzu's approach to winning a competitive challenge might be called "smaller, faster, better," to borrow the terminology from modern management.

Whenever Sun Tzu says, "make good use of war," he means to think strategically—think about what has the greatest chance of success over the long term. This means paying careful attention to the economics of the situation. In meeting any specific challenge, we keep our investments small and ongoing costs small. We act quickly, before our opponents can act against us. We "feed off the enemy"; that is, we find a way to make the challenge pay for itself.

To make this strategy work, we have to avoid getting bogged down. Over the course of our competitive careers, we will face many challenges. What seems critical today may seem relatively unimportant tomorrow. We don't build up large inventories, stockpiles of supplies, or resources that we don't need over the long term simply to meet the challenge of the moment. We should travel light, without encumbering ourselves with excess baggage. The less baggage we have, the faster we can respond to new challenges. We must be prepared to take what the competition gives us. We cannot know beforehand what will work for certain. We can put ourselves in a position to take advantage of whatever the future brings us.

Lesson 47: The Effect of Geography

How should geographic distance affect the selection of a contest?

A.   You want to compete in the broadest arena possible.

B.   You want to compete in an outside area that is close.

C.   In the modern economy, all contests are global.

D.   Distance should not matter.

> *The nation impoverishes itself shipping to troops that are far away.*
> *Distant transportation is costly for hundreds of families.*
> *Buying goods with the army nearby is also expensive.*
> *High prices also exhaust wealth.*
> *If you exhaust your wealth, you then quickly hollow out your military.*
> *Military forces consume a nation's wealth entirely.*
> *War leaves households in the former heart of the nation with nothing.*
>
> THE ART OF WAR 2:3.1-7

Answer: B. You want to compete in an outside area that is close.

Positioning is the key to success because distance is an inescapable cost. Transportation and communication are always more difficult over longer distances. In many areas, they can account for more than half the costs involved. Distance is the most basic barrier to entry in meeting any competitive challenge. Even the smallest organization starts with the special advantage of location in serving its local customers or supporters.

Those who worry about competitors half a world away are basically admitting that they are so inferior that their tremendous advantage of locality doesn't matter. They are saying that even with the costs of transportation and communication, they cannot do as good a job as a distant competitor. Sun Tzu would say that because of the costs of distance, free trade is not nearly as big a danger to local workers as is poor education.

The Internet, faxes, and phones may make national and global communication less expensive than traditional forms of communication. Nevertheless, distance still equals cost. Products must be shipped. Customers must be supported. Language and cultural barriers must be overcome. If we are going to find success, we are more likely to find success close to home, based on what we know, without the additional costs of traveling to some distant place and tackling areas we know nothing about.

Lesson 48: Your Chances of Success

All things being equal, what are your chances of success in meeting any new challenge?

A.   You should expect to win all new challenges.

B.   You should expect to win most new challenges.

C.   You should expect to win a new challenge for every one you lose.

D.   You should prepare to lose most new challenges.

> *War destroys hundreds of families.*
> *Out of every ten families, war leaves only seven.*
> *War empties the government's storehouses.*
> *Broken armies will get rid of their horses.*
> *They will throw down their armor, helmets, and arrows.*
> *They will lose their swords and shields.*
> *They will leave their wagons without oxen.*
> *War will consume sixty percent of everything you have.*

THE ART OF WAR 2:3.8-15

Answer: D. You should prepare to lose most new challenges.

We all face many challenges in life, both large and small. New challenges come along every day. We all make many plans to accomplish many exciting things. We are unrealistic if we expect most of our plans to succeed. Most of the new ideas we try will fail. Eight out of ten new businesses go out of business within their first two years. As we move from what we know into areas in which we have a lot to learn, we should expect to fail.

If we expect failure when we are meeting new challenges, we should prepare to tolerate a complete failure. We should expect to lose our investment. We shouldn't delude ourselves into thinking that we can somehow recover our losses. Failures are usually complete losses.

Why is it important to prepare for failure? We can accept losses by keeping our investment small and the contests quick. Small, quick failed efforts are easier to afford than large ones. We learn from our failures. They move us forward. By failing productively, we can move more quickly toward more successful efforts, which are the only ones that count. One success can pay for many failures.

Lesson 49: Finding Resources

Given the risk of failure, where should you find the resources to compete in a new area or market?

A. You should steal resources from your opponents.

B. You should get financing from your investors.

C. You should get financing from your customers.

D. You should not expect to find any financing.

Because of this, the intelligent commander's duty is to feed off the enemy.

THE ART OF WAR 2:4.1

Answer: A. You should steal resources from your opponents.

Many people starting a business want to know where to get financing. They want to know about venture capital, bank loans, private investors, and so on. They think that if they just had enough investment capital, their business idea would surely work. They think that if they just knew where to find more money, then their success would surely follow. More investment makes success more certain, doesn't it?

The unspoken and foolish assumption here is that given enough investment, success in meeting a challenge is certain. If we believe what Sun Tzu teaches, we know that success is never certain and that failure is more likely than success. No one should be anxious to take on a crushing debt in starting a business. This is especially true if we hold to Sun Tzu's definition of success, which is making victory pay. The deeper we go into debt in trying to succeed, the deeper the hole we have to dig ourselves out of before our venture can pay off.

Instead of thinking about investing more and risking more in a challenge, we need to focus on making our ventures pay. This is what Sun Tzu calls "feeding off the enemy." We can get the resources we need from our opponents in many different ways. In business, we can take away their customers, distributors, and employees. In politics, we can take away their supporters and contributors. In sports, we can take away their sponsors, fans, and so on.

We do not focus on beating our opponents. Instead, we focus on taking support and rewards from them.

Lesson 50: The Most Valuable Resources

What resources are the most valuable?

A.   Those that you create for yourself.

B.   Those that you take from the competition.

C.   Those that you can protect.

D.   Those that you can depend on.

> *Use a cup of the enemy's food.*
> *It is worth twenty of your own.*
> *Win a bushel of the enemy's feed.*
> *It is worth twenty of your own.*

THE ART OF WAR 2:4.2-5

Answer: B. Those that you take from the competition.

Competition can take many forms. In the contests of real life, there are win-win situations in which our success depends on the success of others. There are also lose-lose situations in which the only way to win is to avoid the battle. However, many of the challenges we normally face are zero-sum games in which there is only one winner. Only one applicant can fill a job opening. Only one politician can win an election. When we are competing in zero-sum games, weakening our opponents' positions works much like strengthening our own. This is why negative ads are so common in election campaigns.

When we are playing a zero-sum game, our economic strategy must include the effect of our actions on our opponents. We not only want to reduce our costs, but we want to increase our competitors' costs. We want to take resources from them whenever possible.

In the challenges we face in everyday life, we often don't know who our opponents are. As job applicants, we often don't know who else is applying for the job. As suitors, we often don't know who else someone we are romantically interested in is seeing. We know that we are in a strategic battle, but our actual opponents are often invisible. Sun Tzu clarifies this picture. Everything that can be of benefit to us can also be of benefit to our competition and vice versa. It doesn't matter who our opponents are or where they are. If we do not win some benefit, we must assume that it goes to the competition. If we do win some benefit, we can see it as taking from the competition.

Lesson 51: Managing Costs

How can you best manage the costs of meeting challenges so as to positively affect the outcome of the contest?

A.   You must keep your expenditures low.

B.   You must keep your opponents' costs high.

C.   You must invest only in what will return the investment.

D.   You must focus on getting resources from the competition.

> *You can kill the enemy and frustrate him as well.*
> *Take the enemy's strength from him by stealing away his supplies.*
>
> THE ART OF WAR 2:4.6-7

Answer: D. You must focus on getting resources from the competition.

Here we come to the core of Sun Tzu's advice on managing the costs of competition. All the warnings about the risks of competition come down to this. We want to increase our resources while cutting off the resources going to the competition. The *best* way to do this is to take resources from our opponents. For example, at Clearbridge, not only do we want bookstores to carry our *Art of War* books, we also price our books to discourage anyone from buying other versions. We do not want bookstores to have any reason to carry our competitors' inferior versions.

Winning sales, distributors, employees, and investors from business competition defeats and discourages opponents. It weakens them as future opponents. It is good when we win sales, distributors, employees, and investors for ourselves. It is even better when we take them from our competitors.

Many strategies that don't seem to make sense on the surface make sense once we consider their effect on our opponents. Businesses cannot make money giving away product. If, however, by giving away product we starve our competition, we win a great deal. This was exactly the strategy that Microsoft used in competing with Netscape. Microsoft still doesn't get any income from its Internet Explorer, but that doesn't matter. It removed Netscape from the scene as a future opponent. We can see from this example that Sun Tzu is right. We can kill opponents by frustrating them. This is why resources taken from the competition are so much more valuable than those we generate on our own.

Lesson 52: The Key Competitive Battles

Which competitive campaigns are the most important in determining your eventual success?

A.   Campaigns for position.

B.   Campaigns for dominance.

C.   Campaigns for resources.

D.   Campaigns for people's minds.

> *Fight for the enemy's supply wagons.*
> *Capture his supplies by using overwhelming force.*
> *Reward the first who capture them.*
> *Then change their banners and flags.*
> *Mix them in with your own to increase your supply line.*
> *Keep your soldiers strong by providing for them.*
> *This is what it means to beat the enemy while you grow more powerful.*
>
> THE ART OF WAR 2:4.8-14

Answer: C. Campaigns for resources.

There are many ways we can improve our position. We can grow our organizations. We can force our opponents to back down in face-to-face challenges. We can establish our superior position in people's minds. Position, dominance, and control of people's minds are extremely important in Sun Tzu's system of strategy. However, these are not usually won through competitive campaigns.

Sun Tzu teaches us to attack "places that opponents must defend." These places represent supply lines, sources of food and water, and any other resources necessary to continue the battle. Our first plan of attack should be to take away our competition's resources.

Sun Tzu gives us this simple formula for attacking an opponent's resources. First, we identify the opponent's resources. Next, we find a resource that is guarded lightly enough that we can take it with overwhelming force. Then we put together the effort to win it. When we have won it, we share the rewards with those who helped us in the process. Then we add that resource to our own supplies. Finally, we advertise our victory. All of this weakens the enemy, both physically and psychologically, while making us stronger.

Lesson 53: Your Key Ability

What is the key to your ability to win the competition's resources?

A.   Your knowledge.

B.   Your strength.

C.   Your leadership.

D.   Your planning.

> *Make victory in war pay for itself.*
> *Avoid expensive, long campaigns.*
> *The military commander's knowledge is the key.*
> *It determines if the civilian officials can govern.*
> *It determines if the nation's households are peaceful or a danger to the state.*

THE ART OF WAR 2:5.1-5

Answer: A. Your knowledge.

This stanza summarizes the central lessons of this chapter. First, we must make victory pay. It isn't enough to win. Our success must have a payoff. Next, to get to that payoff, we must control our costs. To do that, we must avoid expensive, long campaigns, but controlling costs isn't enough. We must also win resources from our opponents. This should be our real focus in meeting competitive challenges. The key to winning resources is knowledge.

Sun Tzu teaches that knowledge is the single most important resource in strategy. It can be used to replace all other resources. We see this theme repeated over and over again in Sun Tzu's work. Success comes primarily from knowledge and information. We must know what resources are available. We must know which of them our competition has left unguarded. With that knowledge, we know where we must focus our efforts.

Often people starting a business want to know how to get venture capital or a loan from a bank. They are looking in the wrong place for resources. Investment capital is usually very difficult to win, or, in Sun Tzu's terms, very strongly guarded. Debt is expensive and lasts a long time. The easiest resources for a business to win are customers and distribution channels. Most business competitors take these resources too much for granted to protect them well. These are the resources that new businesses usually capture first.

Chapter 3

謀攻

Planning an Attack

In this chapter, Sun Tzu discusses the issues that we must address before we start a competitive campaign. The topics are unity, focus, and the intersecting roles of a military commander and the nation's leader. The central idea of this chapter is that unity and focus are the source of true power. No matter how large and seemingly powerful, an organization that is divided and unfocused is actually weak.

Sun Tzu puts the typical view of competition into a larger context. Most people think that power comes from size: a bigger force is stronger than a smaller one. In the media, only big celebrities, big government, big corporations, and big events make the news. Sun Tzu sees this view as too narrow. Size is something of an illusion. It looks powerful, but it isn't necessarily. It is what is going on beneath the surface—the cohesion and devotion of the force—that determines strength.

An army of any size can win, but, in Sun Tzu's words, that force has to have the right attack strategy. Our size relative to our competitor's determines the strategy we choose. Sun Tzu is very specific about the strategy we must use given the relative size of our competitor. Sun Tzu also reemphasizes the critical importance of the right competitive attitude. Though he counsels us to avoid destructive conflict, he doesn't want us to think that this means we can avoid competition. Indeed, he tells us that we must always be seeking those competitive situations in which we are certain to win.

The chapter ends with a discussion of politics and its divisive effects on competitive organizations. Political issues arise from competing interests within organizations. They most likely arise when we plan our attack, that is, movement into a new area. We must work carefully to avoid allowing these divisions to cripple our efforts.

Lesson 54: Understanding Strength

How can you tell strong competitors from weak ones?

A.   Strong competitors are smart; weak ones are dumb.

B.   Strong competitors are experienced; weak ones are novices.

C.   Strong competitors are united; weak ones are divided.

D.   Strong competitors are large; weak ones are small.

> *Everyone relies on the arts of war.*
> *A united nation is strong. A divided nation is weak.*
> *A united army is strong. A divided army is weak.*
> *A united force is strong. A divided force is weak.*
> *United men are strong. Divided men are weak.*
> *A united unit is strong. A divided unit is weak.*
>
> THE ART OF WAR 3:1.1-11

Answer: C. Strong competitors are united; weak ones are divided.

Sun Tzu redefines the idea of strength for strategic purposes. The natural mistake is to consider size and strength as the same thing. Sun Tzu teaches that this view is totally wrong. Size doesn't matter. Large forces can be beaten by smaller ones. The difference that determines strength is not in size but in unity and focus.

Scale—that is, large differences in size—does matter, but it determines the particular strategy we use, not whether or not a given force is strong. This topic is covered later in the chapter.

In the translation, we use the word "united," but Sun Tzu actually used the Chinese ideogram for the number "one," contrasting it with the character that means "divided" or "broken." He meant "unity" or "oneness" but he also meant focus and single-mindedness. In the original Chinese, the key concept is *quan*, which means "completeness" or "wholeness." He means unity of purpose, ideas, and people. A related idea, *zhuan*, means "concentration" or "focus." By this measure, a company focused on selling one type or category of product alone is stronger than one that sells many different types of products. A nation in which everyone strongly agrees on basic principles is stronger than one that is deeply divided. In a real competitive battle, such division of purpose and focus creates weaknesses and openings for competition.

Lesson 55: Your Strategic Goals

What should your strategic goals be?

A.   To use your strength to win the key battles you fight.

B.   To use your strength to win most battles you fight.

C.   To use your strength to win every battle you fight.

D.   To use your strength to avoid battle.

> *Unity works because it enables you to win every battle you fight.*
> *Still, this is the foolish goal of a weak leader.*
> *Avoid battle and make the enemy's men surrender.*
> *This is the right goal for a superior leader.*
>
> THE ART OF WAR 3:1.12-15

Answer: D. To use your strength to avoid battle.

Again, Sun Tzu wants to undermine our natural preoccupation with beating our opponents. Competition is not about conflict. Long-term success cannot come from fighting costly battles. Indeed, according to Sun Tzu's method, conflict is the *failure* of successful competitive strategy. Conflict is dangerous and destructive. Think of this in terms of animals competing for mates in nature. The most successful males are not those who win numerous battles with competing males; rather, they are those who discourage others from challenging them. This is why the various forms of sexual display, reflecting Sun Tzu's idea of deception or illusion, become so important in animal courtship. Display takes the place of actual battles.

So, in planning to meet a challenge or move into a new competitive arena, we seek to put ourselves in a position in which others will be discouraged from competing with us. Ideally, we want them not to challenge us, to surrender the position that we desire. Opponents can concede to us for a number of reasons, but they all boil down to just one. We must make the cost of fighting us *seem* greater than the value of the prize.

Too many willing competitors overestimate the value of competition (the prize) while underestimating the cost (the price). Their mistake leads us to good strategies in competition. We can discover areas or niches that others consider worthless. We can develop positions that others view as unassailable. These two approaches give us the rewards of competition without the cost of conflict.

Lesson 56: The Best Attack Strategy

What is the best attack strategy?

A.   Attack while the opposition is still planning.

B.   Attack the opposition's partnerships.

C.   Attack the opposition's people.

D.   Attack the opposition's strongholds.

> *The best policy is to attack while the enemy is still planning.*
> *The next best is to disrupt alliances.*
> *The next best is to attack the opposing army.*
> *The worst is to attack the enemy's cities.*
>
> THE ART OF WAR 3:2.1-4

Answer: A. Attack while the opposition is still planning.

This is a fundamental rule in Sun Tzu's method. We want to make our move into a new area—Sun Tzu's definition of attack—before any of our potential opponents are prepared. By claiming our territory, displaying our strength and commitment, and establishing a strong defensive position, we want to change our competitors' plans and discourage them from coming into conflict with us. This requires quick decisions and misleading others. Every other form of attack is less desirable than a preemptive strike. The purpose of a preemptive strike is to win a position without a battle.

If we cannot make a preemptive strike, the next best attack is indirect, one that breaks apart alliances. Remember that strength comes from unity and focus. By dividing opponents into opposing groups or distracting them with competing goals, we undermine their unity and focus. This attack weakens the enemy and also discourages battles. The last two types of attacks, targeting opposing forces and fortifications, are always more costly.

The problem with the economics of market niches is that once a niche becomes popular (what Sun Tzu calls "contested ground") there are too many willing competitors. However, the marketplace offers infinite territory. Fighting over popular, established territory is simply a failure of imagination. The only legitimate attack is to go after new territory that no one else has yet discovered. Getting to that area first gives us time to build up our position and develop the value of the territory. Competitors should realize the value of our position only when that position is unassailable.

Lesson 57: Attacking Strong Positions

If you must attack an opponent's strong points, how do you do it successfully?

A.   You must take time to build enough strength to attack.

B.   You must encircle the city and cut off its supplies.

C.   You must swarm the city with overpowering force.

D.   You must never attack an opponent's stronghold directly.

> *This is what happens when you attack a city.*
> *You can attempt it, but you cannot finish it.*
> *First you must make siege engines.*
> *You need the right equipment and machinery.*
> *You use three months and still cannot win.*
> *Then, you try to encircle the area.*
> *You use three more months without making progress.*
> *The commander still doesn't win and this angers him.*
> *He then tries to swarm the city.*
> *This kills a third of his officers and men.*
> *He still isn't able to draw the enemy out of the city.*
> *This attack is a disaster.*

THE ART OF WAR 3:2.5-15

Answer: D. You must never attack an opponent's stronghold directly.

A basic strategic principle is that an attacking force must be several times larger than the defending one to win an entrenched position. Because of this fact, Sun Tzu's view is simple: we can always find better and more productive uses for our time and efforts than attacking an opponent's strong points.

Again, this is an idea that is commonly violated in the real world by those who don't understand strategy. Businesses are always trying to copy leading products and directly challenge other companies for market leadership. The result is that most of these challenges fail, wasting a lot of money in the process.

Why directly challenge a strong position controlled by an opponent when the world is full of opportunities? Sun Tzu sees this common tendency as a lack of vision and initiative. The appeal of established positions is that they are proven. However, no position is guaranteed to be valuable in the future. The way to undermine a strong position is to establish a stronger position elsewhere. This approach is much less expensive in terms of time and effort.

Lesson 58: Overcoming Strong Opponents

How then can you overcome your opponents if you cannot attack their strong points directly?

A.   You must not go after opponents; you must simply avoid them by changing your position.

B.   You must first collaborate with your opponents and then turn against them.

C.   You must lure opponents into a series of small competitive challenges that you are sure to win.

D.   You must keep hidden from your opponents and secretly build your position.

> *Make good use of war.*
> *Make the enemy's troops surrender.*
> *You can do this fighting only minor battles.*
> *You can draw their men out of their cities.*
> *You can do it with small attacks.*
> *You can destroy the men of a nation.*
> *You must keep your campaign short.*

THE ART OF WAR 3:3.1-7

Answer: C. You must lure opponents into a series of small competitive challenges that you are sure to win.

Though strategy doesn't focus directly on beating opponents, we shouldn't mistakenly think that Sun Tzu preaches total avoidance of conflict. As we advance our position, we must eventually confront and overcome our opposition. However, we must pick the time, place, and nature of those confrontations.

Initially, we build up our position while avoiding meeting our opponents in head-to-head contests. We may also avoid competition by changing our position, but we cannot actually discourage opposition until we demonstrate that others cannot challenge us. Until we win in direct challenges, our potential opposition doesn't know how strong—united and focused—we are. The secret is meeting opponents only in situations in which we are certain to win—that is, when we have more *local* power in small battles that are quickly decided in our favor.

Lesson 59: The Competitive Attitude

What attitude should you have about overcoming opposition?

A.   You must attack opponents only after they have threatened you.

B.   You must be totally dedicated to overcoming all opposition.

C.   You must see attacking opponents as a necessary evil.

D.   You must bide your time, protect your resources, and outlast all opposition.

> *You must use total war, fighting with everything you have.*
> *Never stop fighting when at war.*
> *You can gain complete advantage.*
> *To do this, you must plan your strategy of attack.*
>
> THE ART OF WAR 3:3.8-11

Answer: B. You must be totally dedicated to overcoming all opposition.

We want to avoid direct conflict, but this doesn't mean that we aren't totally dedicated to overcoming all opposition. We must push against our limits continually. We must always be looking for ways and places in which we can undermine those who oppose us. Sun Tzu advises patience in the sense that we must await our opportunities, but he also wants us to embrace the competitive challenge and never lose sight of it. Just because we don't risk our resources in conflict doesn't mean we shouldn't be using everything we have every day to undermine our opponents and their position.

For example, software leader Microsoft has been criticized for being too aggressive, but Sun Tzu's definition of "too aggressive" is attacking in situations in which we might lose. Microsoft has traditionally used every tool at its disposal to dominate its competitors. In business, the approach has worked flawlessly. It is not its size or its monopoly position that gives Microsoft its success. Microsoft's success comes from its relentlessness. If the company made any mistake in that effort, it wasn't its aggressiveness but its initial ignorance about appeasing the forces of government.

The successful people in life are those who never quit. They keep on coming, but they don't waste their efforts in battles that they can't easily and quickly win. They are always advancing their position. It may take them years to completely undermine their opponents, but they keep building their position until they do.

Lesson 60: Deciding Attack Strategy

What information is the basis of your attack strategy?

A.   Your knowledge of the relative size of your opposition.

B.   Your knowledge of your opponent's goals and plans.

C.   Your knowledge of the psychology of your opponents.

D.   Your knowledge of the local terrain.

> *The rules for making war are:*
> *If you outnumber the enemy forces ten to one, surround them.*
> *If you outnumber them five to one, attack them.*
> *If you outnumber them two to one, divide them.*
> *If you are equal, then find an advantageous battle.*
> *If you are fewer, defend against them.*
> *If you are much weaker, evade them.*
>
> THE ART OF WAR 3:3.12-18

Answer: A. Your knowledge of the relative size of your opposition.

Organizational size is not the basis of strength. However, relative size determines our basic strategy. We are looking for *local* superiority. We can target and beat much larger opponents, but we must divide to conquer them. In each situation, our strategy must be designed to minimize destructive conflict and create a situation in which the competition will be forced to "surrender" to us.

Local superiority is situational. Even a small organization can put ten times more resources into a specific situation than a much larger one can. Our strategy must be to arrange situations in such a way that we are the dominant force. Unless we have five times the force, we aren't in a position to attack. We still have more work to do.

This local superiority is often difficult to measure. Competition in business can be measured in sales, or, more precisely, market share, but the "market" depends how we define a group of customers. Markets can be defined and divided many different ways. The same is true of any other competitive arena. What we are searching for is a way to define and divide the ground in a way that gives us absolute, unquestionable superiority in our particular area. This requires knowledge of the battleground and our opponents' exact position in it.

Lesson 61: The Challenge of Size

Can you win the competitive battle simply by amassing the largest force?

A.   This should be your basic strategy.

B.   Large forces are expensive to build and costly to support.

C.   Both large and small forces have strengths and weaknesses.

D.   Small forces are better suited to small targets.

> *Small forces are not powerful.*
> *However, large forces cannot catch them.*
>
> THE ART OF WAR 3:3.19-20

Answer: C. Both large and small forces have strengths and weaknesses.

Size cuts both ways. Large opponents have more resources, but they cannot move or change quickly or easily. This is no less true today than it was twenty-five hundred years ago.

The advantages and disadvantages of size are the basis of all competition. The power of the large counters and is countered by the swiftness of the small. Philosophically, Sun Tzu clearly prefers the agility of speed over the power of size. This is because his strategic focus is on the future rather than the past. Large forces, in general, are too costly to support and take too long to assemble. With agility, we can create situations in which we have the necessary superiority of forces at a given place and time even though our total forces are much smaller than our opponent's forces.

Remember, every business that is big today once started as a small company working in a small niche, running away from larger competitors. The fact that these companies survived to become large shows that they were successful at never confronting a large competitor directly. Instead, they avoided direct confrontations, competing in areas where their larger competitors were at a disadvantage.

Large competitors are good in large competitive arenas, whereas small competitors are successful in small niches. There are many more small niches than there are bigger ones. For example, large companies make up only a small, and currently shrinking, part of the economy. In this, the competition of the marketplace is like nature: there are many more mice in the world than elephants.

Lesson 62: The Role of Stakeholders

After you make a decision, what is the role of those who have a vested interest in your success?

A.   You should encourage them to challenge your decision.

B.   You must make sure that they approve your plans.

C.   You are in charge, and they should support you.

D.   They must finance you.

> *You must master command.*
> *The nation must support you.*
>
> THE ART OF WAR 3:4.1-2

Answer: C. You are in charge, and they should support you.

Sun Tzu wrote in a feudal era. The will of the state or nation was the will of the duke, king, or emperor. The people of the nation were not consulted. Despite the deference of the times toward rulers, Sun Tzu thought that these rulers should keep out of military matters. Once a ruler hired a commander, the ruler's role was relegated to supporting that commander until he was dead or replaced.

In modern organizations, even the most powerful CEO or business owner has a number of people to whom he or she must answer, such as bankers, outside investors, stockholders, and unions. Even the president has to answer to Congress, the press, and the American people.

Still, Sun Tzu's advice is applicable. The people who rely on the success of the decision-maker cannot continually second-guess his or her decisions. Doing so is simply too divisive. Ideas are discussed, but once decisions are made the debate and criticisms must end and action must begin.

Decision-making isn't easy. When we are in charge, we must make decisions. Those who depend on us must trust and support us. We must step up to the challenge without worrying about winning complete consensus. No decision is perfect. Consensus won't make the decision better. Endless debate simply delays decisions. The future holds an infinite number of possibilities. We should keep those who depend on us informed, but they cannot continually second-guess us. Every decision cannot generate recriminations simply because few decisions are perfect.

Lesson 63: Decision-Making

Why shouldn't those who are directly affected involve themselves in high-level strategic decisions?

A. They will destroy the strength of the organization.

B. They will hurt the confidence of their leaders.

C. They don't have the right priorities or concerns.

D. They don't know the true nature of the situation.

> *Supporting the military makes the nation powerful.*
> *Not supporting the military makes the nation weak.*
>
> THE ART OF WAR 3:4.3-4

Answer: A. They will destroy the strength of the organization.

Sun Tzu puts the problem into a context anyone should be able to appreciate. The ultimate result of weakening the control of the commander is weakening the organization as a whole. Decisions have no value unless they are executed in a timely manner. Remember what makes an organization strong? Strength comes first from unity. The organization's leader must have command. If his or her decisions are executed, those decisions are more likely to prove good ones. The organization and its members will do well. If members and other stakeholders fail to execute their leader's decisions, they weaken the entire organization.

This is a matter of priorities. For a competitive organization, nothing is as important as unity. Good leaders inspire trust, and good followers are willing to trust. Making the "right" decision is never as important as maintaining organizational focus and unity. If a leader's decisions are continuously questioned, debated, and not supported, the organization is damaged. It doesn't matter how good or bad the decision is; we do the organization proportionally more damage than the benefit that could ever be derived from the best possible decisions. Bad decisions can be corrected. Weakened organizations cannot be rehabilitated.

A good way to spot likely winners in any challenge is to find organizations with strong leaders. To spot losers, look for companies with no one willing to make tough decisions.

Lesson 64: The Mistakes of Politicians

What mistakes do followers make in involving themselves in decision-making and criticizing their leader's decisions?

A.   They are too aggressive in risking competition.

B.   They are too fearful about risking competition.

C.   They are too confused, not knowing what to do.

D.   They are at once too aggressive, too fearful, and too confused about what to do.

> *Politicians create problems for the military in three different ways.*
> *Ignorant of the army's inability to advance, they order an advance.*
> *Ignorant of the army's inability to withdraw, they order a withdrawal.*
> *We call this tying up the army.*
> *Politicians don't understand the army's business.*
> *Still, they think they can run an army.*
> *This confuses the army's officers.*

THE ART OF WAR 3:4.5-11

Answer: D. They are at once too aggressive, too fearful, and too confused about what to do.

In business, investors, bankers, stockholders, employees, and other stakeholders know exactly what they want. They want to make money and not lose it. In government, competing politicians know what they want. They want more power. No matter what the nature of the organization, stakeholders are driven by both greed and fear. These emotions have nothing to do with running a competitive organization. Greed makes us too aggressive. Fear makes us too conservative. Switching back and forth between these two emotions creates confusion.

Our decisions must be based upon the situation we are in at the moment, but strategy means doing what works over the long term. Too much immediate concern for eventual gains or losses takes the focus off of action and creates doubt, uncertainty, and paralysis.

Organizational politics arise from competing goals within the organization. To be successful, we must be focused on our external goals. Politicians can lose sight of the critical importance of their organization's success in trying to meet their own personal goals.

Lesson 65: Clarity of Authority

How do other decision-makers in an organization view the involvement of followers in decision-making?

A.   They see it as taking the burden of decision off their shoulders.

B.   They see it as improving understanding within the organization.

C.   They see it as increasing the freedom in the organization.

D.   They see it as improving teamwork and commitment.

> *Politicians don't know the army's chain of command.*
> *They give the army too much freedom.*
> *This will create distrust among the army's officers.*
>
> THE ART OF WAR 3:4.12-14

Answer: C. They see it as increasing the freedom in the organization.

Americans and most other people see freedom as a good thing. Certainly freedom of choice is a good thing, but within organizations roles must be clear and well defined. The involvement of followers in decision-making creates an ever-active court of appeals. If some don't like their leader's decisions, they can question those decisions and the endless debates begin. Running an organization is a balancing act in which some people are always going to be unhappy with some decisions. Their ability to go over the head of their leader creates distrust in the organization. No one ever knows for sure what decisions are final and when.

Once more, unity is what gives an organization strength. The organization must be focused on its competitive goals. However, the larger reality is that everyone in the organization has his or her own individual goals. Since everyone depends upon the organization, we subordinate our individual goals to the larger shared goals. We each play our own role. We have decisions that we can make and we have decisions that we must accept and execute. This is what defines the chain of command.

Sun Tzu knows what happens to an organization when the chain of command isn't clear. He knows that some of the organization's officers, many of whom think that they are smarter than the commander, will begin to put their own ideas and priorities first. Without a clear commander, everyone is fighting for power and recognition within the organization instead of fighting the competition outside it.

Lesson 66: Internal Political Battles

What is the eventual result of internal political battles within an organization?

A.   A new, stronger commander will emerge.

B.   The entire organization is weakened, inviting destruction.

C.   Competition slows and grows more expensive.

D.   Competition waits until order is restored.

> *The entire army becomes confused and distrusting.*
> *This invites invasion by many different rivals.*
> *We say correctly that disorder in an army kills victory.*

THE ART OF WAR 3:4.15-17

Answer: B. The entire organization is weakened, inviting destruction.

When people are free to debate decisions, the organization opens itself to internal politics. Everyone begins fighting for his or her individual self-interests. There is no happy outcome.

In a well-run organization, the success of individuals depends on the success of the organization as a whole. In poorly run organizations, certain individuals can be extremely successful even though the organization itself is failing. Poorly run organizations generate constant internal political battles because everyone distrusts the system. Distrust and conflict between different managers create distrust and conflict between different divisions. A strong, united organization becomes a divided, weak one.

Internal strife within an organization encourages external competition. The sharks smell blood in the water. The pace of competition actually speeds up as opponents try to take advantage of a poorly run competitor.

People who instigate and engage in internal political battles often feel as though they are helping their organizations. By discrediting a leader whom they do not agree with, they hope to create an environment in which a new, better leader can arise. Even assuming that their intentions are good, this type of change for the better almost never happens in this way. What usually happens is that the existing leader is weakened and the organization is weakened, often completely disabled.

Strong, united, focused leadership is vital to the success of an organization. Weak, divided, distracted leadership is almost always fatal.

Lesson 67: The Factors in Success

How many factors are important in planning for movement into a new competitive arena?

A. There are five major factors.

B. There are three major factors.

C. There are seven major factors.

D. There are nine major factors.

> *You must know five things to win:*
> *Victory comes from knowing when to attack and when to avoid battle.*
> *Victory comes from correctly using large and small forces.*
> *Victory comes from everyone sharing the same goals.*
> *Victory comes from finding opportunities in problems.*
> *Victory comes from having a capable commander and the government leaving*
> *   him alone.*
> *You must know these five things.*
> *You then know the theory of victory.*

THE ART OF WAR 3:5.1-8

Answer: A. There are five major factors.

Here, Sun Tzu summarizes the basic ideas in this chapter in a slightly different order than he presented them. He began the chapter by discussing the strength of unity, which he calls here "sharing the same goals." The chapter then covers when to attack—when enemies are still planning, the first topic listed here. The chapter then discusses how relative size determines our strategy of attack—that is, "how to use large and small forces." The chapter then emphases that both large and small forces have their abilities and liabilities, teaching us how to "turn problems into opportunities." The chapter ends with a discussion of not second-guessing the commander—that is, "having a capable commander and leaving him alone."

All five of these issues are tied to the five original factors in war. Philosophy is sharing the same goals. The climate determines when to attack and when to avoid battle. The ground is the basis for turning problems into opportunities. Leadership means trusting the leader and leaving him or her alone. Methods relate to using both large and small forces correctly.

Lesson 68: The Basis of Success

What is the basis for Sun Tzu's theory about when and how to move into a new area to assure success?

A.   It is a theory of size and unity.

B.   It is a theory of complete command.

C.   It is a theory of force and speed.

D.   It is a theory of knowledge.

> *We say:*
> *Know yourself and know your enemy.*
> *You will be safe in every battle.*
> *You may know yourself but not know the enemy.*
> *You will then lose one battle for every one you win.*
> *You may not know yourself or the enemy.*
> *You will then lose every battle.*
>
> THE ART OF WAR 3:6.1-7

Answer: D. It is a theory of knowledge.

Although we have been talking about unity, strength, speed, force, and the nature of command, Sun Tzu reminds us at the close that this is all really about knowledge. We have to know our focus, our shared goal. This brings us back to our underlying philosophy. We have to know what our opponents are doing and their position. We have to know the relative size of our forces. We have to pick the right tactics to use—our methods. We have to know the right relationship between the commander and those who execute his or her decisions.

According to this strategic view, not knowing our opponents can be costly, but not knowing ourselves can be fatal. To catch competitors unprepared, we have to know what they are planning. To outnumber their forces at the point of attack, we have to know where they are moving. However, to keep our forces united and strong, we have to know that our people value our goals and that they are looking only one place for guidance.

Once again, Sun Tzu repeats his underlying concept that success in competition depends totally upon knowledge and information. In the last chapter, the message was that information reduces costs. In this chapter, the message is that knowledge creates unity, focus, and strength.

Chapter 4

形

Positioning

Though this chapter is simply named "Positioning," the original Chinese name for this chapter is an ideogram *xing*, which means "position," "form," or "shape." This chapter describes a dance that represents the continual search for a strategic advantage. In this dance, we try to gain a relative advantage in position by continually making adjustments to our position. In response to our moves, others change their position. Then in response to their moves, we move again. The process is dynamic and continuous.

As in all dances, the key element is timing. Timing is derived from the key element *tian* (heaven, climate, or weather), which we described in chapter 1. The climate, or tempo of the dance, is beyond our control. Changes and shifts in the larger environment have their own pace. What we control is our reaction to the changing situation. We control how we position ourselves while looking for an advantage.

What do we do when we first meet a challenge? Are our first moves aggressive or defensive? What does an opening or opportunity look like? How can we be certain that an opportunity is real?

When we are on the offensive, how do we act? What do we do when we must defend? What is the goal of defense? When we see an opportunity, what must we do? How important is courage to success? How does positioning assure our success? How can we be certain that we will find an opportunity? What calculations do we make to find the right position?

These are the questions that this chapter addresses. The chapter takes us in a logical circle. It starts with how we are controlled by our situation and have to accept its limitations, but ends showing how we can eventually control that situation and change it by our positioning.

Lesson 69: Initiation

What should your first action accomplish in meeting a challenge?

A. You should first deceive your opponent.

B. You should first create an opportunity.

C. You should first avoid failure.

D. You should first test your opponent's resolve.

> *Learn from the history of successful battles.*
> *Your first actions should deny victory to the enemy.*
> *You pay attention to your enemy to find the way to win.*
> *You alone can deny victory to the enemy.*
> *Only your enemy can allow you to win.*

THE ART OF WAR 4:1.1-5

Answer: C. You should first avoid failure.

Whenever Sun Tzu refers to history in his work, he means observing what usually works over a span of time, or, as we would say today, what works statistically. In responding to a competitive threat or challenge, the best first move is usually defensive. We protect ourselves from change.

The movements described in this chapter are the interplay between defensive and offensive actions. When we initially respond to a change or challenge, we don't know enough about our situation. We do not know if the time is right to move forward. We therefore must assume that we are in an inferior position and defend ourselves. In the competitive dance, the key is survival. We can destroy ourselves if we move forward at the wrong time. So we begin cautiously.

While protecting ourselves, we watch our opponents. We want to see what moves they make. Like a good dance partner, we respond to their moves. We will not get the opportunity to move forward unless others give us the opportunity.

For example, if we are starting a new business, our first moves have to ensure that we are not put out of business, that we have the money to survive. Eighty percent of new businesses go out of business within the first two years. We must give ourselves time to test our ideas and learn. We must act carefully, doing what we know works.

Lesson 70: The Basis of Battle

What is the basic "fight" in any competition?

A.   The fight for superiority.

B.   The fight for knowledge.

C.   The fight for position.

D.   The fight to prevent the opponent's victory.

> *You must fight well.*
> *You can prevent the enemy's victory.*
> *You cannot win unless the enemy enables your victory.*

THE ART OF WAR 4:1.6-8

Answer: D. The fight to prevent the opponent's victory.

As we said at the beginning of this book, Sun Tzu's vocabulary was more precise than our own. Earlier Sun Tzu redefined strength as unity and focus. Now, he redefines the term "fight." We fight to prevent the opponent's victory. We fight to preserve our options and the ability to choose our own course of action. In other words, we fight against domination or control. Fighting is a defensive strategy. This type of battle is a short-term response to threatening changes. Longer term, we focus to create local superiority. We spy to obtain knowledge. We move to new positions, but we fight to defend our position when it is suddenly challenged.

When we fight, we use all our efforts to stay in the game. Fighting is important in Sun Tzu's strategy, but he doesn't use the term as an invitation to conflict. Fighting is always a matter of our own survival. It doesn't guarantee our victory.

Where does victory come from? Sun Tzu considers victory a gift given by one participant in the competitive struggle to another. We cannot win victory unless we find an opening left by others. Victory comes from moving into that opening and advancing our position.

We take what our opponents give us. It is a free choice. The role of choice in our interactions in a free economy is obvious. All actions in free markets are voluntary. As customers, we take what suppliers offer us. As suppliers, we take what our customers offer us. When we move into new territory, others must leave us an opening or opportunity to advance.

Lesson 71: The Creation of Opportunity

How do you create opportunities to win?

A.   By planning a series of logical steps.

B.   By creating weaknesses in your enemy's position.

C.   By knowing your position's strengths.

D.   You don't create opportunities; you see them .

We say:
You see the opportunity for victory; you don't create it.

THE ART OF WAR 4:1.9-10

Answer: D. You don't create opportunities; you see them.

Vision is the central skill addressed in this chapter. Vision means seeing an opportunity, that is, being able to perceive an opening. The key element we are exploring is again *tian*—the climate, the weather, or trends. Weather includes the seasons and timing. We don't control the weather. We can only *see and foresee* the changing of seasons, the tendencies of change, and the trends over time. These trends tell us what to *look* for at any given time. We are not creating the opportunity that we need. We are on watch for it.

The limitations on what we can do are an important element in Sun Tzu's strategic system. We are in a dance. We control our movements but not those of others or the general trends of the time. We must take our cues from what is happening in the larger environment. We must keep time with change, the music of life. We must study the signs of activity. We must sense the direction of momentum. The situation around us is fluid. We respond to what our situation dictates. We must watch carefully and forget about trying to control the dance. We must perceive the tempo of change and see into our future.

Every great idea in business and society has come from this insight into the direction of change. Business innovators don't create the need for their product nor the science that makes invention possible. They see the need for change and the possibility of new solutions. New businesses don't arise from working harder or even better. They are created by vision. Founders of successful organizations are simply the first to see an opportunity and take advantage of it while others are still making plans.

Lesson 72: Watching for Opportunities

What situation clearly identifies an opportunity?

A.   Whether or not you can improve your position successfully.

B.   The complete dedication of those who support you.

C.   The clear weakness of your opponents.

D.   Favorable conditions in terms of the trends and battlefield.

> *You are sometimes unable to win.*
> *You must then defend.*
> *You will eventually be able to win.*
> *You must then attack.*
> *Defend when you have insufficient strength to win.*
> *Attack when you have more strength than you need to win.*
>
> THE ART OF WAR 4:2.1-6

Answer: A. Whether or not you can improve your position successfully.

When we can successfully improve our position, we must do so. In the competitive dance, we have only two possible moves. We can defend, that is, stay where we are, or we can attack, that is, attempt to move forward and improve our position. Which of these courses we choose depends entirely on how certain we are that we can be successful in improving our position. Either we will win a better position or we will fail to do so. If we are certain to improve our position, we must attack. If we cannot improve our position then we must defend.

The attitude of our supporters, the weakness of opponents, and conditions on the field may or may not create a situation in which we can improve our position. Remember, we only improve our position if we are stronger after the move than we were before. Some moves can be unpopular with our supporters and still make us stronger. Other moves have nothing to do with our opponents' weaknesses and strengths. Some openings can be so unopposed that even the conditions of the field are unimportant.

We cannot use force to create or invent an opportunity; it will come to us if we defend well enough. We simply must recognize opportunities when they present themselves. Opportunities may not take the form we expect. Their only distinguishing feature is whether or not they allow us to move forward in such a way as to strengthen our position.

Lesson 73: Defense and Offense

How does your situation in the short term determine your movements?

A.   You must always keep moving in every situation.

B.   You must always move to attack when you need to defend yourself.

C.   You must stop to defend and move to attack.

D.   You must minimize movement in every situation.

> *You must defend yourself well.*
> *Save your forces and dig in.*
> *You must attack well.*
> *Move your forces when you have a clear advantage.*

THE ART OF WAR 4:2.7-10

Answer: C. You must stop to defend and move to attack.

Generally, defensive action means protecting our existing position. When we are suddenly threatened, we must pause in our advance to first shore up our existing position. We must dig in and depend on the strengths of our current position. We must leverage our position and strengthen it. In business terms, defense means we keep our current products but improve them. In political terms, it means continuing with our existing programs but making them better. We keep our existing supporters but deepen our relationships.

Longer term, the best defense is a good offense. We want to fight to win our opponents' territory and not have to battle opponents invading our territory. When faced with an invasion by opponents, we can threaten them with a counter invasion to deter their thrust. However, these are long-term strategies, not short-term reactions to an immediate threat.

Movement is costly in terms of defense. We can only move when we know that defense of our current position is unnecessary. Our current markets and customers are safe. When we can overpower the competition, we must take advantage of the situation and move.

When we face a threat, our first moves are always defensive. We must solidify and build up our existing position. We shouldn't pursue new goals until we are certain we can hold our current advantages. Good organizations first make sure that they build up a dominant, safe position. Then they expand from that solid base outward.

Lesson 74: Ensuring Success

How do you define success when the situation demands that you defend?

A. Success comes from weakening competitors as they attack you.

B. Success comes from growing your forces while you await opportunity.

C. Success comes from taking resources away from your competition.

D. Success comes from preserving your forces until you see an opportunity.

> *You must protect your forces until you can completely triumph.*
>
> THE ART OF WAR 4:2.11

Answer: D. Success comes from preserving your forces until you see an opportunity.

We must recognize what we can control and what we cannot. In a defensive position, we must limit our expectations. Defense means preservation. We minimize our actions when we are defending. We may not be able to get any stronger when we are defending ourselves against an attack. We simply don't want to grow any weaker.

We must take care not to overstep the limitations of our situation. If we are attacked we may weaken the enemy, but we should not invite attack. By being forced into defense, we are delayed from making progress. In business, we never want competitors to come after our existing customers. In politics, we don't want opponents wooing our supporters. Defense is a waiting condition. We are waiting to see the situation change. If those attacking us cannot make any progress, they will eventually give up the battle. We must trust that the situation will change. However, we cannot switch from defense to offense until we see an opportunity to advance.

Few organizations show the necessary patience and focus when they are defending their territory. Even when they are actively attacked, they tend to take their existing position for granted. They try to continue their plans to advance when they should be defending.

We must be patient when we are under attack. We must watch for our opportunities. We waste resources trying to find ways to expand when expansion is a poor decision.

Lesson 75: Taking Advantage of Opportunity

What two things do you need to do to improve your position?

A. You must preserve your men and wait.

B. You must wait and see the opportunity.

C. You must see the opportunity and move your men.

D. You must move your men and willingly sacrifice them.

> *Some may see how to win.*
> *However, they cannot position their forces where they must.*
> *This demonstrates limited ability.*

THE ART OF WAR 4:3.1-3

Answer: C. You must see the opportunity and move your men.

We have already explained how important vision, or the ability to recognize an opportunity, is to our ability to move forward. Seeing an opportunity isn't enough. We must also be able to move to take advantage of that opportunity. Action is always required for success.

Sun Tzu defines our competitive ability by the various skills we must master. The ability to see an opportunity, vision, is one of these key skills. Knowledge and vision are two key skills for any leader. The ability to move to the right position at the right time is another skill. Movement and positioning are the two key skills for any organization. To win a new position, we need to develop both areas of skill.

We have all known people who can see opportunity. They tell us about it. Their predictions prove quite accurate. Still, they never seem to be able to take advantage of the opportunities they see. They can spot a hot stock, but they never have the money to invest in it. They hear about a good job, but they never get to the interview. They are sure they are right, but they never have enough energy to make a commitment to the necessary action. In other words, they are stuck. They cannot move. In Sun Tzu's terms, they are really defending when they should attack.

Success requires action and movement. To be successful in reaching our goals, we must always be prepared to act. We must be eager to act. We must have the courage to act. If we are too cautious to move to a new position, we will never find long-term success.

Lesson 76: The Quality of Skill

How should you think about leaders who always find success despite having more difficulty than they expected?
A.   They should be praised for their perseverance.
B.   They should be praised for beating the odds.
C.   They should be praised for always winning.
D.   They have poor strategic skills.

> *Some can struggle to a victory and the whole world may praise their winning. This also demonstrates a limited ability.*
>
> THE ART OF WAR 4:3.4-5

Answer: D. They have poor strategic skills.

Moving to a better position requires two skills: seeing the opportunity and acting to take advantage of it. When we meet more resistance than we expect, we have a problem with seeing and picking the right opportunities. If we can struggle to success, we show that we know how to act. The ability to act is an important skill, but it is only part of knowing how to move forward correctly. The fact that we get into problems and have to struggle shows that we have much to learn about vision.

This is contrary to the way people normally react to success against the odds. People see success and admire it. Success against the odds seems heroic. Outsiders (and sometimes insiders) don't see the cost of success. If we have to struggle to succeed, success is costing us more than we planned. In real war, our struggles can be measured in dead bodies. In business, our struggles are measured in lost dollars. The longer we struggle, the more costly and less profitable victory is. The goal of strategy is to make victory pay. Sun Tzu doesn't teach heroism. He teaches success.

People may think that someone who can overcome great odds is terrific. This is not what Sun Tzu thinks. He thinks that anyone who goes to battle against great odds is a fool who doesn't understand the true nature of victory. A master of strategy is someone who knows how to slant the odds in his or her favor. We may get lucky and win a few lopsided battles or even be skilled in using resources so we can win those battles, but we cannot make a career from picking the wrong battles.

Lesson 77: The Degree of Difficulty

When you are trained in strategy, how hard is it to see an opportunity to improve your position?

A.   It takes a great deal of analysis and time.

B.   Opportunities are hidden and subtle.

C.   Opportunities are obvious and easy to spot.

D.   Some opportunities are obvious; others are hidden.

> *Win as easily as picking up a fallen hair.*
> *Don't use all of your forces.*
> *See the time to move.*
> *Don't try to find something clever.*
> *Hear the clap of thunder.*
> *Don't try to hear something subtle.*

THE ART OF WAR 4:3.6-11

Answer: C. Opportunities are obvious and easy to spot.

If we are struggling to move forward, we are looking in the wrong place. Situations in which we can easily win are obvious once we are trained in strategy. Often, they are so obvious that they are easily overlooked. The whole point of studying these lessons in strategy is to learn how to recognize opportunities easily.

Human beings have powerful imaginations. We have an inborn ability to recognize patterns. This ability is so powerful that we can see patterns even where none exist. If we look at the night sky long enough and hard enough, we will find clear pictures in random dots. This ability creates a danger. When looking for opportunities, we have to be certain that we don't imagine them. We want clear and certain opportunities that are so clear and certain that they are easily overlooked. Looking for subtle and complex patterns can be extremely risky. We can easily become victims of our own imagination. Too much vision is as dangerous as too little.

When a real opportunity appears, it is obvious. We see a situation in which we can succeed with one hand tied behind our back. When we see this type of opportunity, we know exactly what we should do about it. Every builder of a successful organization must have this clear foresight.

Lesson 78: The Lesson of History

If you study the history of successful battles, what does it teach you?

A.   You have to fight hard to win.

B.   You have to be intelligent to win a reputation.

C.   You have to be courageous to achieve success.

D.   You have to make winning easy to be successful.

> *Learn from the history of successful battles.*
> *Victory goes to those who make winning easy.*
> *A good battle is one that you will obviously win.*
> *It doesn't take intelligence to win a reputation.*
> *It doesn't take courage to achieve success.*

THE ART OF WAR 4:3.12-16

Answer: D. You have to make winning easy to be successful.

We study history to discover what happens over time. Bravery may win one battle. Intelligence or extreme cleverness may win another, but over the course of time we can only be successful if we avoid difficult battles. If we keep picking difficult battles, we will eventually lose. If we keep picking easy battles, we will not only win all of our battles; eventually we will win the war.

Sun Tzu recognizes two types of courage. He respects people who have the courage of conviction. In this vein, he praises courage as a necessary element of leadership. He has less respect for mere physical courage, which can lead us into foolhardy behavior. When courage leads us into battles in which the odds are against us, he considers it a dangerous and deadly state of mind.

The same is true of cleverness. Again, a leader has to be intelligent, but we cannot constantly rely upon getting brilliant inspirations to advance our position. We should be able to advance without being brilliant. Indeed, trying to be too clever can get us into trouble. The real opportunities in life are those than anyone can understand.

Sun Tzu has no respect at all for reputation or fame. He thinks that the crowd is fickle and foolish in judging the quality of people's accomplishments. This is even more true today in our celebrity culture. Ninety percent of the hot, new, exciting people who are highly praised today will be forgotten in a year or two, while those who have true staying power are usually overlooked or forgotten.

Lesson 79: Battles to Avoid

What type of battles should you always avoid?

A.   You avoid any battle that you are not certain to win easily.

B.   You avoid any battle that your government opposes.

C.   You avoid any battle that does not hurt your opponent.

D.   You avoid any battle that your troops don't agree with.

> *You must win your battles without effort.*
> *Avoid difficult struggles.*
> *Fight when your position must win.*
> *You always win by preventing your defeat.*
>
> THE ART OF WAR 4:3.17-20

Answer: A. You avoid any battle that you are not certain to win easily.

We should always consider the dangers and risks of meeting a challenge or an opponent. We must even avoid winning if winning costs us too much, weakening our position instead of strengthening it. Winning a competitive battle that leaves our organization poorer and weaker is foolish. Winning must make us stronger. Strategy means systematically strengthening our position over time.

We must put ourselves in a position or situation in which we are so dominant that meeting challenges is completely safe. Our first responsibility is to protect what we have. In business, we must protect our livelihood and the livelihood of those who work for us. We must protect the interests of customers who depend on us.

The central theme of this chapter is the factor of climate, in Chinese, *tian*, the sky or weather. This idea covers the changes in the seasons and the passage of time. When Sun Tzu says that we "always" win by avoiding defeat, he is telling us that opportunity will present itself over time. The passage of time brings with it many changes and surprises. We cannot know what form opportunity will take. We can be certain that if we survive we will discover a winning opportunity.

The challenge of time is survival. What happens over time is not important if we don't survive. Our job now, therefore, is survival. If we survive, an opportunity to win will come.

Lesson 80: Inevitable Success

How do you assure yourself that an opportunity for success will come eventually?

A.   You simply have to wait until the right time.

B.   You have to position yourself where you cannot lose.

C.   You have to position yourself where you can win.

D.   You have to be careful about seizing opportunity.

> *You must engage only in winning battles.*
> *Position yourself where you cannot lose.*
> *Never waste an opportunity to defeat your enemy.*

THE ART OF WAR 4:3.21-23

Answer: B. You have to position yourself where you cannot lose.

This stanza focuses on the active part we play in assuring our success over time. Though we must wait for an opportunity, we don't *just* wait. We must position ourselves for it. We must put ourselves in a place where opportunity will eventually come. Then, when opportunity does come, we must engage it. Opportunities are common, but recognizing obvious opportunities is difficult. We cannot afford to waste a single one. If we delay action, we lengthen the contest, raising its costs.

We should take special note of how Sun Tzu phrases how we must act when we "engage" or confront the enemy. In a confrontation, we are not acting to win. Our actions should prevent our losing. If we don't lose a confrontation, we will win it. If we don't lose, our opponents eventually will make a mistake and create an opening that we can exploit.

This idea echoes the opening lessons of this chapter. The enemy gives us the opportunity. We cannot create it. We see the opportunity and then we move to take advantage of it. When we accept a challenge, we must avoid any missteps. The situation itself creates our opportunity and our inevitable success. We won't have to.

Our position puts us in the path of opportunity. Opportunity comes inevitably to good positions. Our actions taking advantage of these opportunities put us in a better position to see more opportunities. Our continual advance is how we define success. We do not actually fight for our success; we look for the position that wins it for us.

Lesson 81: Timing the Struggle for Success

When does the real struggle for success take place?

A.   Before you meet the challenge.

B.   When you first move to meet the challenge.

C.   As you meet the challenge.

D.   After you meet the challenge.

You win a war by first assuring yourself of victory.
Only afterward do you look for a fight.
Outmaneuver the enemy before the battle and then fight to win.
THE ART OF WAR 4:3.24-26

Answer: A. Before you meet the challenge.

We must have a winning position before we try to meet any challenge. We must think of competition like a chess game. To win in chess, we must position our pieces correctly long before we challenge our opponent's king. Simply checking our opponent's king accomplishes nothing. It is an empty threat unless we can back it up. We must first put our pieces into proper positions so that we can assure a checkmate. This is the real struggle. It takes place well before the showdown. Only after we have set up a winning position do we accept the challenge and move on to success.

Earlier, Sun Tzu criticized leaders who can see an opportunity but cannot move their people into position to take advantage of it. Seeing and moving to positions is a dynamic process. We must position our resources and then reposition them again. We look for the right constellation of positions or power points in which we have all the advantages. We avoid any direct confrontations that risk our resources outside our focus of power. We keep our moves building a winning position a secret. Eventually, our opponents put themselves within the easy reach of one of our power points. At that time, we cannot be shy. We must move against our opponents.

We build our position by creating our power points in more and more areas that we control. When we have developed power points, we move into positions where our opponents are likely to challenge us. We avoid competitive battles everywhere but in those specific areas. Advancing and developing positions that are impossible to attack—and that make others want to join us—is the basis of all strategy.

Lesson 82: Controlling Success

In meeting a challenge, which of the following can we best control?

A.   We can control the timing of opportunities.
B.   We can control the philosophy that we defend.
C.   We can control when openings are created.
D.   We can control where opportunities will appear.

> *You must make good use of war.*
> *Study military philosophy and the art of defense.*
> *You can control your victory or defeat.*

THE ART OF WAR 4:4.1-3

Answer: B. We can control the philosophy that we defend.

Every one of us is born with a unique position in the world. The difference between our relative success and failure is how well we first defend and then develop that position. Our success depends on our competitive philosophy. Successful philosophies are forward looking and optimistic but realistic. Failing philosophies are either pessimistic or idealistic. Strategy teaches that our philosophy unites and focuses our efforts and that when that philosophy is solid, it is easy to defend the positions that it puts us in.

What do we truly control in finding success? We do not control our initial position or the opportunities that come our way. We also do not control when and where those opportunities occur so we cannot control how we must take advantage of them. What we truly control is our basic philosophical position, which determines what we believe about what is possible in our lives.

Success or failure arises from our decisions. Those decisions arise from our basic philosophy. Our decisions allow us to see certain opportunities while missing others. Even when we see an opportunity, we can decide not to act if that opportunity doesn't appeal to our competitive philosophy. We move forward only when an opportunity meets our philosophical criteria.

Whenever Sun Tzu writes "make good use of war," he is reminding us of our larger goals in competition. Our philosophy defines that larger, shared goal. We must compete for a purpose. We don't compete just to win battles. We must win only battles that serve our larger purpose. We must win battles that lead to success as we define it. We must make victory pay.

Lesson 83: The Success Formula

What is the ultimate basis for calculating whether or not a given move will lead you to success or failure?

A. It depends on how well you make decisions.

B. It depends on how you see your odds of success.

C. It depends on how much you are willing to invest in success.

D. It depends on how far you must go to succeed.

> *This is the art of war.*
> *1. Discuss the distances.*
> *2. Discuss your numbers.*
> *3. Discuss your calculations.*
> *4. Discuss your decisions.*
> *5. Discuss victory.*
> *The ground determines the distance.*
> *The distance determines your numbers.*
> *Your numbers determine your calculations.*
> *Your calculations determine your decisions.*
> *Your decisions determine your victory.*
>
> THE ART OF WAR 4:4.4-14

Answer: D. It depends on how far you must go to succeed.

This is one of the most important passages in *The Art of War*. It is the ultimate success formula for deciding when to move to a new position. It says that our current position on the battleground determines how far we must go to develop a new position. This distance determines the amount of resources we must invest in that move to establish a new position. The distance and the amount of resources required determine our odds of success. Longer, more costly moves are less likely to be successful than shorter, less expensive moves. Our calculation of the odds of our success combined with the potential payoff determines our decision about whether or not to take the chance.

In planning a career move, an accountant may discover that being a veterinarian pays extremely well, but becoming a veterinarian is a huge change for someone who has an education in accounting. An accountant can become a vet but the odds are against it. Strategy suggests that most accountants should look for a better opportunity closer to their current arena.

Lesson 84: Where to Invest Resources

What is the most important consideration in deciding where you should invest your resources in challenging an opponent?
A.   The likelihood of a competitive mismatch.
B.   The advantages that you have.
C.   The barriers that your opponents face.
D.   The quality of your resources.

> *Creating a winning war is like balancing a coin of gold against a coin of silver.*
> *Creating a losing war is like balancing a coin of silver against a coin of gold.*
>
> THE ART OF WAR 4:4.15-16

Answer: A. The likelihood of a competitive mismatch.

When we are competing against opponents in a zero-sum game, we are looking for competitive mismatches. We are looking for situations in which our strengths far outweigh the strengths of our opponents.

This stanza emphasizes the relative nature of "good" in developing a strategy. According to Sun Tzu, nothing is good or bad in itself. Goodness or badness arises from comparison to other alternatives. Silver is valuable and fairly heavy, but that value is meaningless when compared to the relative value or weight of gold. We naturally view our own position as good, but the only relevant question is how it realistically compares with the position of our opponent.

Not only should we look for situations in which we are stronger but situations in which we are several times stronger, just as gold is several times more valuable than silver. In a given situation, we may have advantages. Our opponents may face obstacles. Given an equal investment of resources, we would probably outmatch the opponent, but, for Sun Tzu, this isn't good enough. It still means we might have a difficult battle. We need more than an advantage. We need an overwhelming advantage.

We can move in any direction. In calculating our movements, we can determine the likelihood that we will meet a challenge. We can calculate the likelihood that we will succeed in meeting that challenge easily. These aren't difficult calculations because the contest shouldn't be close. We are looking for complete mismatches.

Lesson 85: The Support of People

When we find an advantageous situation, how important is the support of other people in meeting the challenge?

A.   Always important.

B.   Usually important.

C.   Sometimes important.

D.   Never important.

> *Winning a battle is always a matter of people.*
> *You pour them into battle like a flood of water pouring into a deep gorge.*
> *This is a matter of positioning.*
> *Your decisions determine your victory.*

THE ART OF WAR 4:5.1-4

Answer: A. Always important.

The victory formula begins with the ground and its distances, but in the end our success depends directly upon the reactions of other people. Strategic competition is unique in that it exists only within the dimension of human society. The science of strategy is always about human psychology and our wants and needs.

This chapter began by emphasizing our lack of control. We must initially defend ourselves and watch our situation. We cannot create a winning situation; we can only see it. The winning situation is created by the action of others, by the interactions within society as a whole.

We move to where we have all the advantages. We want to create an imbalance that gives us the momentum (the topic of the next chapter). We want to be so far above our competitors that they cannot challenge us and, more importantly, do not think or feel that they can challenge us. We want to have such a dominant position that ideally our opponents will surrender to us without a battle.

For Sun Tzu, success is always a matter of people. Whether we are talking about organizations, markets, governments, businesses, or armies, we are just talking about people and how they think and feel. We build our success largely in people's minds. If people—our supports and our opponents' supporters—are convinced that we will win, then we will. Just as we cannot lose sight of our goals, we also cannot forget that our success depends on people.

Chapter 5

Momentum

We normally think that momentum is created by winning. We say that people who have won in the past have momentum. However, Sun Tzu offers a deeper vision. He teaches that winning, if it is expected, doesn't create momentum. He teaches that momentum comes from overthrowing expectations and surprising our opponents. For example, in a political election campaign, a surprisingly close loss in a primary can give an underdog a powerful boost of momentum, even though he or she technically lost.

In this chapter, Sun Tzu addresses how to generate momentum when we meet our opponents or a challenge directly. We look for strategic ways to advance our position without direct confrontations, but sometimes confrontations are unavoidable. Unavoidable battles include political elections, negotiations, sales situations, contests for job openings, and so on. Sun Tzu defines battle as action that directly opposes the *movement* of a competitor. Battle is still not direct conflict, but it is one step closer. In meeting our opponents, we still want to avoid conflict if possible. Even when we meet opponents in battle, we have a tool to discourage them from fighting. This tool is the momentum of surprise.

The nature and effects of surprise are the topic of this chapter. *Sun Tzu describes surprise in terms of innovation, finding new and creative ways to address old problems. Remarkably for his time, Sun Tzu saw the world as an endless potential stream of inventions and innovations.* Everyone makes unconscious assumptions about what is possible. Innovation changes the rules about what is possible. Surprise is shocking because it challenges our assumptions, creating fear and uncertainty. When surprise is first used, the emotional impact it creates is more important than the innovation itself.

Lesson 86: Using Direct Action

When can you use direct action against an opponent?

A.   You never use direct action against an opponent.

B.   You use direct action only in smaller conflicts.

C.   You use direct action only in large conflicts.

D.   You use direct action only when you have planned a surprise.

> *You control a large army the same as you control a few men.*
> *You just divide their ranks correctly.*
> *You fight a large army the same as you fight a small one.*
> *You only need the right position and communication.*
> *You may meet a large enemy army.*
> *You must be able to encounter the enemy without being defeated.*
> *You must correctly use both surprise and direct action.*
> *Your army's position must increase your strength.*
> *Troops flanking an enemy can smash them like eggs.*
> *You must correctly use both strength and weakness.*

THE ART OF WAR 5:1.12-18

Answer: D. You use direct action only when you have planned a surprise.

Many people think that the rules change as the scale of competition changes, but the rules of competition are scalable. We find success in our small individual challenges using the same methods that governments use to find success in large international challenges. Large efforts require more organization and communication but the rules are the same.

In Sun Tzu's system, forces of different size naturally avoid direct confrontations because larger forces can beat smaller forces but smaller forces can escape larger ones. Direct conflict between equal forces is usually avoided because the outcome is uncertain. We seek to meet our opponents where our opponents miscalculate the weight of force that we can put into a contest. This is where surprise becomes important. Surprise means that we successfully deceive the opponent about our true force and ability. Sun Tzu teaches that to do this we must use unexpected innovations for which our opposition is unprepared. This is why we say that surprise is an attack on knowledge, outmoding the leader's knowledge of methods—what is possible—rather than the leader's foresight.

Lesson 87: Using Surprise

When do you use surprise in a confrontation?

A. You use it immediately to catch your opponent off balance.
B. You use it at the end of the battle to finish off your opponent.
C. You use it in the middle of the attack to turn the tide of battle.
D. You use it continuously throughout the attack.

> *It is the same in all battles.*
> *You use a direct approach to engage the enemy.*
> *You use surprise to win.*

THE ART OF WAR 5:2.1-3

Answer: C. You use it in the middle of the attack to turn the tide of battle.

When most people read "surprise" in this context, they naturally think surprise attack. This is clearly *not* what Sun Tzu was teaching. His word "surprise" is better translated as extraordinary or unusual action. In the original Chinese, this clearly applies to our methods, one of the five strategic factors. This idea of surprise is closer in meaning to what we call innovation.

Why is it important for a challenge to start conventionally? Our opponents must misunderstand the basis of battle. They must come into the situation confident that they know the rules. To put this in military terms, we want them to be sure that we will be using infantry when we are really planning to unleash our cavalry. If they know that we are planning an innovation, they will be cautious, looking to counter it. If they see that we are using the expected approaches, they will commit themselves to responding accordingly. This sets them up.

We need to set them up because the true strategic power of innovation isn't how well it works initially. Innovation is powerful because it changes the balance of battle. The first firearms weren't that much better than swords. They were slow to load and blew up frequently, killing their users. True innovations are easily countered because of these initial weaknesses. Unleashing them in the middle of battle, however, changes the nature of the confrontation, shocking our opponents. We are prepared for this change, but our competition is not. This creates confusion, uncertainty, and fear in our opponents. Surprise is a powerful psychological tool.

Lesson 88: The Source of Innovation

What is the real source of innovation?

A.   Your leader.

B.   Your environment.

C.   Your opposition.

D.   Your philosophy.

> *You must use surprise for a successful invasion.*
> *Surprise is as infinite as the weather and land.*
> *Surprise is as inexhaustible as the flow of a river.*
>
> THE ART OF WAR 5:2.4-7

Answer: B. Your environment.

In Sun Tzu's model for competitive systems, the environment—the climate and ground, time and place—offers infinite possibilities. Each position that we take gives us an infinite number of paths to success. Moving to take over an opponent's position—an "invasion"—requires seeing the possibilities for innovation at that unique place and time.

One of Sun Tzu's common themes is that to be successful we must use the "philosophy of an invader," that is, we must go after new territory. If we are not moving forward, we are moving backward. If we are not improving our position, it is becoming weaker.

Moving forward means that we must use the undiscovered riches in new areas. But, uniquely for his time, Sun Tzu didn't see acquiring new territory as a zero-sum game. He saw the ground as infinite. The strategy of competition isn't simply a matter of taking what someone else has. It is a matter of getting more out of what we have, uncovering new possibilities.

The limitless possibilities of the ground are easier to see in our time than in Sun Tzu's. We live in an age of discovery, when people are constantly inventing new territories to conquer. The human genome, the Internet, and wireless networks are just recent examples in the field of technology, but this pace of change also applies to our individual lives. Creativity comes from developing our unique position in a universe of infinite possibility. Our environment offers limitless potential for us to surprise our opponents if we are willing to leverage all the changes around us. Sun Tzu uses the "river" as an analogy for change in general because of its continuous flow.

Lesson 89: Transforming Innovation into Success

What are the requirements to transform innovation into success?

A.   Persistence after failure.

B.   Secretiveness.

C.   Attention to details.

D.   Luck.

> *You can be stopped and yet recover the initiative.*
> *You must use your days and months correctly.*
>
> *If you are defeated, you can recover.*
> *You must use the four seasons correctly.*
>
> THE ART OF WAR 5:2.7-10

Answer: A. Persistence after failure.

These stanzas can be read in two different ways. First, they describe how we should react to the shock of innovation when it is used against us. Though a surprise stops us, we can recover. Second, we can read it as instructions on how to overcome the initial weaknesses in our innovations. Though they can be countered, we can improve them over time.

Notice how quickly in the discussion of surprise and creativity Sun Tzu addresses the issue of failure. Surprise stops and surprise can be stopped. In other words, the shock of introducing new ideas can be overcome over time. Over time, either the innovation's weaknesses will be exploited or those weaknesses will be addressed.

Sun Tzu teaches a form of innovation that is closely tied to trial and error. In earlier chapters, he discussed keeping our attacks small and affordable. In his discussion of surprise, he makes it clear that we should not be dissuaded by the possibility or even likelihood of failures. This is especially true in innovation. Few ideas are instantly successful. Fewer still come to fruition without being built on a foundation of earlier failures.

Sun Tzu saw time as the key ingredient in invention. If our initial innovative idea doesn't work, we must use time—the days and months, and the four seasons—to improve upon it. Some innovative ideas simply fail, but we can still use them as stepping-stones to better ideas that have better chances of success.

Lesson 90: Hearing New Ideas

What is the starting point of creativity?

A.   Inspiration.
B.   Knowledge.
C.   Action.
D.   Position.

> *There are only a few notes in the scale.*
> *Yet, you can always rearrange them.*
> *You can never hear every song of victory.*

THE ART OF WAR 5:2.11-13

Answer: B. Knowledge.

To understand Sun Tzu, we must know a lot about the metaphors he uses. The verse above is the first of three similar verses that seem, at first, largely poetic, but nothing in *The Art of War* is written without a practical application. In this first verse, Sun Tzu demonstrates his own creativity by incorporating his metaphor for information and knowledge—sound and hearing—to say that what we hear is the starting point for creativity.

Knowledge starts with a set of known facts, but ability comes from knowing which facts are useful and how to arrange them. Though music is a creative art, all music is based upon the same limited set of notes. These notes are completely knowable. We can know and name every one. However, despite knowing all the notes, we don't have music until we put them together. The music is the way we put the notes together.

For Sun Tzu, the way we put facts together provides our basic knowledge. People can know the same facts but not put them together the same way. Creativity is our ability to rearrange facts in a new way that works, that is, find a more useful way to arrange them. Simply by rearranging known facts, we can create something completely new. However, before we can do any rearranging, we must have the facts to rearrange—that is, we must know something true about the world.

However, there is also a warning in this idea. New ideas can initially *sound* good, but that doesn't mean that they will prove to be successful. If knowledge were all there was to it, we wouldn't need the next two stanzas.

Lesson 91: Examining New Ideas

What is the second step in the creative process?

A.   Vision.

B.   Comparison.

C.   Calculation.

D.   Hard work.

> *There are only a few basic colors.*
> *Yet, you can always mix them.*
> *You can never see all the shades of victory.*

THE ART OF WAR 5:2.14-17

Answer: A. Vision.

Not all ideas that sound good will look good once we get them on paper. Sun Tzu consistently uses sight as an analogy for envisioning the future. In his second verse about creativity, he moves from hearing, what sounds good, to putting that idea on paper and seeing how it looks in solid terms. His concept of vision isn't the spiritual visions of a mystic, but the foresight of an economic planner. He taught that vision, the ability to see the future, arises directly from our knowledge, not from some magical process. Once we get an idea on paper, we can calculate, draw, measure, and generally figure how realistic it is. Our knowledge is the basis of this process, and the more we know, the more possibilities we can calculate. This is not genius. It just means taking a hard look at the facts.

Again, Sun Tzu makes the point that there is no limit to creativity, even when we are looking at the facts. Vision, like knowledge, is limitless. There are an infinite number of good ideas in the world, but the real secret to vision is our ability to foresee which ones have the potential for success. Calculation doesn't give us the ability to see the future perfectly, but it gives us the ability to see the shades and possibilities of the future.

Sun Tzu didn't define vision as a rare skill. If we are knowledgeable, we see that there are only certain ways that things can work; that is, there are a few basic colors. Because we are human and our knowledge is limited, we don't see infinite possibilities. The few creative ideas that we have can be combined in an endless kaleidoscope of invention, but if we work in a very focused manner, we can see what is likely to work best.

Lesson 92: Testing New Ideas

What is the final test of an innovation?

A.   It is novel.

B.   It is inexpensive.

C.   It is fruitful.

D.   It is newsworthy.

> *There are only a few flavors.*
> *Yet, you can always blend them.*
> *You can never taste all the flavors of victory.*
>
> THE ART OF WAR 5:2.17-20

Answer: C. It is fruitful.

In this final reiteration of the idea of endless innovation, Sun Tzu chooses the analogy of taste. Tasting is his metaphor for testing. His purpose here is to make us think about what we get out of our creativity, how productive it is. To be useful, creativity must produce something of value. In historical terms, this could be plunder, but in modern terms, we think of producing something people want, need, or find pleasing.

Here, Sun Tzu counters the first two analogies about creativity, which are intellectual, by suggesting that we test the idea in a physical way. First, we ask, "How does this idea sound?" Then we put the idea on paper and ask, "How does this look?" The final test is, "Does it work?"

Despite the poetry of this section, Sun Tzu did not believe in adopting a novel strategy for the sake of beauty or as a form of self-expression. He believed that the only justification for the cost of competition was to protect and support the people, and, in a real sense, to feed them. Victory must pay. A strategy must be fruitful to be valuable.

We often see war as destructive. Sun Tzu viewed destruction and even conflict as the failure of strategy. In his time, the immediate purpose of war was to take land away from those who didn't value it and give it to those who did and could make it more productive. The reason his classic work translates so well into the modern era is because this is still the purpose of competition: to take resources from those who use them poorly and redistribute them to those who can generate more value from them.

Lesson 93: Using Innovation

What is the best way to use innovation in meeting a challenge?

A.   Use a new idea to instantly change the rules.

B.   Use a new idea to reinvent all your methods.

C.   Use a new idea to gradually replace conventional approaches.

D.   Use a new idea to leverage proven methods.

> *You fight with momentum.*
> *There are only a few types of surprises and direct actions.*
> *Yet, you can always vary the ones you use.*
> *There is no limit in the ways you can win.*
>
> THE ART OF WAR 5:2.20-24

Answer: D. Use a new idea to leverage proven methods.

Though we translate the title of this chapter as "Momentum," the Chinese character, *shi*, is closer to the idea of "force." In a larger context, Sun Tzu means something like the force of progress. "Momentum" is a close approximation, but our modern idea of the inexorable force of progress and the continual advance of new ideas over old ones is an even better description. What creates the force of progress? Do new ideas mean that we must reinvent everything?

Sun Tzu says no. New ideas never work by themselves. They work only when they are combined with existing, proven methods. As a matter of fact, innovations must work with existing structures in order to work at all. New ideas that require the reinvention of society do not work. Hydrogen powered automobiles are technically possible today, but we will have to develop a whole system for distributing hydrogen before they become practical for ordinary drivers.

Gradually, innovations accumulate, seemingly recreating society, but this doesn't happen from one idea alone and it never happens overnight. The perception of something entirely new created overnight—such as the Internet—is always an illusion. It took hundreds of small inventions accumulated over dozens of years to make the Internet possible.

The final secret in using innovation is knowing how to combine a new idea with existing methods to create the innovation's real value. We must balance new ideas with existing methods to be successful.

Lesson 94: The Basis of Innovation

What is the source of all new ideas?

A.   Commerce.

B.   Science.

C.   Regulation.

D.   Tradition.

> *Surprise and direct action give birth to each other.*
> *They proceed from each other in an endless cycle.*
> *You can not exhaust all their possible combinations!*
>
> THE ART OF WAR 5:2.24-26

Answer: D. Tradition.

Tradition, in the form of existing technology and widely practiced methods, creates the environment that supports and makes a new idea feasible. Over time, if the new idea works, it becomes standard practice. It becomes a part of tradition itself. This tradition creates a new foundation for new advancements and, together with the continual process of innovation, the momentum of progress.

A base of standards makes faster innovation possible. For example, once every company that built computers used different materials, different chips, different designs, and different technologies, and the advance of computers was slow. Dramatic advances cannot arise until competition among all these different methods produces a standard design and technology. This happened in computers with the adoption of Intel processors, the Windows operating system, and standard designs. Once a winning approach becomes the standard, that is, the tradition, a faster cycle of innovation becomes possible.

Without competition, standard techniques—direct action—cannot arise. Without standards, new methods—surprise—are very difficult, costly, and more likely to fail. Usual and unusual give birth to each other. Without the usual, there is no unusual. Without the unusual, there is no progress and no momentum. The evolutionary nature of reality was observed and recorded by Sun Tzu long before Darwin, but to a more practical purpose. Our goal is to use this theory of evolution to create useful innovations.

Lesson 95: Resisting Change

What force can resist the force of progress?

A.   None.

B.   Faith.

C.   Time.

D.   Courage.

> *Surging water flows together rapidly.*
> *Its pressure washes away boulders.*
> *This is momentum.*

THE ART OF WAR 5:3.1-3

Answer: A. None.

As we have said before, water is Sun Tzu's metaphor for change. The force of change is likened over and over again to the force of water. Small changes are like drops of water. A single drop changes nothing, but drop after drop over time changes everything.

Sun Tzu has defined momentum as combining innovative ideas with proven standards. Momentum isn't just winning consistently. It is surprising others in the process. In using momentum, we confront our competitors with surprise after surprise, change after change. Change creates pressure on people. Over time, people adjust to new standards, but they cannot resist change. If they are not given time, people cannot adjust; they can only break.

The best weapon in competition is speed. This is especially true when using innovation and creativity. Standards are important because they make faster innovation possible. The faster we can innovate, the faster we can change, and the more difficult it will be for our opponents to keep up. The constant pressure of change is irresistible over time.

People talk about the force of progress in a general sense as a tide that carries us all along. Sun Tzu saw another possibility. He saw that individuals and organizations could use the force of a new idea, properly combined with existing methods, to pressure their opponents. When we meet an opponent or meet a challenge, we want the pressure of change on our side. In any given meeting, we want our opponents to be surprised. Over the course of many meetings, we want to wear our opponents down by the pressure of continuous change.

Lesson 96: The Key to Innovation

What is the most important characteristic of an innovation?

A.   Its size.

B.   Its novelty.

C.   Its timing.

D.   Its direction.

> *A hawk suddenly strikes a bird.*
> *Its contact alone kills the prey.*
> *This is timing.*

THE ART OF WAR 5:3.4-6

Answer: C. Its timing.

There are three critical ideas in Sun Tzu's concept of timing.

The first issue is the suddenness of the strike. As taught by Sun Tzu, speed is the essence of warfare. Good timing requires that we use the speed of innovation as a weapon. We seek to pressure the opposition simply by our pace of change. It doesn't matter how novel the innovation is; it is the pace of change that impacts our opponents. It is the speed of the hawk that kills. Most organizations, especially larger ones, have problems dealing with a fast pace of change. This is another advantage that smaller organizations have over larger ones.

The next issue is striking power. To be successful, our strike must damage our opponents. Innovation inside our organizations may seem important because it affects us, but the timing of innovation must be felt by our opponents to have impact. The change must hit our opponents and shock them. It must have enough weight and substance to be felt and recognized.

Finally, our timing must prevent our opponents from going where they are headed. We release surprise to prevent those who oppose us from making progress. Our innovations should deflect our opponents from the path of their progress, preventing them from following that path. Many industries are affected by change, but most changes are foreseen and taken in stride. Organizations have time to adjust to them without having to develop a new plan. Timing means unleashing change at a time when it forces people to change their plans. Our timing should destroy their plans.

Lesson 97: Unleashing Innovation

When should you challenge opponents with your innovations?

A.   As soon as possible to get the innovations' benefit.

B.   When your innovations will get an opponent's attention.

C.   Only when using innovations will impact the battle.

D.   Continuously to pressure your opponents.

> *You must fight only winning battles.*
> *Your momentum must be overwhelming.*
> *Your timing must be exact.*
>
> *Your momentum is like the tension of a bent crossbow.*
> *Your timing is like the pulling of a trigger.*

THE ART OF WAR 5:3.7-12

Answer: C. Only when using innovations will impact the battle.

The topic of this chapter is meeting our opponents directly in battle. As we continuously improve our position, we do pressure opponents, but that pressure is felt irrespective of specific meetings. We should continuously improve our processes and procedures, but the best possible time to unleash those changes is when we are confronted by an opponent who expects to be able to challenge us successfully.

We should time our surprises so that we can use them to effectively change people's minds. We should keep gradual improvements secret, gradually building up the tension and power of their release. We should then promote them when they make a difference in the market, when they will change customers' minds. Imagine being challenged by a rival at work and being in the position to name a dozen important things you accomplished that your opponent knew nothing about. This is the power of timing.

Continual improvement is important, but only when surprisingly revealed during a confrontation. Individually, most of our accomplishments aren't very impressive. Sun Tzu teaches strategy as a science of small advances. Small accomplishments seem trivial taken by themselves but can be impressive when taken all together. Again, until their revelation can make a real difference during a confrontation, these changes should be played down.

Lesson 98: Controlling the Course of Events

How can we make sure that meeting a challenge goes according to plan?

A.   By taking all contingencies into account.

B.   By keeping our plans simple.

C.   By keeping our plans secret.

D.   By assuming that it won't go according to plan.

> *War is very complicated and confused.*
> *Battle is chaotic.*
> *Nevertheless, you must not allow chaos.*
>
> *War is very sloppy and messy.*
> *Positions turn around.*
> *Nevertheless, you must never be defeated.*

THE ART OF WAR 5:4.1-6

Answer: D. By assuming that it won't go according to plan.

Competitive challenges cannot be truly planned. Opposing plans from different people collide with results that no one can predict. Those who think that they can foresee exactly how any confrontation will progress are simply wrong.

Sun Tzu teaches us to keep our plans simple. His philosophy emphasizes adaptability and positioning rather than planning. Keeping plans secret is a great idea. It prevents others from attacking our plans, but, more importantly, it also leaves us free to change our plans. Once plans are published, we are committed to them. Changing our plans is viewed as failure for us and victory for our opponents.

Instead of struggling to make sure that everything happens according to plan, we must expect to be surprised. We must assume that we don't have control over everything that happens. We will succeed at implementing some plans and fail at implementing others. As Sun Tzu says, positions turn around. This shifting type of change is completely predictable because it is the nature of competition.

If competition is chaotic, how can we prevent chaos? If it is always messy and uncertain, how can we prevent our failure? The answer to these questions is the topic of the next two lessons.

Lesson 99: Dealing with Chaos

If competition is chaotic, where does control come from?

A.   Control is impossible.

B.   It comes from human nature.

C.   It comes from discipline.

D.   It comes from aggressiveness.

> *Chaos gives birth to control.*
> *Fear gives birth to courage.*
> *Weakness gives birth to strength.*

THE ART OF WAR 5:4.7-9

Answer: B. It comes from human nature.

Even our opponents want a sense of order. Competition among people creates chaos, but that chaos itself creates a human need for order. Human nature seeks to identify patterns. We want to make sense of confusion. The greater the chaos, the more we desire order. It is this human desire for order that makes it possible for us to take control of events even during hostile confrontations.

The same is true of courage. Uncertainty creates fear. The greater our uncertainty, the greater our fear. At some point, we need to escape from this fear. We find the courage to make changes because, though change is normally frightening, any change is less frightening than the uncertainty of chaos. Any predictable outcome, even death, is preferable to constant fear.

Everyone has weaknesses. We are all well aware of our personal weaknesses. Strength comes from accepting our weaknesses and learning how to use them and compensate for them. We are weak because we are small, but we learn to use our small size by becoming more focused. We are unknown, but we learn to use our obscurity to promote mystery. We are all novices, but we learn to use our newness as the source of a fresh perspective. We can learn to see that every possible weakness is also a potential strength.

The chaos of competition makes our success possible. Without it, our innovations would have little or no impact on the competitive battle. We must not fear chaos but embrace it. Our fear can give us courage. Our limitations are the source of human strength.

Lesson 100: Planning for Chaos

How do you plan to control the chaos of competition?

A.   You plan structure.

B.   You plan surprises.

C.   You plan attack.

D.   You plan defense.

> *You must control chaos.*
> *This depends on your planning.*
> *Your men must brave their fears.*
> *This depends on their momentum.*

THE ART OF WAR 5:4.10-13

Answer: B. You plan surprises.

Sun Tzu defines momentum as meeting a challenge (battle) prepared to unleash a surprise. Chaos makes people desire order, but a plan for order doesn't give us control over chaos. The way we take control of chaos is to feed into it. We can change the rules of competition through surprise, unleashing our innovations. We don't know what will happen when we introduce this surprise into a confrontation, but we are always better prepared for whatever happens than our opponents are because we control the timing of the surprise's introduction.

What is important here is our relative control. We cannot control everything that happens in a confrontation, but we know that we plan to throw our opponents off balance by changing the rules using a surprise. We still cannot control the results, but we are better prepared than our opponents.

By planning to introduce innovations, we are prepared to seize the initiative. For one critical moment, we will control the momentum of the contest. The knowledge that we plan a change gives our people courage. Our fortune in the marketplace will rise and fall, but by preparing surprises for the competition we put ourselves in the driver's seat while the market adjusts to the change. When we know we can spring a surprise, we go into the contest with more confidence. We have more faith in our position and eventual success. The planned surprise makes it possible for us to be more aggressive and courageous when facing adversity.

Lesson 101: The Source of Advantage

What is the source of your strengths and weaknesses in competition?

A.   Your position.
B.   Your innovation.
C.   Your leadership.
D.   Your knowledge.

> *You have strengths and weaknesses.*
> *These come from your position.*
>
> *You must force the enemy to move to your advantage.*
> *Use your position.*
> *The enemy must follow you.*
> *Surrender a position.*
> *The enemy must take it.*
> *You can offer an advantage to move him.*
> *You can use your men to move him.*
> *You use your strength to hold him.*

THE ART OF WAR 5:4.14-23

Answer: A. Your position.

Though this particular chapter is about using creativity and innovation during confrontations, we must not forget the basic rules of strategy. We overcome our opponents by holding a superior position. Innovation is important because it strengthens our position. The goal of using surprise during battle is to secure an even stronger position.

Dominant positions prevent battle, that is, direct confrontations. If our position is strong enough, potential competitors will avoid us. Battle results from the failure to secure a completely dominant position. When we find ourselves facing a challenge, innovation helps us secure a dominant position. It is this position that will make us successful, not the innovation itself.

Innovation can also take us from one dominant position to another. Like innovation, advancing our position is a continual process. Our goal is to keep one step ahead of our opponents. We can let them have past positions that we have abandoned. It puts them at a disadvantage.

Lesson 102: Getting the Most from People

How do you get the most out of people in meeting a serious challenge?

A.   By inspiring them.

B.   By appealing to their self-interest.

C.   By surprising them.

D.   By using momentum.

> *You want a successful battle.*
> *To do this, you must seek momentum.*
> *Do not just demand a good fight from your people.*
> *You must pick good people and then give them momentum.*
>
> THE ART OF WAR 3:5.1-4

Answer: D. By using momentum.

Battle comes from not having a position that is too dominant to challenge. We wouldn't meet a serious challenge unless we thought we could succeed. Others wouldn't be competing against us unless they thought they could beat us. We find success in these situations by controlling the momentum of the battle. We do this by introducing timely surprises into the unavoidable confusion of battle.

In meeting a challenge, too many leaders simply demand that their supporters try harder. Too many leaders expect their supporters to work harder and smarter than their opponent's people work. In situations in which opponents choose to meet in battle, they are fairly equally matched. In many situations, it seems that success goes to the competitors whose people put in a better effort. But simply exhorting our people to try harder is never enough. After all, our opponents are also exhorting their people to work harder as well. Success is not just a matter of motivation and inspiration.

We can control the outcome if we plan to use innovation, that is, meaningful surprises in battle. Our ability as leaders to introduce creative solutions gives our people a sense of power and control. They feel better prepared and more confident in the future because they know they will be seizing the initiative. It is this confidence that gets the best work out of them. People put in more effort when they feel part of a winning endeavor. We get the best work out of our supporters by giving them the confidence that we will win in any confrontation.

Lesson 103: Dealing with Pressure

In high-pressure situations, how do you get people to follow your directions?

A.   By asking them to do what is natural.

B.   By making your directions simple.

C.   By using the proper incentives.

D.   By using the proper punishments.

> *You must create momentum.*
> *You create it with your men during battle.*
> *This is comparable to rolling trees and stones.*
> *Trees and stones roll because of their shape and weight.*
> *Offer men safety and they will stay calm.*
> *Endanger them and they will act.*
> *Give them a place and they will hold.*
> *Round them up and they will march.*

THE ART OF WAR 3:5.5-12

Answer: A. By asking them to do what is natural.

In most situations, we want to keep our instructions to our people simple and give everyone the proper incentives to do what is required, but in the pressure of battle we must do more. We must leverage our people's natural emotions. As humans, our natural tendency is to follow the path of least resistance. In facing difficult challenges, the path of least resistance is defined by momentum, that is, by who is being surprisingly successful.

If we want people to stay calm, we comfort them. We prepare surprises to blunt an opponent's attacks and exhibit our control of the situation. This increases our followers' sense of security and keeps them from getting nervous. They can see that momentum is on our side.

Fear and a sense of belonging are the emotions that drive people. Fear allows people to accept change because the fear of loss is stronger than the fear of change. If we need people to move forward, we must create a sense of danger. If we put people in a valuable position, they will be afraid of losing it and will work to keep it. A sense of belonging enables everyone to work together. A big part of giving people a sense of momentum is highlighting the progress of their advance so that they can act appropriately.

Lesson 104: Making People Powerful

If you must combat an opponent's action with an action of your own, how do you ensure success?

A.   Use proven techniques.

B.   Use surprise.

C.   Use deception.

D.   Use momentum.

> *You make your men powerful in battle with momentum.*
> *This is just like rolling round stones down over a high, steep cliff.*
> *Use your momentum.*

THE ART OF WAR 3:5.13-15

Answer: D. Use momentum.

Remember, momentum is created by starting with standard, proven techniques and then surprising the competition in the course of the battle. Good methods, good decisions, and even deception have a way of evening out in competitive situations. Conflicting claims among opponents create chaos and confusion in the minds of decision-makers.

To cut through the confusion of battle, we need a surprise that forces everyone to reconsider the situation. An expected win doesn't create momentum. A surprising win does. Small improvements that have been secretly refined over a period of time are unleashed when they will make a difference in the outcome of a critical contest. The upset result changes the sense of momentum in the overall contest.

By changing the focus of the battle, we seize control of the situation. This control gives our people more certainty and confidence. It makes them both more calm and more aggressive. People naturally want to be on the side with momentum. An underdog with momentum is more powerful than a favorite who has lost it. A shift in momentum makes our opponents uncertain and confused. We use this situation to press forward and strengthen our position. We seize the momentum in the battle. A big enough surprise can even make our opponents rethink their challenge, avoiding direct conflict entirely. Our momentum carries us forward to secure a stronger position in the future.

Chapter 6

虛實

Weakness and Strength

This chapter is about the unity of two seemingly opposing concepts. We can express these opposing concepts in a variety of ways: weakness and strength, emptiness and fullness, ignorance and knowledge, neediness and satisfaction. In the original Chinese, they are expressed as *xu* and *sat*. *Xu*, or weakness, includes the concepts of emptiness, ignorance, and neediness. *Sat*, or strength, is the same as fullness, knowledge, and satisfaction. Both concepts—weakness and strength—are united and dependent upon each other. Like *yin* and *yang*, they are a necessary union of opposites. Sun Tzu sees them as a single, complementary whole describing the structure of opportunity in the real world.

The unity of these opposing concepts is critical. Strength gives birth to weakness. Weakness gives rise to strength. The ideas are opposites, but they are complementary. Each relies on the other.

Weakness and strength are combined in every competitor and every situation. We all have many strengths and we all have many weaknesses. Even the battlefield has weak points and strong points. More importantly, our strengths and weaknesses do not exist on their own; they arise from the strengths and weaknesses of others. Strength and weakness are relative values, defined by our relationships with our environment and our opponents. The last chapter discussed how surprise, not success alone, creates momentum. This chapter shows how we discover opportunities by examining the interaction between various strengths and weaknesses.

Here, we learn why there is one and only one best focus for our activities at any given point in time. We learn why we must continually adjust to dynamic changes in our competitive environment as empty positions are filled and full positions are emptied.

Lesson 105: Winning a New Position

When should you stake out a new competitive position?

A.   Before anyone else recognizes its value.

B.   When others begin to suspect its value.

C.   After its value begins to be recognized.

D.   When its value is broadly accepted.

Always arrive first to the empty battlefield to await the enemy at your leisure. If you are late and hurry to the battlefield, fighting is more difficult.

You want a successful battle.
Move your men, but not into opposing forces.

THE ART OF WAR 6:1.1-4

Answer: A. Before anyone else recognizes its value.

Nature abhors a vacuum; human nature prefers crowds. According to Sun Tzu, the emptiness of the ground gives us a position of strength. Since strategy is all about advancing positions, this is the first and most important way that emptiness creates strength. When we see a new market that nobody wants, or a new customer no one is doing business with, or even a new method that no one else is using, we are likely to feel uncomfortable pursuing it. It takes courage to be the first to move to a new position. Most people don't have that courage, but those who do get strength from their moves.

Instead of pursuing empty ground, most of us are happy to jump on the me-too bandwagon. We are more comfortable doing what everyone else is doing and buying a product that everyone is buying, and businesses offer a new, improved version of an existing product or market to the same customers everyone else is selling to. No matter how often we are told that we cannot be successful following the crowd, human nature loves to flock.

Successful strategy is always the strategy of the pioneer. We do not find safety in following the crowd. We find only potential conflict. This is the first lesson of emptiness. Empty areas offer greater opportunities than full ones. If we want to find opportunities, we must have the courage to avoid the crowds. The most important key in developing an unbeatable position is to discover that position first, before others see its value. We don't fight other people for the positions that have already been discovered.

Lesson 106: Manipulating Opponents

How do you manipulate opponents into positions of weakness?

A.   By using force.

B.   By deceiving them.

C.   By understanding their needs.

D.   By waiting.

> *You can make the enemy come to you.*
> *Offer him an advantage.*
> *You can make the enemy avoid coming to you.*
> *Threaten him with danger.*

THE ART OF WAR 6:1.5-8

Answer: C. By understanding their needs.

People always have needs. We are never completely strong or completely satisfied. Humans are weak. If we didn't have weaknesses, we wouldn't have needs. Advantage exists because humans always have needs. No matter how strong we are (or think we are), we all still have weaknesses and needs. If we were perfectly strong, we would be safe from all harm. Danger and disadvantage are also created by our needs.

Once we understand human needs, we can use our opponents' needs to move them. Sun Tzu taught that people act either from greed or fear—that is, from their weaknesses. As customers, we have needs. Businesses exist to satisfy those needs. As workers, we make our living satisfying needs. In our roles as spouses, parents, and children, we are continuously addressing the needs of others. If we understand these needs, we use them strategically to get what we need by giving others what they need.

Positioning is critical to any strategy. Our ability to move people, both our supporters and our opponents, is fundamental positioning. This ability comes from our understanding of human needs. We do not get our ability to move people from our strength; we leverage the weakness of others to move them. If we push people, they will naturally just push back. We want to pull rather than push others. We want to attract people to support us and lure our opponents into weak positions. Our strength comes from our ability to gain supporters and move opponents into relatively weaker positions.

Lesson 107: Dealing with an Opponent's Strength

How can you use the strength of your opponents?

A.   You can block their strength.

B.   You can copy their strength.

C.   You can use their strength against them.

D.   You can convert their strength to weakness.

> *When the enemy is fresh, you can tire him.*
> *When he is well fed, you can starve him.*
> *When he is relaxed, you can move him.*
>
> THE ART OF WAR 6:1.9-11

Answer: D. You can convert their strength to weakness.

Not only do we all have weaknesses, but our strengths and those of our opponents—especially in the sense of fullness—are only temporary. The ground (*di*) is the source of strength, but the climate (*tian*) changes, and, over time, every strong position grows weaker. The ground and climate are linked in the same way that strength and weakness are linked. Both are complementary opposites that together form a whole.

Strength is temporary because even when we are satisfied our needs eventually reassert themselves. Fullness (strength) is a temporary state. When we eat a meal, we are full, but we will get hungry again. When we accomplish a task, we are satisfied, but new tasks are always waiting. Fullness constantly transforms back to emptiness. Think of this as Sun Tzu's law of entropy, an early and practical foreshadowing of the scientific principle.

When we work to undermine our opponents' strength, we are working with the forces of nature. A large part of strategy is getting the forces of nature on our side. We don't want to fight gravity, so we seize the high ground. We don't want to work against the current in a river, so we position ourselves upstream. We can use the natural process of needs reasserting themselves in the same way that we use weakness to move people. People are temporarily satisfied, but we can easily make them dissatisfied. We can use time to change their feeling from satisfaction to need.

This temporary feeling of fullness is a target for our efforts. We must learn to sharpen people's sense of their needs. We must help make their needs tangible. When we do, we can move them.

Lesson 108: Using Emptiness and Fullness

How do we use emptiness and fullness to move to new positions?

A.   You leave old positions quickly and fill new ones carefully.

B.   You leave old positions slowly and fill new ones quickly.

C.   You move through filled areas quickly and easily.

D.   You defend with emptiness and attack with fullness.

> *Leave any place without haste.*
> *Hurry to where you are unexpected.*
> *You can easily march hundreds of miles without tiring.*
> *To do so, travel through areas that are deserted.*
> *You must take whatever you attack.*
> *Attack when there is no defense.*
> *You must have walls to defend.*
> *Defend where it is impossible to attack.*
>
> THE ART OF WAR 6:2.1-8

Answer: B. You leave old positions slowly and fill new ones quickly.

Strategy means that we are always looking to advance our position. We do not have to abandon old positions in order to establish new ones. Established positions are inherently stronger than new ones. When we abandon an existing position, we should do it gradually as our resources are best used elsewhere. In business, this is especially true in moving from an existing market to a new one. Businesspeople must be careful not to abandon existing customers quickly. These transitions are best made gradually.

However, we want to use all possible speed to move into new positions. The faster we establish a new position, the sooner we can get strength from it. We don't have to carefully plan such moves. Strategy requires us to be opportunistic, seizing opportunities as they appear.

When it comes to movement, emptiness makes speed, a form of strength, possible. Again, the emptiness (weakness) of the land is the source of our strength. Not all empty areas offer good positions, but we can move through these areas quickly to find positions that can support us.

Our ability to attack depends on the openings (emptiness) that the enemy leaves us. Our ability to defend depends on the fullness (strength) of our defenses.

Lesson 109: Using Strength and Weakness

What skill gives your opponents the ability to utilize strength and weakness?

A. Knowledge.
B. Vision.
C. Movement.
D. Position.

> *Be skilled in attacking.*
> *Give the enemy no idea of where to defend.*
>
> *Be skillful in your defense.*
> *Give the enemy no idea of where to attack.*
>
> THE ART OF WAR 6:2.9-12

Answer: A. Knowledge.

Our strengths and weaknesses come from our position, but we need knowledge to identify the right positions. Of course, knowledge and ignorance are other forms of strength and weakness. In Sun Tzu's system, knowledge specifically means knowing the ground. In the cycle of skills, knowledge leads to vision. Vision leads to movement. Movement creates a new position, which results in new strengths and weaknesses.

People can have strong positions without recognizing it. Their weakness comes from ignorance. This ignorance is another form of emptiness, the need for knowledge. This means that knowledge is strength. It is another form of fullness. Knowledge gives us the ability to satisfy our need to know how to position ourselves.

People's ignorance leaves us the openings that allow us to improve our position. People's ignorance creates needs that we can identify and satisfy. Our ability to move against our opponents or serve customers in business depends upon our superior knowledge. This knowledge is focused in a specific area, making us strong in a specific time and place.

Strength in our position depends upon superior knowledge of our battleground, our competitive arena. To be powerful at work, we must know every aspect of our job and organization better than anyone else. If we are ignorant in any aspect of our position, we leave an opening for attack. Our ability to defend our position comes from the completeness of our knowledge.

Lesson 110: Moving to New Positions

When you initially move to a new position, how do you make it known?

A.   You shouldn't make it known.

B.   You should let only your allies know.

C.   You should let only your opponents know.

D.   You should let everyone know.

> *Be subtle! Be subtle!*
> *Arrive without any clear formation.*
> *Quietly! Quietly!*
> *Arrive without a sound.*
> *You must use all your skill to control the enemy's decisions.*
>
> THE ART OF WAR 6:3.1-5

Answer: A. You shouldn't make it known.

When we initially move into a new area, we want to keep everyone ignorant of our intentions. When we are shifting our positions, we don't want anyone, friend or enemy, to know our strategy. We may not even have a clear plan when we first make the move. Sun Tzu teaches that we shouldn't have to have a plan when we establish new positions. It takes time to learn about the potential of our new position. Knowledge allows us to identify weakness and strength, and knowledge takes time to acquire. This is why Sun Tzu tells us we can move to these empty positions without a clear plan.

If the position proves valuable, we can establish it. At that point, both allies and opponents will discover our new position soon enough. If the new area doesn't prove to be successful, we want our failure to remain unnoticed.

Controlling information is the key to Sun Tzu's strategy. Remember, sound is Sun Tzu's metaphor for knowledge. Keeping quiet is synonymous with controlling information. If we can control information, we can control the decisions that others make. If we can control other people's decisions, we control the balance of power.

In our age of constant promotion, Sun Tzu's consistent advice on keeping quiet speaks against the popular wisdom. Isn't the secret to success promoting and publicizing our ideas and plans? The simple answer is no. Success depends on good strategy, not on promotion. Strategy depends only on controlling our position. Promotion is useful only at the right time.

Lesson 111: Moving against Strength

If the new position proves to be well defended, what do you do?

A.   You must put in more resources.

B.   You must get creative.

C.   You must be persistent.

D.   You must withdraw quickly.

> *Advance where they cannot defend.*
> *Charge through their openings.*
> *Withdraw where the enemy cannot chase you.*
> *Move quickly so that he cannot catch you.*
>
> THE ART OF WAR 6:3.6-9

Answer: D. You must withdraw quickly.

When we move to new areas, we are looking for positions that have been overlooked by the competition. We are looking for emptiness and weakness. To be successful, we must see what others have missed. Success comes from going where people's needs have been unsatisfied.

Exploration of new areas is always risky. If we discover that the new area is well defended (*strong* and *full*, in Sun Tzu's terms), we must withdraw quickly. We should think of our initial movements into new areas as probes—tests for emptiness. If we don't find emptiness and need, we want to keep our expenses and commitments to a minimum. This is why businesspeople probe new markets by test marketing before committing to them. Test marketing is usually done very quietly. Moving into new areas secretly makes it much easier for us to withdraw should these areas not prove to be successful.

We move into new areas quickly, but we can also withdraw from them quickly. Speed is the essence of warfare. Weakness is closely related to speed. Speed is only possible if we are moving through emptiness and weakness, but small, weak forces move faster than large, strong ones. We can move quickly through empty areas and into new positions if they are open. We can also move quickly if we keep our initial movements small. If the new positions prove not to be open, we must be able to move quickly out of them. This means that our commitment to that area must also be weak.

Lesson 112: The Timing of Battle

If you want to meet a challenge of your opponents, what do you do?

A.   You should go to the place they are.

B.   You should go to the place they need.

C.   You should avoid all battles.

D.   You should welcome all battles.

> *Always pick your own battles.*
> *The enemy can hide behind high walls and deep trenches.*
> *I do not try to win by fighting him directly.*
> *Instead, I attack a place that he must rescue.*
> *I avoid the battles that I don't want.*
> *I can divide the ground and yet defend it.*
> *I don't give the enemy anything to win.*
> *Divert him from coming to where you defend.*

THE ART OF WAR 6:3.10-17

Answer: B. You should go to the place they need.

When the time is right to engage in a direct challenge, we use the principle of weakness and strength to do so correctly. We call this strategy *diversion*. Using diversions, we avoid confrontations where and when our opponents want them and instead set up battles that we will win.

First, we never move directly against our competitors' strength. We never move against areas where they are expecting an attack and have had time to prepare to defend themselves. Such defended areas of strength are relatively small. Strength requires support. The resources that provide support come from a much broader area. As members of society, we all unconsciously depend upon many different forms of support. Because support areas are so numerous, most support resources are undefended and often go unrecognized.

The resources that we need are our weaknesses. The resources that our opponents need are their weaknesses. Since we and our opponents depend on a number of different resources, we need only find those that are undefended in order to undermine our opponents.

To focus our attack on these needed resources, we must understand our opponents and their support network.

Lesson 113: The Key to Strength

What is the key to creating strength?

A.   Imagination.

B.   Vision.

C.   Ability.

D.   Focus.

> *Make other men take a position while you take none.*
> *Then focus your forces where the enemy divides his forces.*
> *Where you focus, you unite your forces.*
> *When the enemy divides, he creates many small groups.*
> *You want your large group to attack one of his small ones.*
> *Then you have many men where the enemy has but a few.*
> *Your larger force can overwhelm his smaller one.*
> *Then go on to the next small enemy group.*
> *You can take them one at a time.*

THE ART OF WAR 6:4.1-9

Answer: D. Focus.

Once we identify the key area of a key weakness, we must focus all our resources on it. This is what creates strength. This is an extension of the discussion about unity, focus, and strength in the third chapter. When we can focus on one key area where we see weakness, we become strong in that area and successful in filling the emptiness that defines its weakness.

Focus is difficult for most people. There seem to be many different areas that need attention. Sun Tzu taught that there is always just one key opening where the weakness is greatest. If we can identify it and focus on it, we are able to break through easily and make the best progress.

Instead of thinking of this focus point as an opening, we can think of it as a weakness, a constraint that limits our growth. Organizations are pipelines for productivity. Production passes through many stages (in business, these are design, manufacturing, marketing, sales, distribution, etc.); each has its own maximum capacity. One area is always the key constraint, limiting the total flow of production. For many businesses, the constraint is marketing and sales. For the lucky few, it is the ability to produce. We must identify the constraint and focus on it. Open it, and our position improves.

Lesson 114: Overcoming Larger Opponents

How do you overcome large opponents and large problems?

A.   Addition.

B.   Subtraction.

C.   Multiplication.

D.   Division.

> *You must keep the place that you have chosen as a battleground a secret.*
> *The enemy must not know.*
> *Force the enemy to prepare his defense in many places.*
> *You want the enemy to defend many places.*
> *Then you can choose where to fight.*
> *His forces will be weak there.*

THE ART OF WAR 6:5.1-6

Answer: D. Division.

Again, ignorance is weakness and emptiness. Physical size is never a problem for Sun Tzu. Size is a matter of perspective. Anything that is large must have many parts. Instead of looking at the whole, we need to look at the parts. Since we can break large problems—or opponents—into many parts, we can choose the parts we want to tackle. For Sun Tzu, the ability to discern different parts was a necessary component of a leader's vision.

Our opponents will naturally divide their resources among different interests. We don't have to force this division to happen. It happens naturally because most people fail to develop a focus. Instead, they try to do too many different things at once.

All the challenges we face can also be divided into bite-sized tasks. We then should select the easiest of those tasks to tackle first. Over time, we can whittle any problem down to size, not by facing it directly but by taking it apart.

We must keep our focus a secret. Our knowledge is our strength. If our opponents know that we are targeting a specific area, we are inviting them to unite their resources against us. Focus is usually a reaction to a challenge, not a long-term plan. If opponents don't know where we are focusing our efforts, they cannot counter our efforts.

Lesson 115: Preventing Weakness

How do you prevent weakness somewhere in your organization?

A.   You cannot prevent weakness.

B.   You must divide your resources evenly.

C.   You must train your people well.

D.   You must know your weaknesses.

> *If he reinforces his front lines, he depletes his rear.*
> *If he reinforces his rear, he depletes his front.*
> *If he reinforces his right flank, he depletes his left.*
> *If he reinforces his left flank, he depletes his right.*
> *Without knowing the place of attack, he cannot prepare.*
> *Without knowing the right place, he will be weak everywhere.*
>
> THE ART OF WAR 6:5.7-12

Answer: A. You cannot prevent weakness.

Though Sun Tzu is talking about the opposition here, the original Chinese is more abstract, more like an equation. Its advice can be applied equally to either the enemy or our own organization. Neither we nor our opponent can be everywhere. We cannot do everything. Resources are limited. No matter how large or small our organization is, we must make choices about how we distribute our resources. If we ask people in any part of our organization, they will tell us that they have too few resources for what needs to be done. The world that we compete in is always much too large for the resources that we actually have. No matter how strong we are, we still have weaknesses.

Weakness and strength are part of every organization. Focus does not change this. We can focus on the bottlenecks in our organization, but in doing so we weaken other parts of our organization. We must be aware of this. We are always juggling resources, doing a balancing act.

This is also true for our competitors. If we know where they are focusing their resources, we know where their strengths are, and we also know where their weaknesses might be. This is why Sun Tzu wants us to keep our own focus a secret. We don't want others to know where our strengths are and where our weaknesses might be.

Lesson 116: What Our Opponents Defend

What do you want your opponents to defend?

A.   Their strengths.

B.   Their weaknesses.

C.   Their resources.

D.   Their decisions.

> *The enemy has weak points.*
> *Prepare your men against them.*
> *He has strong points.*
> *Make his men prepare themselves against you.*

THE ART OF WAR 6:5.13-16

Answer: A. Their strengths.

If our competitors defend their strengths, they leave their weaknesses open to attack. In the world of challenges, our opponents have strengths and we have strengths. We both also have weaknesses. What matters in the outcome is how we focus our strengths in the competitive environment.

To advance our position and take away our opponent's territory, we want to aim our strengths at the weaknesses of the competition, that is, at the needs of the market. We must not aim our strengths at the strengths of the competition. We should never seek to beat others at their own game. Our goal should be to turn the game around, taking what others see as unimportant and making it important.

In doing this, however, we don't want to have our competitors strengthen their weak points. Instead, they must feel as though their strengths are being threatened. People are naturally proud of their strengths. They are quick to defend them because they are confident in defending them. Politicians campaign in areas where they are popular. Businesspeople advertise products that are already selling well. We want them to follow this natural inclination. We don't want to do anything to disturb this natural tendency.

People have weaknesses because they consider some areas of their responsibility relatively unimportant. As challengers, we have to make those areas our focus without our opponents realizing it. These areas are critical to the contest.

Lesson 117: The Ability to Focus

What gives you the ability to focus where you must?

A.   Position.

B.   Innovation.

C.   Leadership.

D.   Knowledge.

> *You must know the battleground.*
> *You must know the time of battle.*
> *You can then travel a thousand miles and still win the battle.*
>
> THE ART OF WAR 6:6.1-3

Answer: D. Knowledge.

Sun Tzu defines "battle" as meeting a specific challenge or a specific opponent. This meeting occurs at a specific time and place. In politics, for example, we know clearly when the election takes place and who our opponents are.

In other competitive arenas, the location of the battle is not always clear. In business, for example, we may not know who is buying our product and against whom we are competing. Sun Tzu taught that a vague idea of competition is an illusion. Competition is real, solid, and specific. It occurs at specific times and places. For a businessperson, the battle among opponents takes place whenever a customer makes a decision about what to buy and a judgment about the value of products and services.

The more we know about the specific battles we face, the more successful we will be. Ignorance is weakness. The less we know about the specific time and place of battle, the weaker we are. For some competitors, such as salespeople, this is easy because they work one-on-one with the decision-makers, but no matter what our form of competition, we must work to know where and when competitive decisions are made. The more details we have about the specifics, the more effective our strategy will be.

We must choose the battleground and climate, where and when we want to compete. We choose the territory that we want to win. Perhaps more importantly, we choose where we don't want to compete. Often it is what we avoid doing that makes us successful. We succeed when we compete under the best possible circumstances.

Lesson 118: Knowledge of Situations

When do you know enough about your battleground?

A.   You never know enough.

B.   When you know more than most people.

C.   When you know more than your opponents.

D.   When you are satisfied with your knowledge.

> *The enemy should not know the battleground.*
> *He shouldn't know the time of battle.*
> *His left will be unable to support his right.*
> *His right will be unable to support his left.*
> *His front lines will be unable to support his rear.*
> *His rear will be unable to support his front.*
> *His support is distant even if it is only ten miles away.*
> *What unknown place can be close?*

THE ART OF WAR 6:6.4-11

Answer: C. When you know more than your opponents.

For Sun Tzu, our knowledge and abilities are judged relative to the knowledge and abilities of our opponents. There are an infinite number of facts, but knowledge is finite. We cannot know everything about other people's decisions, but we can work to know more than our opponents know. Nothing is completely full.

This is why deception and bluffing are so important. Ideally, we want our opponents to think that our challenge will take one form when, in reality, the real competitive battle will take another form entirely.

This happens all the time in business competition. When Starbucks started opening coffee shops, did any existing coffee company or coffee shop chain understand how its competitive arena was being redefined? When Dell started selling computers directly to consumers, did the other major manufacturers realize that the ground of competition had changed?

Innovation can take many forms, but one of the most important innovations comes from redefining the time and place of battle, that is, redefining the battlefield. We must see openings that our competitors are unable to see. When we focus on these areas, the size and strength of our opposition simply doesn't matter. Our opponents are unable to succeed against us.

Lesson 119: The Value of Size

When does your relative size compared to your opponents' size matter in a strategy?

A.   Size never matters.

B.   Size matters in the opponents you choose.

C.   Size matters over the long term.

D.   Size matters at a specific time and place.

We control the balance of forces.
The enemy may have many men but they are superfluous.
How can they help him to victory?

We say:
You must let victory happen.

The enemy may have many men.
You can still control him without a fight.

THE ART OF WAR 6:6.12-18

Answer: D. Size matters at a specific time and place.

Over the long term, the general size of our opponent doesn't matter strategically at all. There are many times when choosing large opponents is a strategic advantage, especially since they have to defend many different areas, and we can easily focus on one of them.

Size does matter when we meet an opponent in battle at a specific time and place. General overall superiority doesn't matter. Only local superiority does. This is the meaning of focus. It gives us that local superiority that we need. The secret of using strength and weakness, fullness and emptiness, and knowledge and ignorance is setting up the right confrontations. We want to put our resources where our opponents have the fewest resources. We want knowledge where they are ignorant. It is the balance of one against the other in a specific time and place that makes the difference.

We may want our initial contests to be relatively small, but in every specific competition we need to have overwhelming force on our side. Even the smallest companies can be "bigger" and more knowledgeable in a narrow situation. These narrow situations are what we look for in order to develop them as stepping-stones to success.

Lesson 120: The Balance of Power

When is balancing strength and weakness important?

A.   In your planning.

B.   In your actions.

C.   In your positioning.

D.   In all of the above.

> *When you form your strategy, know the strengths and weaknesses of your*
> *plan.*
> *When you execute, know how to manage both action and inaction.*
> *When you take a position, know the deadly and the winning grounds.*
> *When you battle, know when you have too many or too few men.*
>
> THE ART OF WAR 6:7.1-4

Answer: D. In all of the above.

Strength and weakness, fullness and emptiness, knowledge and ignorance are very powerful concepts that we continuously use in strategy. We must ask ourselves about this balance at every phase of competition. We must think about this balance when we are planning. We must question this balance when we are advancing our position. We must know about it when we are choosing a battlefield. We must wonder about it whenever we confront our opponents.

All strategies have weaknesses and strengths. We find that it is easy to see what is good about our plans, but we must know the weaknesses of our plans just as well. It is these weaknesses that we must guard against.

This awareness is even more important when we are considering action, moving into a new territory. Often what we don't do is more important than what we choose to do. Since time is limited, when we choose a course of action, we are also choosing what we will not do, at least at this time. This choice is often unconscious. We must make this decision for inaction consciously instead of unconsciously.

Sometimes we must simply choose not to act. We must choose to decline a confrontation with our opponents. We must choose to wait to be attacked rather than to attack. Choosing these forms of inaction is as important as choosing action.

Lesson 121: The Key Weakness

What is your opponents' most important form of weakness?

A.   Emptiness in one of their positions.

B.   Ignorance of the position that you desire.

C.   Their need for resources.

D.   Their lack of overall forces.

Use your position as your war's centerpiece.
Arrive at the battle without a formation.
Don't take a position in advance.
Then even the best spies cannot report it.
Even the wisest general cannot plan to counter you.
Take a position where you can triumph using superior numbers.
Keep opposing forces ignorant.
Everyone should learn your location after your position has given you success.
No one should know how your location gives you a winning position.
Make a successful battle one from which the enemy cannot recover.
You must continually adjust your position to his position.

THE ART OF WAR 6:7.5-15

Answer: B. Ignorance of the position that you desire.

Toward the end of his chapters, Sun Tzu often puts his topic in a larger context. Positioning and knowledge are together the heart of his strategic system. Weakness takes many forms, but no form of weakness is as important to our success as our opponent's ignorance. Strategic positioning in Sun Tzu's system is the way we win a payoff in meeting a challenge. It is the step in strategy that creates strength, either by generating revenue or creating an immediate advantage over our opponents. Our opponents should never understand how we plan to use a desired position against them to make ourselves successful. Their ignorance of our desired position makes them vulnerable while it protects us.

In business, this specifically means that we don't let our competitors know how we plan to make money out of a given market. In politics, it means that they shouldn't know how we plan to leverage a certain issue. In advancing our career, it means that rivals shouldn't know what type of future position we hope to advance to.

Lesson 122: The Key to Strength

What is the key to taking advantage of strength and weakness?

A.   Flexibility.

B.   Organization.

C.   Training.

D.   Planning.

> *Manage your military position like water.*
> *Water takes every shape.*
> *It avoids the high and moves to the low.*
> *Your war can take any shape.*
> *It must avoid the strong and strike the weak.*
> *Water follows the shape of the land that directs its flow.*
> *Your forces follow the enemy, who determines how you win.*
>
> THE ART OF WAR 6:8.1-7

Answer: A. Flexibility.

As we have said before, water is Sun Tzu's metaphor for change. In this lesson, his focus is on our ability to adjust to change. When meeting a challenge or opponent in a dynamic environment, we cannot predict the exact choices our opponents will make. This means that we cannot predict exactly where weakness and strength will appear. Openings can appear in an instant. We must be continually ready to take advantage of these openings when they occur.

In other words, no quality of our plan is as important as being opportunistic. When a weakness in our opponents appears, we must be ready to take advantage of it. Perhaps more importantly, we must be patient and wait until the needed opening appears. When those opportunities appear, we must reshape our plans and our organization to take advantage of those opportunities. We shouldn't wait for them to conform to our exact requirements. We must conform to the openings that we see.

It is the competitive battlefield and our opponents that create our opportunities. We must naturally flow toward the needs of those around us and the weaknesses of our competition. Our organization and training must support this ability. To a large degree, positioning and our ability to find advantages depend on flowing toward the needs of the market.

Lesson 123: The Choice of Techniques

What are the best approaches for you to exploit your opponent's weaknesses?

A.   Proven approaches.

B.   Standard approaches.

C.   Planned approaches.

D.   Nonstandard approaches.

> *Make war without a standard approach.*
> *Water has no consistent shape.*
> *If you follow the enemy's shifts and changes, you can always win.*
> *We call this shadowing.*
>
> THE ART OF WAR 6:8.8-11

Answer: D. Nonstandard approaches.

The lesson here echoes the previous chapter's discussion of innovation and momentum, but it focuses specifically on being creative in taking advantage of the openings that our opponents give us. We must follow our competition closely in order to see our opportunity develop. When an opportunity arises, we must instantly be ready to take advantage of it. This means being opportunistic. It means being unpredictable. It means doing what our opponents least expect.

The idea of "shadowing" also requires us to mimic our opponents while we are waiting for openings to develop. If they are direct competitors, we must be sure to match their accomplishments, announcements, and new products with accomplishments, announcements, and new products of our own. If meeting the challenge requires us to learn more—for example, through research and development—we must make sure that we never fall behind our opponents in the race for knowledge. We are waiting for an opening, but we must keep up with our competitors and follow their twists and turns. This is a very active form of waiting, on what Sun Tzu calls "open terrain" in a later chapter.

While we are adjusting to our opponents on open terrain, we avoid taking the initiative. We also avoid making a long-term commitment to a plan of action. We don't take the initiative and make a commitment until we see the opening that we need.

Lesson 124: The Choice of Approach

If your approach has worked well in the past, what do you do?

A.   Look for an opportunity to use it again.

B.   Keep using that approach until it stops working.

C.   Use the same approach in different forms.

D.   Find a new approach for each situation.

> *Fight five different campaigns without a firm rule for victory.*
> *Use all four seasons without a consistent position.*
> *Your timing must be sudden.*
> *A few weeks determine your failure or success.*

THE ART OF WAR 6:8.12-15

Answer: D. Find a new approach for each situation.

There is a difference between ten years of experience and one year of experience repeated ten times. Good strategy demands that we continuously advance our position. An approach that has worked before will not work again, because our position has changed. Not only does our position change, but our competitive environment also changes. Our opponents adjust. Old openings close. Every campaign, every new competitive advance demands new methods, new issues, and new approaches.

This is why speed, timing, and the momentum of change are critical for success. Most people and organizations are too slow to change, too fond of past successes to try new ideas. Most armies are refighting their last war rather than dealing with the current situation.

If we want to succeed, we must never hesitate to try new ideas, adopting them if they work and discarding them if they don't work. We must quickly adjust our methods to fit the emerging trends. New concepts arise, especially in today's world, and we must adapt to these changes. We must be capable of adapting more quickly than the competition.

Change is our only constant. Sun Tzu's strategy distrusts long-term, detailed plans. In the dynamic environment of competition, too many factors are changing too quickly. Rather than waste time planning, we should spend our time advancing. We act, defending and keeping up with opponents until we see an opening. When we see an opportunity, we must seize it quickly.

Chapter 7

軍 爭

Armed Conflict

This chapter moves the discussion of strategic confrontations one step further. "Battle" means meeting a challenge or a competitor, but it doesn't necessarily mean conflict. This chapter tackles the specific topic of avoiding conflict or, if it cannot be avoided, dealing with it successfully.

Without understanding strategy, most people think that war or competition consists of only one thing: dealing with hostile, violent confrontations. Sun Tzu called this particular type of competition "armed conflict." Unlike most people, he did not consider it the central fixture of warfare. Strategic warfare means advancing our position, not conflict. In his era and in ours, people mistake the art of war as the art of fighting. They focus too much of their thinking on direct, violent conflict. They confuse fighting with winning. Sun Tzu addresses these misconceptions in this chapter.

In the everyday world, we don't often come to blows with our opponents, but we do have direct, hostile confrontations, which are the modern equivalent of armed conflict. Everyday commerce requires us to face a host of unpleasant, painful confrontations. We have to fire people. We have to deny people what they want. We have lawsuits. We sometimes have to face competitors directly in a sales competition and stop them. What should our attitude toward these hostile confrontations be?

Sun Tzu always wants us to keep our focus on the real prize of strategy: success. Do direct confrontations help us find success or do they hurt us? What is our goal when we get into a confrontation? What are we trying to accomplish? Is the hostile confrontation truly unavoidable? If so, what are the important issues in managing the confrontation? How do we make sure that the confrontation ends successfully? These are the questions that are addressed in this chapter.

Lesson 125: The Source of Disaster

What is the most disastrous situation in competition?

A.   Facing a larger opponent.

B.   Engaging in conflict.

C.   Holding a weak position.

D.   Sustaining a loss.

> *Everyone uses the arts of war.*
> *You accept orders from the government.*
> *Then you assemble your army.*
> *You organize your men and build camps.*
> *You must avoid disasters from armed conflict.*

THE ART OF WAR 7:1.1-5

Answer: B. Engaging in conflict.

People think of competition as a fight, a hostile, violent confrontation—in a word, conflict. Sun Tzu saw that successful strategy depends on avoiding conflict whenever possible. The goal of facing challenges is not conflict. When we "accept orders from our government," our goal is to accomplish something specific relating to advancing our position. For this purpose, we organize our army and our resources. We organize to achieve the goal that we have been given. Sun Tzu wants to make it clear that hostile confrontation, armed conflict, is more often a hindrance to achieving our goal than it is a benefit.

Some people want to fight. They want to beat, embarrass, or hurt people. They want to get even with those who they think have wronged them. These people are not true competitors. They certainly aren't strategists. The goal of strategy is never simply to beat an opponent. Beating an opponent gets us nothing. Sun Tzu's system is completely goal-oriented. His concern, starting from the second chapter, is on making victory pay—that is, making the cost of competition worth the investment we must make in it.

To this end, armed conflict, or hostile confrontation, is extremely risky. Every hostile confrontation courts "disaster," that is, a costly failure. Sometimes hostile confrontations cannot be avoided, but they certainly should never be sought out.

Lesson 126: Avoiding Conflict

How much difficulty should you be willing to go through in order to avoid conflict?

A.   Avoid conflict as long as you don't detour from your plan.

B.   Avoid conflict but do not create problems for yourself.

C.   Avoid conflict even if it creates problems for you.

D.   Avoid conflict unless you are sure to win.

> *Seeking armed conflict can be disastrous.*
> *Because of this, a detour can be the shortest path.*
> *Because of this, problems can become opportunities.*

THE ART OF WAR 7:1.6-8

Answer: C. Avoid conflict even if it creates problems for you.

Sun Tzu considered avoiding hostile confrontations extremely important to long-term success. He saw that people fall into conflict because it is simply the path of least resistance.

Instead of seeing the avoidance of potential confrontation as a problem, Sun Tzu sees it as an opportunity to get creative. People get into conflicts because they are too lazy or too foolish to avoid them. Energetic and inventive leaders can avoid almost all forms of conflict and benefit from the experience.

Why do confrontations occur? Sun Tzu poses two possible reasons.

First, hostile confrontations occur because we are unwilling to change our plans. We hold to our course despite the fact that we see it leading us into conflict. People who are unwilling to change their plans to avoid conflict are going to find themselves embroiled in it. Sun Tzu teaches us that this is foolish. Confrontations are always much more expensive and time-consuming than changing our plans. We are foolish if we are not willing to take detours to avoid confrontations.

The second common reason that we find ourselves in hostile confrontation is that conflict is easy to fall into. People's self-interests naturally collide. Problems exist because everyone has different goals. We have to work to avoid conflict. Sun Tzu suggests that avoiding confrontation is well worth the effort. We discover our best ideas and opportunities in working to avoid conflict. He teaches that those problems that we hate are really the source of our biggest opportunities.

Lesson 127: The Essence of Strategy

Which of the following ideas is more important in strategy?
A.   Taking advantage of opportunity.
B.   Intimidating rivals.
C.   Destroying opponents.
D.   Proving your superiority.

> *Use an indirect route as your highway.*
> *Use the search for advantage to guide you.*
> *When you fall behind, you must catch up.*
> *When you get ahead, you must wait.*
> *You must know the detour that most directly accomplishes your plan.*
>
> THE ART OF WAR 7:1.9-13

Answer: A. Taking advantage of opportunity.

When we seek to create a strategy, we are not looking for a fight. We are looking for an opportunity. There is a huge difference between looking for a fight and looking for an opportunity, but for some reason people confuse them. Strategy is focused on accomplishment, achieving a goal at a minimum of cost. Conflict and destruction raise the costs of winning, decrease the certainty of having victory pay, and must always be avoided.

Sun Tzu says that opportunities are not discovered by using the same methods used by others. We must plan on using new methods to uncover an opportunity. Innovation is easier if we are looking for an opportunity. The search for opportunity naturally takes us to places that others have missed, along routes that others have not taken. Conflict only gets in the way of our search for opportunities. It distracts us from the search for true success, forcing us to focus on simple subjugation.

Even though we are taking advantage of opportunities, we can still execute a strategic plan that focuses on accomplishing a goal. The plan must subjugate itself to the opportunity, being flexible enough to use every opportunity. Planning is often the key in recognizing an opportunity. In executing a plan, we must still keep to our plan and timetable even when we are being opportunistic. In execution, we cannot forget our timing. We cannot let ourselves fall behind, nor should we get ahead of ourselves. To keep our forces together, we must make sure that some don't get ahead of the others.

Lesson 128: Avoiding Hostilities

Should you always avoid hostile confrontation?

A.   You should not avoid confrontation if it creates an advantage.

B.   You should not avoid confrontation if it hurts the competition.

C.   You should never avoid confrontation.

D.   You should always avoid confrontation.

> *Undertake armed conflict when it creates an advantage.*
> *Seeking armed conflict for its own sake is dangerous.*
>
> THE ART OF WAR 7:1.14-15

Answer: A. You should not avoid confrontation if it creates an advantage.

Hostile confrontations are dangerous, often disastrous. They are always costly. However, we can find ourselves in situations in which such confrontations are to our advantage—where the cost of conflict reduces our other costs and allows us to achieve our goals more easily. When hostile confrontations can help us achieve our goals with more certainty, we can engage in them.

Though people are often much too quick to engage in hostile confrontation, we can also be too shy about confrontation. We cannot let our cowardice guide us any more than we should let hostility guide us. We must be guided only by opportunity. Strategy is goals oriented. Though conflict usually takes us further from most goals, when a confrontation brings us to our goal, when we will win much more than we lose, we must directly challenge our opponents.

Because such confrontations are always costly, we should certainly look for ways to avoid them. Again, most confrontations occur not because they offer a true advantage but because people are either too stubborn in sticking to their plans or too lazy to work to avoid them. The work involved in avoiding confrontation is almost always effort well spent. It saves us more than it costs us. We avoid confrontation because it is usually extremely profitable to do so.

The point is that the cost of confrontation is no excuse for fear or cowardice. The cost can be trivial compared to the gain. However, it must be the gain that matters.

Lesson 129: Setting Up Confrontations

How do you set up confrontations in which you can gain an advantage?

A.   You build up your resources.

B.   You act quickly.

C.   You push your people harder.

D.   You cannot set up such confrontations.

> *You can build up an army to fight for an advantage.*
> *Then you won't catch the enemy.*
> *You can force your army to go fight for an advantage.*
> *Then you abandon your heavy supply wagons.*

THE ART OF WAR 7:2.1-4

Answer: D. You cannot set up such confrontations.

As human beings, we are exceptionally good at fooling ourselves about the nature of reality. We want to think that we are in control, masters of the universe. We aren't. We want to think that we can create our opportunity to beat our opponents. We cannot. Unfortunately, competitive situations are based on a competitive reality that is beyond the control of any one party. Our environment is bigger than we are.

The fundamental principle of strategy is that we cannot create our opportunities. Our environment and our opponents must create opportunities for us to take advantage of. We certainly cannot create opportunity out of conflict because conflict is costly. It is so costly that both parties often lose. One may win the battle, but in many conflicts the costs are so high that even the winner is often a loser.

People often get so interested in beating their opponents that they think only about the damage that they can inflict. In this state of mind, we forget about the punishment that we will also absorb in the process. We forget about the costs. We forget that our opponents are not going to make it easy for us to damage them.

Sun Tzu wants us to remember our goals, to focus on making victory pay. In trying to create an opportunity by damaging our opponents, we forget that our opponents are also planning on damaging us. This endangers our position. It causes us to forget about protecting ourselves and our resources when it is those resources that keep us strong.

Lesson 130: Chasing Opportunities

How can you catch up to a weaker but quicker opponent to be successful?

A. Don't stop day or night.

B. Use many routes at the same time.

C. Let your strongest lead.

D. You cannot.

> *You keep only your armor and hurry after the enemy.*
> *You avoid stopping day or night.*
> *You use many roads at the same time.*
> *You go hundreds of miles to fight for an advantage.*
> *Then the enemy catches your commanders and your army.*
> *Your strong soldiers get there first.*
> *Your weaker soldiers follow behind.*
> *Using this approach, only one in ten will arrive.*
> *You can try to go fifty miles to fight for an advantage.*
> *Then your commanders and army will stumble.*
> *Using this method, only half of your soldiers will make it.*
> *You can try to go thirty miles to fight for an advantage.*
> *Then only two out of three get there.*

THE ART OF WAR 7:2.5-17

Answer: D. You cannot.

Sun Tzu's point is simple. Success cannot come from violating the principles of strategy. One of those principles is that smaller forces are less powerful but larger forces cannot catch them. We can try a lot of different techniques to beat these laws of nature, but, no matter what we do, it will cost us. That cost will show up somewhere else in our competitive efforts.

There is a natural balance at work. When we push our people, we trade speed for unity. We can give up our strength for speed. We cannot create an advantage and shouldn't try to. The enemy must leave us an opening to give us an advantage. If an opening isn't there, we cannot create it. The power to command people is easily confused with the power to make things happen. As leaders, it is our responsibility to direct people to success. We are abusing our power if we arrogantly think that we have the power to force our people to create success for us.

Lesson 131: Success without Resources

What is the risk in pushing on without resources?

A.   You will fail completely.

B.   You will suffer a serious setback.

C.   You will fall behind the enemy.

D.   You will not be as successful as you think.

If you make your army travel without good supply lines, your army will die.
Without supplies and food, your army will die.
If you don't save the harvest, your army will die.

THE ART OF WAR 7:2.18-20

Answer: A. You will fail completely.

We must remember that the first goal of competition is survival. The most serious mistakes that we can make in competition are those that risk destruction. Sun Tzu clearly puts the mistake of going forward without resources into this critical class of potentially fatal mistakes. We work to advance our position and win more territory because our control of the ground is our source of resources. Without resources, we can do nothing.

We can win in armed conflict, but pressing for an advantage without resources and searching for successful confrontations is worse than foolish. It is totally self-destructive.

In the long term, beating opponents in direct conflict is relatively unimportant. The strategic goal is always advancing our position so that we control better and more productive territory. Over the long term, success always comes down to economic strength. We cannot sacrifice our resources and expect to win. Protecting our source of income, our resources, and supporters provides for the future. If we manage our organizations well, we preserve our ability to compete in the future. We survive. Survival should be the first and foremost goal of anyone striving for success.

If we keep ourselves financially strong, we are in a much better position to compete than if we simply seek situations in which we can beat our opposition. The purpose of competition is never simply beating the competition. The purpose of strategy is survival, growth, and prosperity—nothing more, nothing less.

Lesson 132: Knowledge Is Power

What is the most important knowledge in advancing your position?

A.   The battleground.
B.   The competition's position.
C.   The trends of the time.
D.   The skills of your organization.

> *Do not let any of your potential enemies know of what you are planning.*
> *Still, you must not hesitate to form alliances.*
> *You must know the mountains and forests.*
> *You must know where the obstructions are.*
> *You must know where the marshes are.*
> *If you don't, you cannot move the army.*
> *If you don't, you must use local guides.*
> *If you don't, you cannot take advantage of the terrain.*

THE ART OF WAR 7:2.21-28

Answer: A. The battleground.

To use strategy, we must understand the battleground on which we are competing. Where does our income come from? What is the source of our resources? What is the basis of our financial strength? In other words, what is the foundation of our ability to survive? Winning the ground gives us the wherewithal to move forward. In business, this means winning sales from the marketplace. In politics, it is getting donations from voters. In every competitive arena, we are competing for the support of the ground.

Controlling and understanding the ground is paramount in our ability to survive and prosper. It is the ground that potentially gives us an advantage, not our ability to push ourselves or others. We must avoid confrontation with the competition unless we have an advantage. Since that advantage comes only from the ground, our own efforts must focus on winning the ground. To do that, we must know how to take advantage of the ground.

To gain the advantages of a marketplace, we must not hesitate to make alliances with others who control some part of it. We must not hesitate to employ those who are familiar with the territory. We must know especially the problems and difficulties encountered in dealing with specific competitive arenas. This is what gives us an advantage.

Lesson 133: Upsetting the Competition

How do you upset your competition?

A.   By confrontation.

B.   By bluffing.

C.   By observation.

D.   By consolidation.

> *You make war using a deceptive position.*
> *If you use deception, then you can move.*
> *Using deception, you can upset the enemy and change the situation.*
> *You can move as quickly as the wind.*
> *You can rise like the forest.*
> *You can invade and plunder like fire.*
> *You can stay as motionless as a mountain.*
> *You can be as mysterious as the fog.*
> *You can strike like sounding thunder.*

THE ART OF WAR 7:3.1-9

Answer: B. By bluffing.

We don't disturb our opponents by direct confrontation. They see a battle coming and prepare for it. We can seek strength and advantage from the ground, but if our competitors understand what we are doing, they should not be upset by it. They should expect it. If they understand what we are trying to win from our position, they will try to counter us, but that doesn't upset their plans. Only by bluffing can we catch our opponents off guard. Only by bluffing can we upset their plans.

We must disguise our opportunities and plans. As Sun Tzu said in the first chapter, we must make our opponents misread our situation. Everything we do sends a signal. If everything we do makes sense based on our knowledge, our opponents can read our situation from our actions. Sometimes we must do what doesn't make any sense based on our knowledge so we can send a confusing signal to our opponents.

We must never let other people, even our supporters, know exactly what our opportunities are and how much they will benefit us. We must keep our methods for generating value a secret. We must not let others know what we are trying to achieve until we have achieved it.

Lesson 134: Fertile, Empty Ground

When you discover fertile, empty ground, what should you do?

A.   Unite your forces.

B.   Divide your forces.

C.   Wait for your opponents.

D.   Defend your position.

> *Divide your troops to plunder the villages.*
> *When on open ground, dividing is an advantage.*
> *Don't worry about organization, just move.*
> *Be the first to find a new route that leads directly to a winning plan.*
> *This is how you are successful at armed conflict.*
>
> THE ART OF WAR 7:3.10-14

Answer: B. Divide your forces.

When we face our opponents, we must unite our forces, but when we find an open area, an area overlooked by our opponents, we should do the opposite. We should divide our forces, finding as many sources of revenue as possible from the new fertile ground. In business, when we find open, underdeveloped markets, we must waste no time in addressing as many of their needs as possible and getting as much out of them as we can. In politics, when we discover groups of overlooked voters, we can divide our focus among many of them.

Notice how the discussion has switched from confronting the competition to getting the benefits out of our competitive arena, the ground. What started as a discussion about direct confrontation and armed conflict has turned into a discussion about finding open, empty areas that we can profit from and that the competition doesn't know about.

How do we win armed conflict? By avoiding it entirely. Instead, we find areas that can enrich and strengthen us. Then, instead of uniting our forces to face the enemy, we can spread our resources throughout the territory to generate the greatest possible support from the ground. Winning the support and wealth of the ground advances our position, makes us stronger, and makes it impossible for our opponents to win.

Lesson 135: Priorities during Conflict

When conflict is unavoidable, what must be your first consideration?

A.   Communication.

B.   Direction.

C.   Resources.

D.   Vision.

> *Military experience says:*
> *"You can speak, but you will not be heard.*
> *You must use gongs and drums.*
> *You cannot really see your forces just by looking.*
> *You must use banners and flags."*
>
> THE ART OF WAR 7:4.1-5

Answer: A. Communication.

The best way to win from direct conflict is to avoid it entirely, but what about when we cannot avoid it? Employees must sometimes be fired. Rivals must sometimes be confronted. Mistakes and those who made them must be addressed. These are the situations that Sun Tzu explains in developing the strategy of conflict.

In a hostile confrontation, the first key is communication. Remember that battle—all meetings of opponents—is confused and messy. In making our plans, we must expect confrontations to be chaotic. We generally try to gain the initiative in battle by preparing surprises in advance that will give us momentum during the meeting and ward off conflict, but none of this planning will work without good communication. We cannot win in hostile confrontations if we do not have the support of others. We must seek that support and communicate exactly what is happening and what we need.

Within our immediate organization and the larger arena of our potential supporters, the key element of the communication system is visibility. Successful organizations all have good reporting and measuring systems that make all conflict within the organization visible. We do not want our competitive threats, problems, and challenges hidden within our organization. We also need strong visibility among our potential supporters. We need to use every tool at our disposal to communicate our message to those in our competitive arena whose support we desire.

Lesson 136: The Purpose of Communication

What is the purpose of good communication?

A.   Creativity.

B.   Unity.

C.   Discipline.

D.   Order.

> *You must master gongs, drums, banners, and flags.*
> *Place people as a single unit where they can all see and hear.*
> *You must unite them as one.*
> *Then, the brave cannot advance alone.*
> *The fearful cannot withdraw alone.*
> *You must force them to act as a group.*

THE ART OF WAR 7:4.6-11

Answer: B. Unity.

Unity is important in competition in general, but during hostile confrontation unity is critical. The key to unity is our philosophy, the shared values that define our competitive position. In any direct confrontation, we must continually remember to communicate our philosophy. In verbal confrontations, this often means raising the dialogue to larger, more universal issues rather than discussing details. We must insist that people recognize and embrace the organization's philosophy. Once people accept the importance of the underlying philosophical issues, they are more willing to support other people who share the same value.

Sun Tzu's system respects the dynamics of an organization. It recognizes that people have different skills and abilities. These differences among people are less important than our ability to work with others. Given good communication systems, we can take advantage of our people's strengths while minimizing their weaknesses.

Sun Tzu taught that unity depends on both what people see and what they hear. He teaches us to use symbols, graphic displays, and visual presentations to get people's attention and make ideas concrete. He teaches us to make our message loud and difficult to ignore. We must be subtle and secretive in our planning, but we must be extravagant at communicating our mission, assignments, and progress within our own organization.

Lesson 137: Communication Methods

What is the most important consideration in choosing your methods of communication?

A.   The type of organization.
B.   The type of confrontation.
C.   The type of opponent.
D.   The type of environment.

> *In night battles, you must use numerous fires and drums.*
> *In day battles, you must use many banners and flags.*
> *You must position your people to control what they see and hear.*
>
> THE ART OF WAR 7:4.12-14

Answer: D. The type of environment.

This lesson means that we must adjust our communication strategy to our environment. Our competitive environment has two components: time and place, heaven and earth, climate and ground—in Chinese, *tian* and *di*. Climate changes, and it is beyond our control. Different positions on the ground offer different advantages and disadvantages, but we get to choose our position. When we choose the ground, that is, our competitive arena, we have to realize that the ground comes with a specific climate.

We must recognize these two different aspects of our competitive environment in planning how we communicate.

From the beginning, we must adjust our communication to what we can and cannot control. We must recognize that time passes. Time changes the conditions under which communication can take place. Conditions can be as different as day and night. Conditions change over longer periods of time. Every competitive area has its own seasons. We must adjust our communication strategy to these changing conditions. We must foresee and adjust to the trends of the time in communicating our message. We must leverage changes in fashion to emphasize our message.

Finally, we must recognize that the size of our organization also affects communication. Organizations that are small and centrally located have less difficulty in communication than those that are large and spread out. Communication is like our ability to move in this regard.

Lesson 138: Key Elements in Communication

When communicating, what is the most important content in your communication?

A.   The value of your ideas.

B.   The timeliness of your information.

C.   The accuracy of information.

D.   The emotion in your ideas.

> *You control your army by controlling its emotions.*
> *As a general, you must be able to control emotions.*
>
> THE ART OF WAR 7:5.1-2

Answer: D. The emotion in your ideas.

Communication should provide information that is valuable, timely, and accurate, but more important than any of these is its emotional content. Too often, people focus on the tangible content in communication, but they overlook the fact that its emotional content is critical.

People choose to support us or work with us because they feel that it is in their best interest. This is an emotional decision. As humans, we use our emotions to predict an uncertain future. We develop logical arguments to back up our feelings. Our feelings come first. Our emotions are the basis for our actions. This is especially true in the highly emotional world of direct confrontations.

We must continuously consider the emotional content of everything we communicate. Though the topic here is communicating with our supporters, we must also be aware of the emotions that we are communicating to our opponents. All communication has emotional impact as well as intellectual impact. This is something that women are usually more aware of than men are. As leaders, we can never afford to treat our people as if they were automatons, machines that automatically do our bidding. We must tailor every message to satisfy our people's emotional needs.

When we think about communication, our first consideration is the emotional impact of our messages. How do we want people to feel? Do we make our supporters feel as if the situation is under control? Do we make others optimistic about the future? Do we give them faith in our decisions? These are the critical issues in communication.

Lesson 139: Timing Confrontations

When should you engage in a direct confrontation?

A.   At the beginning of the day.

B.   Before midday.

C.   In the afternoon.

D.   At the end of the day.

> *In the morning, a person's energy is high.*
> *During the day, it fades.*
> *By evening, a person's thoughts turn to home.*
> *You must use your troops wisely.*
> *Avoid the enemy's high spirits.*
> *Strike when he is lazy and wants to go home.*
> *This is how you master energy.*

THE ART OF WAR 7:5.3-9

Answer: D. At the end of the day.

Given the emotional nature of direct confrontation, we must consider not only the emotions of our people and allies but also the emotions of our opponents. We can affect people's emotions through communication, but we all go through emotional cycles that are related to time. This is in the realm of heaven, which is beyond our control. We can use these cycles to time our confrontations to target our opponents' emotional weak points.

The general rule of Sun Tzu's strategy is that we don't want to fight unless it will win more than the usually large costs of conflict. In situations in which conflict is unavoidable, we want to minimize the fight in our opponents. One way to do this is to time our battles so that they take place at the end of the day when people have less fight in them.

The end of the day is just one example of a time when our opponents don't want to fight. We could also force a confrontation right before a holiday when people are looking forward to getting away. We could pick a time when our opponents aren't feeling well. We might pick a time after they have gotten some bad news that discourages them. Any event that weakens their resolve and depresses their spirit makes them a good target for a confrontation. Our goal is not to create a fair fight but to minimize the cost of the battle as much as possible. This is the basic idea of attacking weakness.

Lesson 140: Emotions during Confrontation

What should your emotional state be during a confrontation?

A.   Relaxed.

B.   Angry.

C.   Impatient.

D.   Aggressive.

> *Use discipline to await the chaos of battle.*
> *Keep relaxed to await a crisis.*
> *This is how you master emotion.*

THE ART OF WAR 7:5.10-12

Answer: A. Relaxed.

Conflict and confrontations aren't pleasant. We shouldn't expect them to be pleasant. They aren't simple. They aren't painless. We must be prepared for the unpleasantness that is bound to occur. The way to minimize our losses in these situations is to remain calm.

Many people cannot face a confrontation unless they work themselves into an emotional state. This is a form of cowardice. If we hide behind our emotions instead of simply doing what must be done, we are making ourselves weaker when we need strength the most. Our emotional state can make an employee firing, an argument, or a criticism that much more confused and chaotic. We must battle chaos with control. By remaining calm during conflict, we can defuse much of the chaos in these situations.

We don't seek confrontations unless we can gain from them. We generally want to avoid conflict because it is so costly. Still, we all know that conflict in life is sometimes unavoidable. We must face the challenge of conflict when it is to our advantage, rather than running from it. Sometimes opponents must be challenged. People must be called to account. When these situations are advantageous, we shouldn't worry over the fact or feel bad because they cannot be avoided. We must simply accept their necessity and do what must be done. We should not take pleasure in it any more than we should hate it. We should be emotionally prepared for the unpleasantness of confrontation. We must expect the confrontation to turn ugly. If we keep ourselves cool and businesslike during such situations, we can turn these conflicts to our advantage.

Lesson 141: Preparation for Confrontation

What should you do to prepare yourself and your people for a confrontation?

A.   Get out of your normal environment.

B.   Refuse to let yourself get comfortable.

C.   Pamper yourself.

D.   Avoid preparing for the event.

> *Stay close to home to await a distant enemy.*
> *Stay comfortable to await the weary enemy.*
> *Stay well fed to await the hungry enemy.*
> *This is how you master power.*

THE ART OF WAR 7:5.13-16

Answer: C. Pamper yourself.

In hostile confrontations, it is our emotional edge that can make the difference between success and failure. We want to time our confrontations so that our opponents are at their weakest. This isn't only a matter of picking the right time of day. It is also a matter of picking the right conditions. Conversely, we want battles to take place when we are at our strongest.

When we can choose the site for a confrontation, we want to choose a site where we are comfortable. We want the battle to take place in our chosen space, a place where we know the ground, and where we feel comfortable and our opponent feels uncertain and ill at ease. We want to fight for the opponent's territory, but conflict should occur in a site where we are more comfortable than our opponent can be.

We want hostile confrontations to take place at a time when we are rested and our opponents are tired. If we are planning a confrontation late in the day, we should get extra rest during the day to make sure that we are ready for it. If we have to travel to the battleground, we should arrive as early as possible, rest, and get comfortable with our surroundings.

It isn't a bad idea to eat well before facing a hostile confrontation. We want to give ourselves not only the physical but emotional energy we need to be successful. Hostile confrontations that create a real advantage should be rare enough events that we can afford the luxury of pampering ourselves before the showdown. Pampering ourselves and our supporters increases our organization's unity and power.

Lesson 142: Your Opponent's Condition

What should you do when your opponent seems relaxed and well prepared for a confrontation?

A.   Delay the confrontation.

B.   Suspect appearances.

C.   Accept the inevitable.

D.   Confuse the situation.

> *Don't entice the enemy when his ranks are orderly.*
> *You must not attack when his formations are solid.*
> *This is how you master adaptation.*
>
> THE ART OF WAR 7:6.1-3

Answer: A. Delay the confrontation.

Even when hostile confrontations are inevitable, we can still control their timing. When the situation in any way favors our opponents, we should delay the confrontation until our opponent is weakened. Given the paramount importance of emotion in the success of these encounters, we must pick a time that works in our favor as carefully as we pick a winning position.

We must have trust in Sun Tzu's concept of weakness and strength. Sun Tzu teaches that all strength degrades over time. All situations under heaven change. Our opponents may be orderly and well prepared now, but they won't always be. An opportunity in which we have the emotional advantage will inevitably arise in the future.

Our potential mistake here is impatience. Since we usually dread these encounters, we often have to work ourselves up to face the challenge. When we reach an emotional state and feel ready, we naturally want to get the conflict over with regardless of the circumstances. This is a huge error. We may be ready for the confrontation, but if the opponent is just as ready we should wait. This is why we must be relaxed and patient rather than emotional and hurried.

Adaptation has many different shades of meaning in Sun Tzu's system, but in the context of direct confrontation, it means waiting patiently until the right opportunity presents itself.

Lesson 143: Action during Confrontation

In a confrontation, what must you do?

A.   Defend any position.
B.   Disregard normal rules of competition.
C.   Beat your opponent on every issue.
D.   Never put your opponent's back against a wall.

> *You must follow these military rules.*
> *Do not take a position facing the high ground.*
> *Do not oppose those with their backs to a wall.*

THE ART OF WAR 7:6.4-6

Answer: D. Never put your opponent's back against a wall.

Often Sun Tzu ends a chapter with a summary of the basic rules of war, reviewing his principles in the context of the chapter's topic. He ends this chapter looking generally at how we deal with direct hostile confrontation.

The first rule is basic positioning. We never want to take an opponent on when we have a weaker position. In a violent confrontation in particular, attacking strong positions is simply too costly. In a conflict, we want to force our opponent to defend not one but many different positions. We can then attack the positions in which we have the greatest advantage.

We can take this general advice about military battles down to the level of an ordinary argument. A verbal conflict between people usually raises a number of issues. We do not need to win every point to be successful. We should avoid attacking the strongest arguments against us. We can cede some points and still succeed in getting what we want out of the argument.

Another important element in strategy is not to force people to fight to the death. We always want to leave them a way to save themselves or just save face. The end of this stanza reemphasizes this point. Our goal in a confrontation is not to destroy our opponents entirely. If we attempt to completely destroy them, if we put their backs up against a wall, we are only asking for a more costly battle, one that can never create a benefit. By conceding their best points, by respecting their strongest positions, we are telling them that they can lose this particular battle without being destroyed.

Lesson 144: Confrontations' Dangers

In a direct confrontation, what must you avoid doing?

A.   Following those who are fleeing.

B.   Taking gifts your opponents offer you.

C.   Fighting the enemy's weakest forces.

D.   Taking defensive positions.

> *Do not follow those who pretend to flee.*
> *Do not attack the enemy's strongest men.*
> *Do not swallow the enemy's bait.*

THE ART OF WAR 7:6.7-9

Answer: B. Taking gifts your opponents offer you.

This lesson is as familiar as the story of the Trojan horse. We must be suspicious of everything that happens during hostile confrontations. When our opponents are planning their side of the encounter, it is almost certain that they have thought of a few ways to mislead us into making a mistake. We must be continually suspicious of deception and traps.

We can and should follow those who are really retreating, but we don't want to follow those who are simply pretending to flee. How do we tell the difference? We must sense why our opponents are backing down. Are they backing down because they have to or because they have a plan? During a conflict, a concession is often not really a concession. It is a setup. We are being positioned to face a tougher battle than we have already faced.

The last chapter taught that momentum comes from surprise, not simply from winning. That chapter advised us to prepare surprises for our enemies. We were told to lure enemies into traps by offering them positions that they would like. Here we are reminded that our opponents can use the same strategies. We must not accept bait that lures us into a weaker position or forces us to face our opponents' strongest arguments.

The basic assumption here is that in a conflict our opponents are not going to give us anything. If we don't win the position or the point, we don't want it. Gifts are always traps, especially during a hostile confrontation.

Lesson 145: Escaping Confrontations

What should you do when opponents try to escape?

A.   You should stop them.

B.   You should let them go.

C.   You should kill them.

D.   You should cut them off.

> *Do not block an army that is heading home.*
> *Leave an escape outlet for a surrounded army.*
> *Do not press a desperate foe.*
> *This is the art of war.*

THE ART OF WAR 7:6.10-13

Answer: B. You should let them go.

This is the logical, if—for many—uncomfortable, end point of Sun Tzu's system for dealing with direct conflict and violent confrontation. We do not want such confrontations. When they are unavoidable, we must accept them and manage them as well as we can, but when the enemy loses the confrontations, we have no interest in completely destroying our opponents. There are two parts to this logic.

First, we don't want to put our opponents in a position in which they must fight to the full extent of their abilities. We must not make any battle a matter of life or death for our opponents. This will simply increase the intensity, violence, and destruction inherent in the situation. Destroying people completely is much more expensive than simply winning the confrontation.

Second, strategy is about advancing our position, not beating opponents. Sun Tzu teaches that there is no inherent benefit in destroying any particular force or enemy. We may win a better position by besting them in a hostile confrontation, but it is the position that is important. Today's enemies may be tomorrow's enemies, but they may also be tomorrow's allies. We must respect our enemies and not give them more reasons for future hostility. We want to provide our opponents with a way to save their self-respect. If possible, we want them to retreat rather than fight the battle to the end. Some confrontations may be inevitable, but winning the position offered by winning the confrontation is all we want.

Chapter 8

九變

Adaptability

Those who have not studied Sun Tzu usually think of strategy as a form of planning, but in this chapter, Sun Tzu makes it clear that strategy requires us to continually change our plans. Strategy is not planning as much as it is a systematic process. Strategy follows a consistent set of rules. It uses well-defined methods, but it also teaches us to continually adjust our plans to meet the unique, specific situations that we encounter. Sun Tzu teaches that competitive systems are dynamic and constantly changing. Like competition itself, successful strategies must be dynamic—willing to and capable of change. Sun Tzu's concept of adaptability, the topic of this chapter, teaches that we succeed by adapting to our circumstances.

Sun Tzu's system of strategy mandates opportunism. No matter what our plan, we must take advantage of certain types of opportunities when they present themselves. Though strategy teaches flexibility, we have to know and use its well-defined rules to be successful.

Situations change quickly. We must react instantly to those changes in an appropriate way. In earlier chapters we discussed the general rules of strategy, but from this point on we focus on very specific rules for advancing our position in particular situations. As those situations arise, we must quickly recognize them and react appropriately.

This chapter makes it clear that adaptability does not mean that we can do whatever we want in every situation. Creativity is an important part of strategy, but the rules of strategy are as certain as the rules of geometry. Since adaptability depends entirely on the discernment of the leader, the end of this chapter addresses the potential weaknesses of a leader and how those weaknesses can lead to our downfall.

Lesson 146: The Key Constraints on Strategy

What are the most important limiting factors on your strategy?

A.   You are constrained by your government's commands.

B.   You are constrained by your position and the situation.

C.   You are constrained when surrounded by the enemy.

D.   There are no constraints in strategy.

> *Everyone uses the arts of war.*
> *As a general, you get your orders from the government.*
> *You gather your troops.*
> *On dangerous ground, you must not camp.*
> *Where the roads intersect, you must join your allies.*
> *When an area is cut off, you must not delay in it.*
> *When you are surrounded, you must scheme.*
> *In a life-or-death situation, you must fight.*
> *There are roads that you must not take.*
> *There are armies that you must not fight.*
> *There are strongholds that you must not attack.*
> *There are positions that you must not defend.*
> *There are government commands that must not be obeyed.*

THE ART OF WAR 8:1.1-13

Answer: B. You are constrained by your position and the situation.

The point of this stanza is that our position and our situation determine the boundaries within which we must plan our strategy. Strategy means leveraging our position in the environment to advance our position. In this process, we are dependent on the ground and our initial position. In the original Chinese, the term for the ground, *di*, means at once our battleground, the terrain, and our situation and condition.

The topic of this chapter, adaptability, serves as an introduction to the next three chapters, which offer very detailed prescriptions for dealing with specific situations. In this stanza, the first three lines echo the previous chapter, but the next ten lines reference situations discussed in detail in the next three chapters. The ten situations listed here are not, as we might first think, the specific issues discussed in this chapter. They are selected to illustrate the fact that what we can and cannot do is determined by our specific situations, not our wants and desires.

Lesson 147: The Goal of Adaptability

What is the purpose of knowing how to adapt?

A.   Accomplishing your goals.

B.   Finding better goals.

C.   Planning your campaign.

D.   Planning a surprise.

> *Military leaders must be experts in knowing how to adapt to win.*
> *This will teach you the use of war.*
>
> THE ART OF WAR 8:1.14-15

Answer: A. Accomplishing your goals.

All strategy starts with a goal. At the beginning of this chapter, Sun Tzu says that we are given "orders from the government." From Sun Tzu's perspective, these orders define our goal. We get our goals from a variety of sources, but no matter what the source, we need clear goals. Without them, we don't know what we are attempting to accomplish in our competitive campaign. Our plans are built around our strategic objectives.

Sun Tzu teaches that to meet our objectives we must be willing to abandon our plans. The purpose of our plans is to accomplish our goals. Too often, we forget that our plans are not goals in themselves but only a means to an end. We cannot lose sight of our goals.

In a competitive campaign, we must always be searching for opportunities. We plan from what we know, but our knowledge is limited. This is especially true of our knowledge of the future. We cannot let our plans blind us to the opportunities that arise over time. A true leader plans from his or her knowledge, but a leader must also have vision. We must continually be looking for opportunities that are unplanned. Sun Tzu taught that the competitive environment is always full of opportunities. Our problem is that we fail to see them.

Our opportunities arise from our situation. Even the worst situations contain opportunities. Bad situations—being surrounded, for example—force us to find hidden opportunities. Our plans and expectations can blind us to our true situation and the opportunities that are everywhere around us. Leaders have to be different from regular people. We must know our situation and how to search for the opportunity hidden within it.

Lesson 148: Blind to Opportunity

When you know your competitive arena, what prevents you from seeing your opportunities?

A.   Your fear.
B.   Your lack of discipline.
C.   Your lack of confidence.
D.   Your closed mind.

> *Some commanders are not open to making adjustments to find an advantage.*
> *They can know the shape of the terrain.*
> *Still, they cannot find an advantageous position.*
>
> THE ART OF WAR 8:1.16-18

Answer: D. Your closed mind.

In Sun Tzu's system, vision is the ability to see opportunities. The primary obstacle to vision is a closed mind. We must develop an open mind to recognize our opportunities. The Chinese concept is *tong*, which means both expert and open. Experts are those with open minds, people who are open to new ideas. *Tong* also means unobstructed. We create our own mental obstacles that prevent us from seeing how we can move forward and improve our position.

Vision comes from our knowledge, but certainty acts as a barrier to vision. We make assumptions about what is and is not possible. Our confidence can be an obstacle when we think we know it all. We can never know the terrain completely. The ground has infinite possibilities. We can never have too much knowledge, but we should never have too much faith in our knowledge. Our sense of certainty is a barrier to vision.

The danger in knowing is that we can stop looking. We think that we already know all the twists and turns of a given situation, so we stop searching for new possibilities. We stop wondering. We are no longer curious. We stop asking questions. There are two problems with this approach. First, our knowledge reflects the past, not the present. If we stop looking, we lose touch with the process of constant change. Second, we miss the critical points of detail. By definition, opportunities are easy to overlook. If they were not, others would have seen them already. To see opportunities, we have to study the conditions closely.

Lesson 149: Taking Advantage of Opportunities

When you see a new opportunity, what is required to take advantage of it?

A.   More information.

B.   A new plan.

C.   A change in approach.

D.   More resources.

> *Some military commanders do not know how to adjust their methods.*
> *They can find an advantageous position.*
> *Still, they cannot use their men effectively.*

THE ART OF WAR 8:1.19-21

Answer: C. A change in approach.

The step that follows vision is action. However, new opportunities require us to change our methods to take advantage of them. To advance our position, we must change ourselves and what we are doing. Change is difficult for most people. People get comfortable in their habits. They want to keep doing what they have always done before. Change means uncertainty. Most people are afraid of making changes. Strategy is part economics, part mathematics, and part psychology. Resistance to change is part of the psychology Sun Tzu expects from people.

Leaders must be change-masters. We must be comfortable with continually adjusting our methods. We must be constantly looking for ways to improve what we are doing, but we must also be willing to completely change the entire approach when the situation calls for it.

Bill Gates offered a great example of change leadership when he reorganized Microsoft to adjust to the rise of the Internet. He realized that stand-alone desktop computing was a dead end, a "cut off" position. He reacted by changing the whole structure of his organization and its methods to move out of that position and become a networking company. Many large companies die because they cannot make these changes.

Today, we call an organization that can change and evolve a "learning organization." Our methods, systems, and organization must continually adapt to new opportunities as we discover them. Like dinosaurs facing a climatic change, those of us who cannot adapt to ever more dynamic competitive environments are destined to fail and disappear.

Lesson 150: Consistent Results

To achieve consistent success, what should you use?

A.   Consistent methods.
B.   Creative planning.
C.   Standardized systems.
D.   Direct confrontations.

> *You must be creative in your planning.*
> *You must adapt to your opportunities and weaknesses.*
> *You can use a variety of approaches and still have a consistent result.*
> *You must adjust to a variety of problems and consistently solve them.*
>
> THE ART OF WAR 8:2.1-4

Answer: B. Creative planning.

Strategy deals with finding success under the chaos of competitive conditions. Normal logic dictates that consistent methods or standardized systems produce consistent results. This is true in a controlled productive environment where the focus is on manufacturing or production. Rules for working in a competitive environment, however, are different from those that work a controlled environment. In a competitive environment, we do not control what happens. To achieve consistent results in a competitive environment, we must be flexible in our methods. We must be creative to adjust to continually changing conditions.

In a production environment, we control all the factors that determine consistency. We set standards and achieve consistent results through our ability to control our environment. Competitive environments are inherently different from controlled environments. Sun Tzu describes them as chaotic. Competitive environments are large, open arenas in which many different people are working toward their differing goals. The environment is made of the infinite ground and the changes in climate. This environment is always beyond our control.

To gain control in a competitive environment, we vary our methods to meet current conditions. We plan surprises so that our opponents' plans are thrown off course. Creative plans are not set in stone. We continually adjust these plans to meet the dynamics of the evolving situation.

Lesson 151: Potential Opponents

How do you adapt your methods for potential opponents?

A.   React to your potential opponents' moves.

B.   Challenge your potential opponents.

C.   Wait for your potential opponents.

D.   Predict your potential opponents.

> *You can deter your potential enemy by using his weaknesses against him.*
> *You can keep your enemy's army busy by giving it work to do.*
> *You can rush your enemy by offering him an advantageous position.*
>
> THE ART OF WAR 8:3.1-3

Answer: B. Challenge your potential opponents.

Here, we focus our methods on our potential enemies. As we have said, the larger competitive environment is beyond our control. However, this doesn't mean our opponents or potential rivals are beyond our influence. We can control some aspect of this chaotic environment by taking the initiative, challenging our potential opponents, and forcing them to react to us rather than putting ourselves in a position where we have to react to them.

The larger context here is adaptability. We adapt to our situation to find an opportunity. We use that opportunity to seize the initiative from our opponents. This creative planning is what gives us consistent results.

Adaptability doesn't mean giving our opponents the lead. As we adapt to the dynamics of the situation, we want our opponents to be forced to deal with the challenges that we set for them. We want to determine the agenda rather than leave our opponents free to develop their own agenda. We adjust to the moves of our competitors, but we don't passively allow them to determine what we do. When the opportunity arises, we must challenge opponents and make them work. If we don't put them in this situation, they will force us to react to their challenges.

In this stanza, the Chinese term Sun Tzu uses includes not only our enemies but our potential enemies and allies as well. We can set the agenda for everyone we are working with. The only way that we can predict competitive behavior is to try to control it. We want to exert this control over as many parties that we can influence as possible.

Lesson 152: Defending Valuable Ground

If you hold valuable ground, how can you defend it against the competition?

A. By size and strength.

B. By readiness and positioning.

C. By guile and deception.

D. By control and command.

> *You must make use of war.*
> *Do not trust that the enemy isn't coming.*
> *Trust your readiness to meet him.*
> *Do not trust that the enemy won't attack.*
> *We must rely only on our ability to pick a place that the enemy can't attack.*
>
> THE ART OF WAR 8:4.1-5

Answer: B. By readiness and positioning.

All strategy depends on developing positions that we can defend. Making good use of strategy means planning for a changing situation. The enemy is coming eventually. We are going to be challenged. Since change is inevitable, we must prepare for it.

Holding onto an advantageous position is always difficult. We must never think that any position is safe from a competitive challenge. If we are large and dominant, our competitors will look for small pieces of our territory that they can take away. If we control a small niche, others will try to take it away. We should try to keep our position a secret, but others will eventually discover it.

If we expect eventual attack, we must use whatever time we have to entrench ourselves in our territory. We need to build barriers to entry. We can and must do whatever we can to make it difficult if not impossible for anyone to win the position.

Our ability to defend is largely determined by our initial decisions about what positions to develop. Some positions are naturally easier to defend than others are. Other positions are naturally open to attack. Sun Tzu discusses these different types of positions in more detail in later chapters. The point here is that our ability to make the adjustments necessary to defend a position depends largely on how wisely we pick a position.

Lesson 153: Vulnerable Leaders

If competitors put themselves in a position where they can be destroyed, what should you do?

A.   Destroy them.

B.   Avoid them.

C.   Ignore them.

D.   Suspect them.

> *You can exploit five different faults in a leader.*
> *If he is willing to die, you can kill him.*
>
> THE ART OF WAR 8:5.1-2

Answer: A. Destroy them.

Earlier in this chapter, we examined two weaknesses in using adaptability. These weaknesses were the inability to see an opportunity and failure to adjust methods. Now we end the chapter examining five potential character flaws in leaders. Like other conditions that arise in strategic situations, these five character flaws demand a specific response on our part when we encounter them in opposing leaders. These five flaws are the extremes of the five strengths of a leader: intelligence, trustworthiness, caring, courage, and discipline. We must adjust our plans to take these flaws into account.

The first and most serious of these weaknesses is the willingness to lose everything. This is an excess of courage, complete and irrational fearlessness. This weakness may sound relatively rare, but it is more common than it seems at first. We must recognize it, especially in ourselves, to defend against it. Leaders who are willing to lose everything do not deserve to lead, so Sun Tzu suggests that we eliminate them.

Some people would rather die than be wrong. They will risk everything to prove themselves right. These people will risk everything to avoid even minor setbacks. Because they are willing to risk everything, these people often put more resources into a battle than winning the battle is worth. They lose even when they win.

When dealing with these people, we must destroy them. We cannot be cowed by their aggressiveness. The battle may not be worth the effort to them, but it gives us the opportunity to eliminate a dangerous and foolish competitor.

Lesson 154: Fear of Destruction

What should you do if competitors are afraid to risk everything in order to win?

A. Capture them.
B. Destroy them.
C. Respect them.
D. Ally with them.

> *If he wants to survive, you can capture him.*
>
> THE ART OF WAR 8:5.3

Answer: A. Capture them.

Some leaders have the opposite problem of complete fearlessness. Instead of risking too much, they are afraid to risk anything. For Sun Tzu, this is the destructive extreme of intelligence. Our natural and intelligent concern for losing and dying can take a destructive turn. Leaders with this flaw are always too afraid of losing. They don't mind losing a battle. Instead of worrying about winning, they are always looking for ways to cut their losses.

We can hold these leaders captive to their fears. Once we know that these leaders are overly cautious, we can easily use their fears against them. Since these leaders are afraid to risk too much on any given battle, all we have to do is keep raising the stakes. This is like raising the bet in poker against a player that we know we can frighten out of the hand. It doesn't matter if we put in more than the battle is worth because we know that our opponent will back down and it will not cost us anything.

Strategy teaches us to calculate the value of meeting every challenge. We need to gauge our investments correctly. Strategy also teaches us to take small, incremental steps toward our goals. Part of this calculation requires that we know the psychology of our opponents. We have to adjust our basic methods based on the types of competition we face. Strategy means calculating all the factors in the competitive environment. If the opposing leader is too aggressive or too fearful, we must adjust our methods to meet that particular type of challenge. To meet fearful opponents, we must be more aggressive than we would normally be to effectively counter their approach.

Lesson 155: The Opponent's Emotions

What do you want your opponent's emotional state to be during competition?

A.   Relaxed.

B.   Angry.

C.   Happy.

D.   Fearful.

> *He may have a quick temper.*
> *You can then provoke him with insults.*
>
> THE ART OF WAR 8:5.4-5

Answer: B. Angry.

In the middle of the last chapter, Sun Tzu told us that we need to control our emotions and remain relaxed during confrontation. In the second to last chapter, we will revisit this topic again. We make the best decisions when we are relaxed and patient. We make the worst possible decisions when we are angry.

Some people are easily angered. According to Sun Tzu, this response comes from an excess of discipline or strictness. These strict, controlling people become angry when they are challenged. Once people become angry, their behavior becomes aggressive and wild. They are no longer fighting for gain or for their goals; they are fighting to punish their enemies.

Temperamental leaders often find that their short fuse works to their benefit. Many people are afraid of those who are easily angered. Many treat temperamental people more cautiously, giving them what they want.

However, if we are skilled at strategy, we should never be afraid of making our opponents angry. The secret is picking the right time and place to enrage them. At the wrong time and place, our opponents' anger makes their reactions more predictable. Temperamental people make mistakes. Over time, they lose the support of their people.

If we discover that opponents are easily angered, we should use this flaw against them when the time is right. We can lure them into situations that they cannot win. We can damage the respect that others have for their judgment by enraging them.

Lesson 156: Using an Opponent's Pride

What should you do if your opponents are overly proud of their reputation?

A.   You should flatter them.

B.   You should embarrass them.

C.   You should confuse them.

D.   You should earn their respect.

> *If he has a delicate sense of honor, you can disgrace him.*
>
> THE ART OF WAR 8:5.6

Answer: B. You should embarrass them.

Trustworthiness in a leader is a strength. However, when leaders are too concerned with their honor, this strength becomes a weakness. Sun Tzu warns us that we must never fight for ego or fame. He knew that a great many people do fight to satisfy their egos. People with delicate senses of honor have inflated egos. We can use their inflated egos to cloud their judgment, obscuring their real goals. People are seduced by the sense of power and glory that they can get from achievement. The more success they have, the more enticing ego gratification can be.

Sun Tzu distinguishes here between two forms of egotism. Some people are so egotistic that their actual success or failure makes no impression upon their sense of self-worth. These people do not have the delicate sense of honor that Sun Tzu is talking about here. Sensitive people with a delicate sense of honor are in some way insecure. They need to be successful to feel good about themselves.

In a competitive environment, this sense of honor is too fragile to survive. No matter how good we are, facing real challenges means that we must deal with failure. No one wins every battle. People who need to be pure and perfect are easy to embarrass and humiliate.

Strategic success requires humility. Those who lack humility will be tested by failure. We can embarrass these people in any number of ways. We know that they have a high opinion of themselves and this makes them easy to predict. They are easily set up for a trap in which they will be embarrassed. Once embarrassed, they are more likely to give up.

Lesson 157: Devotion to Individuals

What should you expect if your opponents are completely devoted to specific individuals who are working for them?

A.   Their people will be loyal to them.
B.   Their people will create problems for them.
C.   Their people will make them strong.
D.   Their people will all be excellent.

> *If he loves his people, you can create problems for him.*
>
> THE ART OF WAR 8:5.7

Answer: B. Their people will create problems for them.

Leaders must care about their followers, but even this strength can become a weakness when it becomes too strong. There are two different potential problems with excess love for followers. The first is caring too much about specific individuals. The second is caring too much about what other people think about us.

As leaders, we are often in the difficult position of having to choose between the good of our organization and our devotion to specific individuals. In these situations, the good of the organization—that is, the best interests of everyone—must take precedence over the best interests of specific individuals. We can't play favorites. This is why it isn't a good idea to hire friends or relatives. When leaders put their concern for individuals above the needs of their organization, it always creates dissension. These organizations suffer because everyone knows that the organization is being run for the benefit of a few special people.

We also can't worry about doing what makes people happy in the short term. Leadership is not a popularity contest. Decision-making isn't a popularity contest. The success of competitive organizations depends upon leaders making difficult decisions. If leaders are too concerned about the opinions of their people, they will be unable to make the right choices when situations call for tough decisions. Leaders cannot be indifferent to the opinions of their people. We all need the support of others, but that support in the long term comes from making the right decisions even when they are difficult and not from doing what is popular.

Lesson 158: The Five Weaknesses

Where should you look for a leader's five weaknesses?

A.   In your opponents.

B.   In yourselves.

C.   In your supporters.

D.   In all of the above.

> *In every situation, look for these five weaknesses.*
> *They are common faults in commanders.*
> *They always lead to military disaster.*

THE ART OF WAR 8:5.8-10

Answer: D. In all of the above.

When these weaknesses appear in our opponents, we must know how to exploit them. If our opponents take risks or are afraid of risks, we can respond appropriately. If they are easily angered, we can upset their judgment. If they are fighting for egotism, we can make competition too painful for them. If they play favorites within their organization, we can use this against them.

If we have these weaknesses ourselves, we need to counter them. If we tend to be fearless, we must be more careful. If we tend to be too timid, we must try to be more aggressive. If we tend to be easily angered, we must calm down. If we tend to care too much about what people think of us, we must remember our goals and stop trying to win popularity contests. If we have special friends or relatives within our organization, we should make it clear that we will never favor them. They have to stand on their own.

We should also look for these same weaknesses in those whom we work with, people who are our followers and supporters. We must tell people when we think they are too aggressive or too timid. We must counsel people who have problems with anger. If they have problems with their ego, we should make it clear that the organization will not tolerate it. If they are playing favorites, we must call them on it. If we cannot correct their behavior, we must eliminate them from our organization. These problems only create more problems with time.

Lesson 159: True Defeat

How do you truly overcome your opponents?

A.   By overpowering their men.

B.   By taking away their territory.

C.   By destroying their leadership.

D.   By countering their philosophy.

> *To overturn an army, you must kill its general.*
> *To do this, you must use these five weaknesses.*
> *You must always look for them.*

THE ART OF WAR 8:5.11-13

Answer: C. By destroying their leadership.

Strategy doesn't always depend on destroying opposition. Often, we can advance our position irrespective of what others are doing. We can win territory and find success without specifically defeating any competitor.

However, when it becomes necessary to defeat an opposing organization to succeed, we should know that we can only truly destroy that opposition by destroying its leader. An organization exists in opposition to us as long as its leadership is opposed to us. We can beat this group in confrontation after confrontation. We can win territory from this opponent. No matter what we do, as long as an opposing leader is not destroyed or discredited, he or she will rise again to oppose us. The only way to make sure an opposing organization is dead is to cut off its head.

This is not to say that we want to engage in personal battles. As long as individuals do not make it their business to continually frustrate us, we should ignore them. Personal battles are just obstacles on the road to success.

We only attack the leaders of opposing organizations when it is certain that we must eliminate an opponent in order to make progress. When faced with this situation, we must know the leader of the opposing organization. We must specifically know that leader's strengths and weaknesses. We must then adapt our strategies to target the specific weaknesses of that leader. By definition, an opposing leader must have the five strengths of a leader to be a strong opponent. The question is which of these strengths can be turned into a liability.

Chapter 9

行軍

Armed March

Strategy is about advancing our position. To do this, we must move into new areas. This is what Sun Tzu calls a strategy of invasion. This is one of the longest chapters in *The Art of War*. It takes a detailed look at how we adapt to specific situations that we encounter when we are moving into unfamiliar territory.

Though originally written about specific situations faced by armies in the field, this chapter works extremely well as a series of analogies. It works because of the deep, fundamental connection between the natural world and the competitive environment in modern society. When Sun Tzu discusses moving through mountains or marshes, on one level he is talking about physically moving through these types of territory. However, each of these situations has an analogue in our social environment. In society, we have mountains, rivers, marshes, and plateaus as well. We also have animals that gather at abandoned camps and startle at approaching armies.

As the chapter continues, the emphasis shifts from understanding the environment to understanding what the competition is doing. We must discern the opposition's intent from its words, actions, and emotions. Sun Tzu provides a great deal of detail to help us understand our competitors' situation and direction. Because human nature has not changed, this advice works equally well in understanding the intentions of our competitors in the business world.

The chapter shifts focus again at the end. We must understand how to handle our people when we are moving into new areas. The final lessons are about getting the most out of our people.

Lesson 160: Key to Movement

What would be your primary consideration when you are moving into a new competitive area?

A.   The territory.
B.   The obstacles.
C.   The trends.
D.   The competitors.

Everyone moving his army must adjust to the enemy.
                                      THE ART OF WAR 9:1.1

Answer: D. The competitors.

This chapter focuses on how to understand a number of situations that we face as we move into new territory. It analyzes a number of different types of terrain and obstacles, but Sun Tzu warns us from the very beginning that we must not forget our opponents. All movement is possible because it is allowed by an opening left by our opponents. As we move into new areas, we are adjusting our position relative to the competition that we face. Positioning is always a matter of using the territory, but when looking to expand our position, we are specifically trying to find a hole left by the competition. Later, the chapter focuses specifically on interpreting opponents' behavior.

As we move into new competitive territories, we are exploring. We suspect that there is an opening in the territory, but we don't know the shape and dimensions of that opening. We wouldn't be involved in that competitive arena unless we were drawn by an opportunity. That opportunity exists only because our potential rivals have overlooked or ignored the possibilities of this area.

As we will see in this chapter, social environments, like physical environments, have different types of terrain. We can call these differences demographics, but the point is that society, like the land, has structure. Sun Tzu advises how to make the best use of these different terrains, but the focus is always on how to best use them to make progress. Later in the chapter, the focus shifts even more clearly to what our competitors are thinking and doing in response to our movement.

Lesson 161: Among the Powerful

When moving into high, rarefied environments, how do you establish a position for yourself?

A.   Go after the highest positions.
B.   Go after the biggest names.
C.   Go into the areas that are easiest.
D.   Go into the areas that are the most difficult.

> *When caught in the mountains, rely on their valleys.*
> *Position yourself on the heights facing the sun.*
> *To win your battles, never attack uphill.*
> *This is how you position your army in the mountains.*

THE ART OF WAR 9:1.2-5

Answer: C. Go into the areas that are easiest.

Mountains are an analogy for any area in which we see a real disparity between the high and the low, the large and the small. In business, there are large companies and small. In society, there are celebrities and regular people. In politics, there are national offices and local offices. In baseball, there are the major leagues and the minors. In the media, there are the major networks, magazines, and papers and everyone else. When we are dealing with the rarefied reaches of society, we are moving through the mountains.

When we are moving through areas dominated by the big players, Sun Tzu's advice is to stay on the path of least resistance and seek out those who assist the powerful rather than dealing directly with powerful people themselves. This is how we stay in the valleys. In business, when we are dealing with large customers, we want to interact with those lower in the hierarchy. In politics, when running for a high office, we should concentrate on wooing the common people—popular groups—instead of getting endorsements from celebrities or other national politicians.

When Sun Tzu tells us "never attack uphill," the general advice is that we should not try to win by fighting against natural forces, especially not fighting the big and powerful. This is a common theme in this chapter, which is about leveraging natural forces. We may not be working with the top people, but we shouldn't attack them either. When fighting in their territory, we want to fight on the side of the most powerful.

Lesson 162: Dealing with Change

When you are faced with an area or situation that is completely fluid and changing rapidly, what do you do?

A.   Use the change.

B.   Avoid the change.

C.   Ignore the change.

D.   Distrust the change.

> *When water blocks you, keep far away from it.*
> *Let the enemy cross the river and wait for him.*
> *Do not meet him in midstream.*
> *Wait for him to get half his forces across and then take advantage of the situation.*

THE ART OF WAR 9:1.6-9

Answer: B. Avoid the change.

Water is also one of Sun Tzu's most common metaphors. He uses it to symbolize change and the incessant force of nature that we cannot oppose. As change, water is a metaphor for our ability to adapt, and, in this context, water is powerful. Like water, we should take a shape that fits the situation that we are in. When the change is a part of the ground, the new area we are moving through, it is a dangerous thing. As a force of change, water can sweep everything in front of it away. As a force of nature, water can be used as a weapon.

The lesson here is that we want to avoid areas or situations that are changing rapidly. In business, this would include industries and organizations that are going through rapid change. If an organization or industry is changing rapidly, we are not likely to make much progress dealing with it, and even when we do make progress, we make ourselves vulnerable both to the change itself and to attack.

The primary way we can use these shifting areas or changing situations is as traps for our opponents. These changes become a weapon. If we wait until our opponents are embroiled in a changing situation, we can attack them more successfully. They will have fewer resources to deal with competitive attacks because much of their organization is still trying to deal with the changes that they are embroiled in.

Lesson 163: During Transitions

How do you meet a challenge successfully when you are in the midst of change?

A.   You can't meet a challenge when you are in the midst of change.

B.   You can defend yourself.

C.   You must attack the enemy.

D.   You must reevaluate your market.

> *You need to be able to fight.*
> *You can't do that if you are in the water when you meet an attack.*
> *Position yourself upstream, facing the sun.*
> *Never face against the current.*
> *Always position your army upstream when near the water.*
>
> THE ART OF WAR 9:1.10-14

Answer: A. You can't meet a challenge when you are in the midst of change.

When we are "at sea," we are surrounded by change. We don't have anything solid and stable to base our position on. These are the positions in which we are the most vulnerable. We cannot really meet a challenge, even to defend ourselves, when we have to cope with change. We should avoid competitive challenges in these situations. This is why management changes, organizational restructuring, political shifts, and especially financial changes must be avoided when we are in any competitive risk at all. We are most vulnerable to our opponents when we are in the midst of dealing with these types of environmental changes.

When we get into a competitive battle in territories that are changing, we need to make sure that the trends of the time—that is, the current—work for us rather than against us. We never want to battle against the current in trying to compete. Generally, we want to avoid change. When it can't be avoided, we must make sure that time is on our side.

Even if we establish positions in fast-changing environments, these positions are quickly washed away. Today's fashions are tomorrow's funny memories. The latest technology today is quickly outdated tomorrow. These positions can be highly profitable for a while, but solid, permanent positions are difficult to establish.

Lesson 164: Dealing with Uncertainty

When you find yourself in an uncertain area or situation, what do you do?

A.　　Move through it quickly.

B.　　Explore the area thoroughly.

C.　　Wait for certainty.

D.　　Pick a battle.

> *You may have to move across marshes.*
> *Move through them quickly without stopping.*
> *You may meet the enemy in the middle of a marsh.*
> *You must keep on the water grasses.*
> *Keep your back to a clump of trees.*
> *This is how you position your army in a marsh.*
>
> THE ART OF WAR 9:1.15-20

Answer: A. Move through it quickly.

If we stand still in some areas, we will get bogged down and start sinking. In these marshes, the secret is getting through them. There are many "marshes" in life, where the ground is uncertain and progress is difficult. In water areas, change is a dominant force. In marshy areas, the pressure of change is less of an issue than the instability of the ground. We know we are in a marsh because our progress bogs down in it. For example, if we ever find ourselves having to deal with the government, we will discover what it is like trying to make progress in marshes.

The main point about marshes is that we must get through them. We can use marshes as stepping-stones to other areas, but we don't take a permanent position in them. Often we find ourselves in a bog without realizing what we are getting into. Legal procedures almost always turn into marshes. When we are trying to make progress, we should stay out of these areas, and, if we find ourselves in marshes accidentally, we should get out of them as soon as possible. Marshes may look like competitive openings because they are empty, but this is because those who go into them sink out of sight.

If we are challenged when we are bogged down, we can defend ourselves only if we stick to our most solid ground—the best and most established positions in the area. These positions are not strong long-term positions, but we can defend them if we are careful.

Lesson 165: Dealing with Equality

When you are in a situation that puts everyone on equal footing, how do you position yourself?

A.   You take a position that you can change.

B.   You take a position that you can defend.

C.   You take a position that brings opponents to you.

D.   You take a position that keeps the danger behind you.

> *On a level plateau, take a position that you can change.*
> *Keep the higher ground on your right and to the rear.*
> *Keep the danger in front of you and safety behind.*
> *This is how you position yourself on a level plateau.*
>
> THE ART OF WAR 9:1.21-24

Answer: A. You take a position that you can change.

The three other terrains we have discussed—mountains, water, and marshes—all have serious defects. Because they are even, solid, and certain, plateaus are the antithesis of all three. A "level plateau" represents any situation in which many different viable positions are available. These areas offer level playing fields. Success is determined by how we handle ourselves and how we develop our position.

When we choose a position on these level playing fields, our first choice should be to take a position that we can change, adjusting to the competition. Since the ground itself is solid, we want the ability to change on it. The various qualities of the ground are less important than our relationship to our opponents and how we adjust to them.

This does not mean that we can totally ignore the ground. We always want to control the high ground. How we define the high ground will change with the situation. Sometimes it will mean having the strongest supporters. Other times it will mean having the best arguments. We want to move forward with the support of the ground behind us.

In these situations, our focus should be on the competition and our challenges. In these situations, we should face our problems—that is, aim ourselves directly at our opponents' supporters, ideas, and resources while we protect our own supporters, ideas, and resources.

Lesson 166: The Lack of Opportunity

Are there any situations in which you cannot outmatch your opponents?

A.   Yes, in fast-changing situations.

B.   Yes, with larger organizations or important people.

C.   Yes, in uncertain situations.

D.   No, you can find an advantage in every situation.

> *You can find an advantage in all four of these situations.*
> *Learn from the great emperor who used positioning to conquer his four rivals.*
> THE ART OF WAR 9:1.25-26

Answer: D. No, you can find an advantage in every situation.

When we are looking for a new position, some areas are simply better than others. Permanent positions in elevated situations (mountains), changing situations (water), or uncertain situations (marshes) are weaker and less stable than positions on plateaus, but under these conditions our opponents must deal with the same handicaps that we face. When we find ourselves faced with a challenge under these conditions, we can make the best of it, besting our opponents. In each of these situations, Sun Tzu explains specifically how we can use them to meet a competitive challenge.

The general rule for positioning is to seek out areas that others have overlooked. In following this basic plan, we can easily find ourselves in areas that are too elevated, fast changing, or uncertain. Sun Tzu looks upon movement into a new area as an experiment. We are never certain of what a territory is like until we explore it. This is why we generally commit ourselves to small, quick, inexpensive explorations.

This doesn't mean that we cannot do better than our opponents under these different conditions. As we advance our position, we can find ourselves in these situations unexpectedly. No matter what situation we find ourselves in, we can always do better than others. All success is relative. This is why, along with explaining the weaknesses of certain types of territories, Sun Tzu always explains how to find an advantage in them. If we meet our competitors in these areas, we can still come out ahead. If our opponents are also in the same situation, they are in danger if they don't know how to use the ground to their advantage.

Lesson 167: Healthy Organizations

What keeps your organization healthy?

A.   Visibility.

B.   Success.

C.   Financial strength.

D.   Surprise.

> *Armies are stronger on high ground and weaker on low.*
> *They are better camping on sunny, southern hillsides than on the shady, northern ones.*
> *Provide for your army's health and place it well.*
> *Your army will be free from disease.*
> *Done correctly, this means victory.*

THE ART OF WAR 9:2.1-5

Answer: A. Visibility.

For those interested in Asian philosophy, in the original Chinese this passage introduces the concept of *yin-yang*, that is, what we know in the West as the male and female principles. In the original form, written twenty-five hundred years ago, the sunny, southern hillside is presented as the male principle, whereas the shady, northern hillside is the female principle. Sun Tzu certainly appreciates the power of female mystery, subtlety, and secrecy in keeping our plans hidden, but for purposes of positioning a healthy organization, he favors openness and visibility, the sunny hillside, the direct male principles.

Sun Tzu teaches that exposure on the sunny hillside keeps an organization healthy. Visibility is health while secrecy within an organization breeds corruption and disease. We want the productivity of our organization to be visible and the chain of command to be easily recognized. Modern management philosophy teaches that making problems visible is one of the keys to solving them. This is very close to what Sun Tzu teaches here. We want to keep the organization out of the shadows for the sake of efficient internal operation as well as our organization's health.

In competitive occupations such as business, entertainment, or politics, visibility also plays a key role of getting attention. However, this stanza is less about communication than it is about the health of the organization.

Lesson 168: Defending Desirable Positions

When you are forced to defend a desirable position, where should you position yourself?

A.   Where you can easily move.

B.   Where you cannot go backward.

C.   Where your opponents approach you directly.

D.   Where you are hidden.

> *You must sometimes defend on a hill or riverbank.*
> *You must keep on the south side in the sun.*
> *Keep the uphill slope at your right rear.*
>
> *This will give the advantage to your army.*
> *It will always give you a position of strength.*

THE ART OF WAR 9:2.6-10

Answer: B. Where you cannot go backward.

Though we cannot make progress passing through cut-off positions—a topic in an upcoming chapter—we can use these positions for defense. These positions have the advantage of making it impossible for people to attack us from behind.

Their second strength is that they provide us with high ground.

We can utilize any high ground, no matter how slight. In business, we establish the high ground when we build up the value of our product. In politics, we establish the high ground when we build up the value of our philosophy. When Sun Tzu talks about keeping an uphill slope behind us, he is talking about using our position to make it difficult for the competition to move against us. We do this by using the strengths of our position against our opponents. With real accomplishments behind us, it is difficult for others to compete with us.

It also makes it difficult for us to abandon what we have developed. It is difficult to abandon real customers, cash flow, or the skills that create them. The high ground keeps us in our position.

We must continually look for ways to develop high ground that is hard to attack.

Lesson 169: The Furor of Change

What do you do when change temporarily disrupts the path that you had identified to establish a new position?

A.   Stop trying to advance and wait.

B.   Look for allies that you can use.

C.   Move quickly out of your current area.

D.   Face the change directly and master it.

Stop the march when the rain swells the river into rapids.
You may want to ford the river.
Wait until it subsides.

THE ART OF WAR 9:3.1-3

Answer: A. Stop trying to advance and wait.

Water always represents change, but there is a metaphorical difference between rivers and rain. When *The Art of War* discusses rivers, it is talking about a place on the ground that is always changing and shifting. Like the fashion industry, rivers are ground that by its nature is always changing. We have a choice of ground, so we should choose to stay away from this constantly shifting form of ground.

When *The Art of War* discusses rain, it is addressing the nature of heaven (*tian*), which is beyond our control. We cannot avoid rain. It comes to us. Rain can change any type of ground into a river. Periods of change come to every area. The best thing we can do during times of change is build up our current position and wait for the change to subside.

The general rule is that we should always move away from existing positions slowly. We should never abandon established sources of strength quickly. We may want to change our competitive direction, but we do this by developing new areas quickly and abandoning existing areas slowly. Our existing position is the firm foundation for making moves to new positions.

When a period of change engulfs our existing business, we may be tempted to get out of that area quickly, to press on with our movement into new areas more quickly. This is extremely dangerous. Instead, we must be patient. The weather will change. We must weather the change until conditions are better for moving.

Lesson 170: Limited Opportunities

What do you do when you find an opportunity that limits your future advance?

A.   Develop the opportunity quickly.

B.   Develop the opportunity temporarily.

C.   Discourage the opposition from pursuing the opportunity.

D.   Encourage the opposition to take the opportunity.

> *All regions have dead ends such as waterfalls.*
> *There are deep lakes.*
> *There are high cliffs.*
> *There are dense jungles.*
> *There are thick quagmires.*
> *There are steep crevasses.*
> *Get away from all these quickly.*
> *Do not get close to them.*
> *Keep them at a distance.*
> *Maneuver the enemy close to them.*
> *Position yourself facing these dangers.*
> *Push the enemy back into them.*

THE ART OF WAR 9:3.4-15

Answer: D. Encourage the opposition to take the opportunity.

We can advance down a path that eventually cuts us off from any future advance. Every actor who has ever worried about being typecast understands this problem. Certain positions make it impossible to move forward in the future. While such an advance may seem desirable at the moment, we will regret taking that path. Instead, we want our opponents to face this problem.

Like actors, businesses, politicians, and other competitors can also be typecast. We are defined by what we do. All successful positions cut us off from *some* future position. A waste management company may well find it impossible to get into the food management business. We must be aware that there are positions that cut us off from *all* other future positions.

The deep assumption here is that we must always keep our options open, leaving ourselves the ability to move in the future. Each position is simply a stepping-stone to future positions. No matter how devoted we are to our current position, we must remain free to move. The best positions give us the most appealing options for future movement.

Lesson 171: Competitive Visibility

How do you deal with areas that lack visibility and make it difficult to recognize opposition?

A.   Avoid them.

B.   Move into them cautiously.

C.   Move through them quickly.

D.   Use them to hide.

> *Danger can hide on your army's flank.*
> *There are reservoirs and lakes.*
> *There are reeds and thickets.*
> *There are forests of trees.*
> *Their dense vegetation provides a hiding place.*
> *You must cautiously search through them.*
> *They can always hide an ambush.*

THE ART OF WAR 9:3.16-22

Answer: B. Move into them cautiously.

Visibility is a good thing. Visibility promotes good communication within an organization and between an organization and its supporters. We want to be where we are visible to our supporters. Our people like it when the operation and rules of our organization are highly visible. We also like it when we can easily see and understand our opponents. When we are in an area where we have difficulty understanding who and where our opponents are, we must be extremely careful.

Notice that Sun Tzu does not tell us to stay out of these areas entirely. Unlike an area that has no longer-term future, these situations are worth exploring. However, we must depart from our regular approach of trying to develop a new area quickly. Instead, we must be careful how we invest in these areas. Is the area open, or is the competition simply hidden?

Information is always the key ingredient in Sun Tzu's system. If we don't know where our opposition is, we need more information before we can make a serious commitment to the new area. Speed is often an advantage, but we can use it only when we know the ground well, especially when we know exactly where the competition is.

Lesson 172: An Opponent's Attitude

If you move into an area where your competitors have a position but they seem to ignore you, what does it mean?

A.   They are secure in their position.

B.   They are afraid of competition.

C.   They are waiting to see what you will do.

D.   They are planning to attack.

> *Sometimes, the enemy is close by but remains calm.*
> *Expect to find him in a natural stronghold.*
> *Other times, he remains at a distance but provokes battle.*
> *He wants you to attack him.*

THE ART OF WAR 9:4.1-4

Answer: A. They are secure in their position.

In this new section, we shift topics. We started the chapter by evaluating the types of territories and conditions that we encounter when advancing our position. Now we change to judging our opponents' reactions.

When opponents act confidently about their existing position even when we are closing in on them, it is likely that they know the situation better than we do and that they are secure in their position. They probably know that we are wasting our time trying to challenge them in that situation. This is even more certain if competitors invite us to challenge them when we have to make significant investments to do so. They are baiting us. In these situations, we must resist the temptation to attack their positions. The fact is that they have advantages that we do not recognize.

The general rule is that we move away from our opponents' strength, not toward it. This lesson goes back to the ideas of weakness and strength. We want to establish strong positions that others covet, not covet the positions that others have established. We must assume that our competitors know what they are doing. Most of our rivals are as rational and intelligent as we are. To assume they aren't is the fatal flaw of hubris. When we are moving into an area that our competitors know better than we do, they have a special advantage. We should assume that their knowledge about that area is superior to ours. If they aren't worried about our presence and invite attack, we are usually wasting our time in that situation.

Lesson 173: An Opponent's Change of Position

When an opponent moves away from his or her existing position, what does it signify?

A.   He or she is planning to attack.

B.   He or she is leaving the area.

C.   He or she is avoiding conflict.

D.   He or she is looking for a stronger position.

> *He sometimes shifts the position of his camp.*
> *He is looking for an advantageous position.*
>
> THE ART OF WAR 9:4.5-6

Answer: D. He or she is looking for a stronger position.

An organization moves or should move for only one reason: it is looking for a stronger position. People do not leave where they are established unless they have a reason. The most likely reason is that there is a problem with their existing situation.

Here, Sun Tzu warns us about an exception to the general rule. The general rule is that we move into open areas. A recently vacated area is open, but it isn't necessarily desirable. If our competitors didn't like that position, we should suspect that there will be problems there for us as well.

This rule is often violated in the business arena, and the results are usually disastrous. When one business moves out of a particular market, other businesses are often naturally drawn in. Nature abhors a vacuum. For example, we often see this situation when one restaurant after another moves into a specific location. Each business fails in turn. When a business moves out of a market, customers in that market look for another supplier. This doesn't mean that they are good customers or that it is a profitable market. We must be suspicious of these situations.

Again, our rivals are rational. If they didn't like a position, it has a flaw. That flaw may not be immediately apparent, but we should expect that our competitors who have experience in that area know something that we do not know. They know the problems more intimately than we do. Because we are different from our competition, there *may* be an opportunity for us in this area, but we must find out what the competitor's problem was in the area in order to make that determination.

Lesson 174: An Opponent's Movement

How can you know best what your competitors are doing if you can't see their moves directly?

A.   By observing the environment.
B.   By listening to your instincts.
C.   By knowing their leader.
D.   By knowing yourself.

> *The trees in the forest move.*
> *Expect that the enemy is coming.*
> *The tall grasses obstruct your view.*
> *Be suspicious.*

THE ART OF WAR 9:4.7-10

Answer: A. By observing the environment.

The topic shifts subtly again. We started by talking about responding to different types of environments. We then addressed making judgments about a situation or position based on our competition's reactions to it. Now, we must judge our competition based upon our observations of reactions in the natural or social environment itself.

The general rule here is that if there is a change in our immediate environment, we should suspect that our opponents might be behind it. If the environment lacks visibility, we have a known problem. Environments that provide very little information should make us cautious and suspicious, but we still shouldn't imagine things. We should prepare to meet a challenge from our opposition even though an attack is not certain.

The underlying message here is that we want facts upon which to base our suspicions. Suspicion is necessary but it is costly. It slows down our progress. Sun Tzu is very concerned about people reacting with too little hard information. He dedicates the entire final chapter of the book to getting solid information from other people because he feels that people are the best source of information. We can, however, get hard information from the environment, and we should always be looking for it. The absence of information is a problem. We cannot assume that it means the absence of competition. We can know, however, that if the environment changes, there is something else causing it to change.

Lesson 175: Sudden Environmental Changes

When neutral parties in a situation suddenly change direction for no apparent reason, what is happening?

A.   You are upsetting them.

B.   It has nothing to do with you.

C.   Your opponents are coming.

D.   Your opponents are working secretly.

> *The birds take flight.*
> *Expect that the enemy is hiding.*
> *Animals startle.*
> *Expect an ambush.*

THE ART OF WAR 9:4.11-14

Answer: D. Your opponents are working secretly.

Ideally, we want information from people who can tell us what is going on in a given situation. However, people do not always tell us what is happening for a variety of reasons. In these situations, people's behavior can also tell us what is going on.

When people change direction, they have a reason. When they won't tell us the reason, we have to assume that someone is working secretly against us. When opponents are working against us, they usually want to keep it a secret. Since they know people talk, they build incentives in their plan to keep people from telling us what is going on. Like the dog that didn't bark in *The Hound of the Baskervilles*, people's silence is strong evidence of what is happening.

While certain forms of competition, such as political battles, are direct, competition in some areas, such as business, is more subtle. Opponents in business are often less obvious than competitors on other battlefields. Ambushes in battle are common enough, but almost all opposition in the business world takes the form of an ambush. In business, relationships are everything. When we move into a new area, we must focus on the reality that our competitors have established relationships. We do not. This makes it easy for established businesses to ambush new ones moving into an area. People won't tell us what is going on out of sympathy. If we don't pay attention to the way people behave, we will have no idea what is going on.

Lesson 176: Subtle Evidence

If you get only tiny, seemingly meaningless bits of information from a new environment, how can you tell what is going on?

A.   By filtering out new from old.
B.   By filtering out truth from fiction.
C.   By the holes in the information.
D.   By the pattern of the information.

> *Notice the dust.*
> *It sometimes rises high in a straight line.*
> *Vehicles are coming.*
> *The dust appears low in a wide band.*
> *Foot soldiers are coming.*
> *The dust seems scattered in different areas.*
> *The enemy is collecting firewood.*
> *Any dust is light and settling down.*
> *The enemy is setting up camp.*

THE ART OF WAR 9:4.15-23

Answer: D. By the pattern of the information.

Again, the key to strategy is knowing how to use information. Sun Tzu teaches that to use information, we must be sensitive to details. In some situations, we don't even need direct evidence to get information about what is happening. Properly analyzing information is often a matter of forensics, noticing specific details that go together to create a meaningful picture.

We can think of dust as the tiny disturbances that arise from the actions of our opponents. Dust particles are the seemingly meaningless rumors or mere indications of the opponent's presence here and there. Sun Tzu's point is that the information itself doesn't have to make any sense. We can glean a great deal merely from the pattern of dust.

Where do these bits of information come from? Are they coming directly from a few people? Are they the top people or people lower down? Are they coming broadly from everywhere? The sources tell us where and how broadly the competition is working. Is competitive activity increasing or is it dying down? This change in pattern reveals a change in activity.

Lesson 177: An Opponent's Communication

When your opponent communicates with you directly, how do you best discern his or her intentions?

A.   By trusting his or her words.

B.   By trusting his or her actions.

C.   By distrusting his or her actions.

D.   By distrusting his or her words.

Your enemy speaks humbly while building up forces.
He is planning to advance.

The enemy talks aggressively and pushes as if to advance.
He is planning to retreat.

THE ART OF WAR 9:5.1-4

Answer: D. By distrusting his or her words.

We all know when we are in competition with other people. We know that our words, actions, and even emotions are being evaluated. To mislead others, we have to become actors. We are all playing poker and want to bluff. We pretend in our words, attitudes, and actions that we are going to do one thing when we are really planning something quite different.

Generally, we can trust actions more than words, but even actions are not a perfect indicator of intention. People commonly feint to make us think that they are doing one thing when they are actually doing another. In every situation, we must look at the words, actions, and emotions of our opponents and ask why they are showing them. By such analysis we can sometimes discern their intentions, but signals are often mixed.

If we have to choose a single signal, the safest course is to distrust people's words. Verbal lying doesn't cost our opponents a thing. Actions have some cost attached to them. Plus, strategy teaches us to keep our true plans a secret, so lying is natural.

We can be fooled by emotional displays. Because we tend to hide our emotions, people trust them more than words, but emotional display is just another form of verbal lying. It doesn't cost a thing, and it can disguise our true intentions. A show of anger is more often a sign that our opponent wants to avoid a battle and is trying to bluff.

Lesson 178: Evaluating Movement

When your opponents change their organizational structure quickly, relying more heavily on speed, what does it mean?

A.   They are preparing to move forward.

B.   They are preparing to withdraw.

C.   They are preparing to move to a new position.

D.   They are preparing to defend their position.

> *Small vehicles exit his camp first.*
> *They move the army's flanks.*
> *They are forming a battle line.*

THE ART OF WAR 9:5.5-7

Answer: A. They are preparing to move forward.

How do we interpret changes in an opponent's formation? Strategically, every competitor has a position. Just like the Chinese term *di* means both the ground and the situation, the Chinese term *xing* means both position and formation. Sun Tzu's concept of *xing* simultaneously means how we are situated on the ground—our position—and how we align our resources to make the most of the ground we hold—our formations. Changes in formation, like all of our opponent's actions, communicate information. The question is, what do they mean?

Speed is a tool for invasion. When opponents restructure their organization to move quickly, they are planning to advance their position. Speed and coordination are important only in an attack. Withdrawals from a position are done or should be done slowly, ideally secretly. Defense is built up patiently. Only attacks require speed and coordination at the flanks.

In business, a leader restructures his or her organization only because he or she is serious about winning a new market or expanding into a new business area. We saw this when Bill Gates restructured Microsoft to refocus his company from desktop computing to networking. He wasn't concerned with simply defending his dominance on the desktop. He was signalling that he was serious about going after new lines of business. This is the type of action that speaks much louder than words. While organizations can restructure, especially to downsize or to defend their territories, those changes emphasize stability and continuity, not speed.

Lesson 179: Evaluating Agreements

When your opponents say that they want to negotiate with you but do not offer a concrete plan, what does it mean?

A.   They are planning an attack.

B.   They are seeking information.

C.   They are in trouble.

D.   They know that an agreement is impossible.

> *Your enemy tries to sue for peace but without offering a treaty.*
> *He is plotting.*
>
> THE ART OF WAR 9:5.8-9

Answer: B. They are seeking information.

In this situation, our opponents are not necessarily planning an attack. They are also not likely looking for an agreement. If they really knew what they wanted in an agreement, they would come with a proposal, hoping to influence the final agreement by acting first. In other words, they would come with a specific offer.

In this situation, when they don't have a specific offer, they either don't know what they want or don't want us to know what they want. Instead, they are using the process of negotiation to find out more information from us. Opening negotiations puts them in a position where they can make contact with us. By not offering anything specific, they are putting us in a position where we have to talk. In such a discussion, they learn at the least what our goals are. Any information they can gather helps them formulate their plans.

To use another example from Microsoft, the software company became somewhat infamous for using negotiations with potential competitors to gather competitive information. Microsoft's people would ask for meetings with representatives from leading companies in areas into which they were planning to move. They used the offer of a potential agreement to open up their competitors and see inside their organizations, but very few of these meetings produced actual agreements. Instead, these meeting were often simply tools for market research in which Microsoft obtained an advanced look at its potential competitors' plans. Lawsuits sometimes resulted, but the tactic worked more often than not.

Lesson 180: Contradictory Signals

When your opponents' actions give contradictory signs about advancing or retreating, what should you think?

A.   Their forces are confused.

B.   Their leaders want to fight, but their men do not.

C.   They are trying to mislead you.

D.   They plan to fight but are afraid.

> *Your enemy's men run to leave and yet form ranks.*
> *You should expect action.*
>
> *Half his army advances and the other half retreats.*
> *He is luring you.*
>
> THE ART OF WAR 9:5.10-13

Answer: C. They are trying to mislead you.

Defense is always less costly than attack. Deceiving or luring a potential opponent into an attack is a powerful strategy. If we can show signs of weakness or uncertainty where no weakness or uncertainty exists, we can lead our opponents into a trap.

When we are on an "armed march," the topic of this chapter, we are looking for new worlds to conquer. We are expanding our reach with the hope of expanding our control. Since that is our intent, we are looking for weaknesses, the openings that create an opportunity. It is said that to a hammer, everything looks like a nail. When an opponent acts confused, we naturally take this as a sign of weakness. However, as every serious poker player knows, feigned confusion is a great way of baiting a trap. It isn't as obvious as feigned weakness or strength. If we are looking for viable opportunities, we will tend to see opportunities whether they are there or not.

This lesson is particularly important in evaluating an ambiguous situation. Is our opposition really in disarray—an easy victim—or are we seeing something more threatening—opponents trying to lure us into a situation in which they can easily beat us? Sun Tzu wants us to always suspect the latter. If our enemy is really in disarray, we should see more tangible signs of it, as we discuss later in this chapter.

Lesson 181: Personal Rewards

What does it mean when all your opponent's people are focused first on their personal situation?

A.   Their organization lacks resources.

B.   Their organization has poor leaders.

C.   Their organization encourages selfishness.

D.   Their organization rewards them too well.

> *Your enemy plans to fight but his men just stand there.*
> *They are starving.*
>
> *Those who draw water drink it first.*
> *They are thirsty.*

THE ART OF WAR 9:5.14-17

Answer: A. Their organization lacks resources.

First, let us consider the nature of individual selfishness. People are motivated by self-interest in all circumstances. When we are focused on the well-being of our organization, it is because we perceive that if our organization is successful, we will be successful. When we focus even more broadly on the general welfare of society, it is because we perceive that we will personally do better in an environment where everyone is doing better. There are no truly unselfish actions. Even Mother Teresa said that she chose to serve the poor because it fulfilled her needs. She said that she had benefited more than anyone else from her generosity.

If people in opposing organizations must focus on their personal needs directly, it tells us that they have lost faith in their organization's immediate ability to provide for them. They may believe in the organization longer term, but for the moment they feel that they must provide for themselves.

When an opposing organization is strapped for resources, its people realize that their positions within the organization are not secure. This breakdown in unity is an invitation to attack that unity. In these situations, we can work to divide an opposing organization, stealing its best people or frightening its supporters away. No one sees any advantage in being part of a losing campaign, and when organizations run low on resources, even the most dedicated supporters begin to lose faith.

Lesson 182: Ignoring Opportunities

When competitors have a clear opportunity but do not take advantage of it, what does it mean?

A.   They are moving in another direction.

B.   They are planning a trap.

C.   They are stretched too thin.

D.   They have poor leadership.

> *Your enemy sees an advantage but does not advance.*
> *His men are tired.*
>
> THE ART OF WAR 9:5.18-19

Answer: C. They are stretched too thin.

This topic is covered again at the end of the chapter, where we look at how we cope with situations in which there is more work than manpower to get it done. Here we focus on recognizing this vulnerability in the competition.

One basic tenet of strategy is that we must take advantage of all possible opportunities. Another basic tenet of strategy is that all resources are limited. No matter how many opportunities we have, we can only do so much. People can only do so much. We cannot continually move from opportunity to opportunity at full speed. Eventually, we have to stop and regroup.

Since all resources, including human endurance, are limited, we have to be selective about the opportunities we invest in. We want to make sure that we use our limited resources in the best possible way. We don't want to be fully committed when an even better opportunity comes along. This is why Sun Tzu teaches that we defend when we don't have enough resources and attack when we have more than enough resources.

We want to recognize this condition in our opposition, because being tired or stretched too thin is a weakness. We can take advantage of this weakness in our competitors. If they are stretched too thin, we know that they can't take advantage of an opening even if we leave it for them. For a little while, we can know where they are and what they are doing. We can take advantage of this situation by giving them more work to do, further overloading their already overtaxed resources.

Lesson 183: Scavengers

What does it mean when apparent scavengers suddenly appear around an opponent's established position?

A.   Your opponent is doing well.

B.   Your opponent has abandoned his or her position.

C.   Your opponent has new partners.

D.   Your opponent is luring you.

> *Birds gather.*
> *Your enemy has abandoned his camp.*
>
> THE ART OF WAR 9:5.20-21

Answer: B. Your opponent has abandoned his or her position.

Organizations seldom announce when they are abandoning a position. If we are wise, we certainly do not make such an announcement. We move out of an old established position slowly. We gradually shift our resources to stronger positions where they can do us more good, but we keep our decision secret. As much as possible, we try to make our transitions invisible.

We can, however, know when an opponent is moving out of a position by observing the type of people who are attracted to that position. Scavengers—that is, those looking for a short-term gain—tend to appear in abandoned positions. We have discussed the vacuum that is left in an area when someone abandons a position. The appearance of scavengers and similar fast-moving opportunists is one of the first signs of this vacuum. These vacated positions are not usually good long-term opportunities, but small scavengers can temporarily feed on what a larger organization has left behind.

When we notice an opponent moving out of a position, we shouldn't be attracted to his or her leavings. Those leavings are literally for the birds. Our more immediate concern should be where he or she is going and why. The reason an opponent leaves an area is because he or she has found better opportunities elsewhere. Since resources are limited, all organizations have to focus on the most profitable, most fertile, longest-term opportunities that they can find. We want to know what those opportunities are, especially if they affect our plans.

Lesson 184: An Opponent's Difficulty

How can you tell when your competitors are really in disarray and not just trying to fool you?

A.   Their people contact you secretly.

B.   Their people act out of control.

C.   Their internal alliances change.

D.   All of the above.

> *Your enemy's soldiers call in the night.*
> *They are afraid.*
>
> *Your enemy's army is raucous.*
> *They do not take their commander seriously.*
>
> *Your enemy's banners and flags shift.*
> *Order is breaking down.*

THE ART OF WAR 9:5.22-27

Answer: D. All of the above.

An opponent can lure us into attacking a position by feigning confusion and a breakdown in organization. How do we know when such a breakdown is actually taking place? Instead of one sign, there are many different signs that indicate real problems within an opposing organization. Any of them can be faked, but a pattern of disorder shows up in many places.

First, it shows up in self-interest. When individuals from a competing company start communicating with us, they are looking at their personal options. This means they are concerned about the condition of their organization.

Next, problems show up in the behavior of the organization's people as a group. If, as a group, they act disorderly and out of control, they have lost faith in their management. They are no longer worried as a group about losing their jobs.

Finally, the alliances within the organization start to change. The leaders within the organization start to turn on one another. They start picking sides and finding scapegoats.

Lesson 185: Extreme Measures

If your opponents are in trouble, what should you be concerned about?

A.   Losing the opportunity to attack.

B.   Encountering the same trouble.

C.   Falling into a trap.

D.   That they have nothing to lose.

> *Your enemy's officers are irritable.*
> *They are exhausted.*
>
> *Your enemy's men kill their horses for meat.*
> *They are out of provisions.*
>
> *They don't put their pots away or return to their tents.*
> *They expect to fight to the death.*

THE ART OF WAR 9:5.28-33

Answer: D. That they have nothing to lose.

We normally expect people to act in their own individual self-interest. We can predict people's behavior because we understand where their interests lie. However, when organizations are pushed into extreme situations, the people within them become more unpredictable and therefore more dangerous.

A broad breakdown in an organization begins among the organization's decision-makers. The pressure of competition puts decision-makers in a position where they have few good decisions to make. They begin to react emotionally. The danger is that this emotion can lead to costly battles that no one can win. The normal calculation of what the battle is worth is forgotten.

When opponents start consuming their assets simply to keep the organization going, they realize that they have nothing left to lose. They have discounted their future. As a group, the organization's members are psychologically capable of anything. People who are willing to fight to the death are the toughest possible adversaries. People are many times more effective when their backs are to the wall and they know that they will gain nothing from defeat.

Lesson 186: Organizational Problems

What is the first sign that your opponent's organization is headed for problems?

A.   Its internal communication slows down.
B.   Its leaders are proud and boastful.
C.   Its methods are aggressive.
D.   Its positioning is weak.

> *Enemy troops appear sincere and agreeable.*
> *But their men are slow to speak to each other.*
> *They are no longer united.*
>
> *Your enemy offers too many incentives to his men.*
> *He is in trouble.*
>
> *Your enemy gives out too many punishments.*
> *His men are weary.*

THE ART OF WAR 9:5.34-40

Answer: A. Its internal communication slows down.

An organization exists only if it has good internal communication. When people within the organization stop talking with one another, problems are unavoidable. Communication too often focuses on messages passed up and down a hierarchy, but that type of communication is often less important than discussion across divisional lines. When people no longer speak to one another, the organization is in trouble. Just having the pace of information flow slow down is enough to break down the unity within any organization.

Leaders too often think that they can address their organizational problems using the right incentives and penalties. While a well-understood framework of incentives and punishments is necessary, changing that structure to address immediate problems is a mistake. Trying to control an organization through incentives is a sign of weakness. New penalties can make existing problems worse. Sun Tzu teaches that organizational strength comes from a shared philosophy or mission. That philosophy must define the shared goals of everyone. It is the basis of all internal communication. It assures that people do the right thing without being told.

Lesson 187: Judging Emotions

What does it mean when opponents' emotional reactions don't seem to make sense in light of their behavior?

A.   They are playing for time.

B.   They are having internal conflicts.

C.   They do not know what they are doing.

D.   They are hoping for a change of luck.

> *Your enemy first attacks and then is afraid of your larger force.*
> *His best troops have not arrived.*
>
> *Your enemy comes in a conciliatory manner.*
> *He needs to rest and recuperate.*

THE ART OF WAR 9:5.41-44

Answer: A. They are playing for time.

Lesson 179 discussed how our opponents can use negotiations to get inside information about our organization. This lesson describes a similar ruse. Here the opponent's purpose is to buy time. In this case, we must sense a mismatch between our opponent's current attitude and his or her behavior.

The larger lesson here again is that people don't do anything without a reason. Even when their behavior doesn't seem to make sense, there is some sense in it. Opponents don't change their approach in a moment without having a good reason. In this case, they are delaying a challenge at least for a short time so that their position can improve in the immediate future.

Why would opponents use attack as a delaying tactic? In lesson 234, Sun Tzu teaches us to use the speed of a small invasion as a method of delaying an opponent's attack with overwhelming force. This lesson is partly a warning that just because our opponents run away in fright, it doesn't mean that they didn't accomplish their goal of delaying the main battle. Since deception is central to warfare, good competitors never pass up opportunities to confuse their opponents. Deceptive reconciliation is a similar bluff, used simply as a means of securing enough time to regroup. Many fierce competitors, including Hitler, routinely used treaties simply as a method of delaying conflict until they were ready for battle.

Lesson 188: Ambiguous Situations

When opponents don't attack for a long time despite indicating that they want a confrontation, what should you do?

A.   Attack them before they build up resources.

B.   Forget about them because they aren't serious.

C.   Get more information about them.

D.   Suspect that they are laying a trap.

> *Your enemy is angry and appears to welcome battle.*
> *This goes on for a long time, but he doesn't attack.*
> *He also doesn't leave the field.*
> *You must watch him carefully.*

THE ART OF WAR 9:5.45-48

Answer: C. Get more information about them.

The rules of strategy teach us that we have to control both what we do and what we don't do. We often succeed simply by avoiding mistakes. This is why this lesson is so important. Many situations are ambiguous. Acting on the wrong assumptions can be disastrous. In ambiguous situations such as the situation described above, we must wait and gather more information because acting inappropriately is a costly error.

In the situation this stanza describes, one possibility is that our opponents want us to attack them—in other words, they are luring us. Lesson 180 discussed the dangers of being lured into a trap. If a trap is being set, we should stay away from our opponents and not fall for the bait.

The other possible interpretation of this ambiguous situation is that our opponents are buying time because they want to build up their forces. The contradiction between their attitude and their behavior fits Sun Tzu's description in the previous lesson of a person buying time. If this is the situation, keeping our distance is the worst thing that we can do.

Faced with two equally likely scenarios, we need more information. This lesson is the final one in this section devoted to diagnosing the competition's condition. It points out the types of conflict we might run into using the other rules we've been studying. When we see such a conflict, we must look at the situation more closely and not get ourselves into trouble that could be avoided.

Lesson 189: The Limits of Expansion

When you are developing a new area, how do you know when you've gone far enough?

A.   You can never go too far.

B.   You find it difficult to get information.

C.   Your people are overworked.

D.   You run out of new directions.

> *If you are too weak to fight, you must find more men.*
> *In this situation, you must not act aggressively.*
> *You must unite your forces, expect the enemy, recruit men, and wait.*
>
> *You must be cautious about making plans and adjust to the enemy.*
> *You must increase the size of your forces.*

THE ART OF WAR 9:6.1-5

Answer: C. Your people are overworked.

When we are on an "armed march," that is, exploring areas controlled by our opponents, we have to understand our own limitations. Strategy teaches us to focus long term on continually improving our position. However, when our resources run low, we have to stop the campaign.

In Sun Tzu's strategic system, we go after new territory whenever we have excess resources that we can use for expansion. We stop that expansion when we run out of resources. Strategically, knowing when to stop is at least as important as knowing when and how to expand.

For Sun Tzu, knowing when to stop is simply a matter of knowing when we have too few people to continue. We must then consolidate our gains and use our position to build up our resources. This takes time. During this time, we must be careful about making plans for new expansion. Instead, our focus must shift back to defense until we can build up the resources that we need to continue expansion. This is a critical phase in every campaign.

Many people think that when they are successful they have to keep going to maintain their momentum. This is where Sun Tzu's definition of momentum as needing the surprise of change is important. If we continue to expand beyond our capabilities, we are headed for failure. The illusion of momentum will carry us only so far.

Lesson 190: The Treatment of Recruits

How do you treat new people recruited into your organization in comparison to how you treat veterans?

A.   You treat new people more severely.

B.   You treat new people more kindly.

C.   You treat new people more patiently.

D.   You treat new people with indifference.

> *With new, undedicated soldiers, you can depend on them if you discipline them.*
> *They will tend to disobey your orders.*
> *If they do not obey your orders, they will be useless.*
>
> *You can depend on seasoned, dedicated soldiers.*
> *But you must avoid disciplining them without reason.*
> *Otherwise, you cannot use them.*

THE ART OF WAR 9:7.1-6

Answer: A. You treat new people more severely.

Since we must add more people when we no longer have enough resources to expand, we must know how to successfully make them part of our organization. The most common mistake that leaders make is failing to challenge their newest recruits. By immediately challenging new recruits, we force them to commit themselves emotionally to the organization.

The great truth about developing relationships is that we must treat new relationships differently than existing ones. When a relationship is new we must be much more serious and strict about testing the relationship. At the beginning of a relationship, we need to establish commitment. New people don't understand our mission or necessarily buy into it. They haven't found their role in the organization. So people must be asked to sacrifice early in the relationship so that they have something to lose by later dropping out of the relationship. Military academies have always understood this.

However, this is the opposite of the way we treat existing relationships. Existing relationships must be based on trust. We must expect our experienced people to understand our mission and their role. If we are too strict in the relationship, we destroy what makes relationships work.

Lesson 191: Esprit de Corps

How do you get people to believe in your organization's mission and develop esprit de corps?

A.   You train them well.
B.   You suffer together.
C.   You honor all agreements.
D.   You win victories.

> *You must control your soldiers with esprit de corps.*
> *You must bring them together by winning victories.*
> *You must get them to believe in you.*

THE ART OF WAR 9:7.7-9

Answer: D. You win victories.

Where does the fabled "esprit de corps" come from? Training is good, but no amount of training creates spirit. For new recruits and old, suffering together creates a bond, but that bond is well short of "esprit." Honoring all our agreements is a necessity for trust, but this too is inadequate. In the end, the only thing that brings people together is shared success. Esprit de corps comes from the sure knowledge that we are part of a winning team.

People don't believe in us and our organization until they see that we are successful. Strategy is a science based upon human psychology. Only by continually advancing our position do we get a sense of progress and continued success. People join an organization because they want to share in its success. Organizations that never advance their position are doomed to fall apart because they have never won anything. Their best people will look for success elsewhere. Strategy as a process of continually making steps forward gives people a sense of progress so that they will be devoted even when the going gets difficult.

If we want to build an organization that will last, one that can grow in good times and bad, we must develop a shared feeling of accomplishment. We must continually engineer strategic wins for our organization. As leaders, we need challenging but achievable goals simply for the sake of building organization spirit. A success need not advance us much to give people a sense of progress and accomplishment, especially when our people are new.

Lesson 192: Earning Obedience

How do you get new, inexperienced people to obey your orders?

A.   By explaining your reasons.

B.   By using incentives.

C.   By making your orders simple.

D.   By using punishments.

> *Make it easy for them to obey your orders by training your people.*
> *Your people will then obey you.*
> *If you do not make it easy to obey, you won't train your people.*
> *Then they will not obey.*

THE ART OF WAR 9:7.10-13

Answer: C. By making your orders simple.

The strategy here is simple. Obedience depends on training. Training depends on simplicity. Simplicity must come first. We start developing new people by making our orders easy to understand. We must make no assumptions about what they know or don't know. We must start at the beginning and build up our people's knowledge one small piece at a time.

To a large degree, this advice follows the design of Sun Tzu's book, *The Art of War,* itself. Like Euclid's *Geometry,* the first chapters of *The Art of War* start with basic principles, and each successive chapter builds on those principles. By starting with a few basic ideas to begin with, we learn their sophistication and depth gradually, as our familiarity with these lessons grows. Though it can take years of reading and rereading to master these lessons, we get a sense of progress by simply understanding the first few pages of the book.

When it came to teaching strategy, Sun Tzu realized that he had to simplify the complexities of its science. In our books, we try to make it even easier to master his ideas. Originally, Sun Tzu hid the sophistication of his system in the dense relationships among its component parts. By simply reading his book, we get a sense of what strategy is. We can increase that knowledge by studying the relationships between the book's concepts as we present them in *The Art of War Plus Its Amazing Secrets.* The purpose of this book is to make understanding those principles an even simpler step-by-step process.

Lesson 193: Keeping It Simple

What is the key to making your commands easy to follow?

A.   Making them as detailed as possible.

B.   Starting with the easiest ideas first.

C.   Understanding how people think.

D.   Repeating them until they are understood.

> *Make your commands easy to follow.*
> *You must understand the way a crowd thinks.*

THE ART OF WAR 9:7.14-15

Answer: C. Understanding how people think.

This final lesson addresses the most common mistake that we can make in training people. Too often, we start with what we know instead of what our audience knows. To build a successful training program, we actually have to forget everything we know. We can then approach our subject from the same viewpoint as a beginner. We have to see ourselves as one of the crowd.

This is, of course, very difficult to do. One of the first steps is to escape from the technical nomenclature of our expertise, or, more simply, to stop using jargon.

Every area of skill develops its own terminology. These special vocabularies are filled with obscure terms and—too often these days—acronyms. For example, in the military a car is know as a POV. Why replace a three-letter word that everyone knows with a three-letter acronym that no one knows? When we are immersed in a specialty, we learn to think in its special terms. Unfortunately, those special terms often act as an obstacle to learning, a barrier to entry.

Having a special language makes us feel special. This specialized language can sound impressive to outsiders. It points to the secret knowledge that we have and that others lack. Unfortunately, it also makes it difficult to explain our ideas to other people.

To teach others, we have to learn to see our special knowledge with fresh eyes and explain it without letting the depth of our knowledge get in the way. We can find simpler terms that capture the basic premise of very complex ideas.

Chapter 10

地 形

Field Position

"Field position" in the original Chinese is *di xing*, literally "ground position," a key concept in classical strategy. Another legitimate translation of *di xing* is "situation formation," which evokes some of the subtlety in this long, detailed chapter. A major theme of this chapter is that every position is temporary. It must be evaluated not only on its own strengths and weaknesses but on how well it serves us in making our next move. A field position must be both useful in itself and useful as a gateway to even stronger positions in the future.

To clarify what a competitive position is in modern terms, we take a position every time we take an action. When we express an opinion, submit a proposal, or suggest an idea, we are taking a tentative position. A business takes a position when it releases a new product or produces a new commercial. Candidates take positions whenever they say where they stand on an issue. Taking a position is a choice. Strategically, it tells everyone what ground we want to defend.

In this chapter, Sun Tzu develops a method of evaluating our potential field positions in three different dimensions. Sun Tzu calls these dimensions obstacles, dangers, and space. These three dimensions are discussed in terms of the six extremes, which allow us to compare the strengths and weaknesses of various field positions before we move into them. Our ability to move to a specific field position comes from both our current location and our abilities. Since our position arises from our capabilities, the discussion of positioning leads naturally to how we manage people and a discussion of organizational weaknesses. The chapter ends by reviewing the concept of victory in terms of field position.

Lesson 194: The Six Characteristics of Position

When you develop a position in a market, how does it affect what you can do next in advancing your position?

A.   Your current position has very little effect on future choices.

B.   Your current position must protect your next move.

C.   Different positions have the same effect on future moves.

D.   Different positions affect your future moves in different ways.

> *Some field positions are unobstructed.*
> *Some field positions are entangling.*
> *Some field positions are supporting.*
> *Some field positions are constricted.*
> *Some field positions give you a barricade.*
> *Some field positions are spread out.*
>
> THE ART OF WAR 10:1.1-6

Answer: D. Different positions affect your future moves in different ways.

Positioning means picking a specific place on the ground. A specific ground position can give us a number of different advantages and disadvantages. In this chapter, we look at one specific class of characteristics: those that determine how our current position affects our future position. This means looking at ground position from a long-term perspective.

Positioning is a skill. Positioning means that we use the territory to find advantage. Our "field position" is the location that we have *currently* chosen to develop. Sun Tzu teaches that we must see each position as a stepping-stone to our next position. Any given position must be evaluated in terms of how easy or difficult it makes our next step.

In the dynamic environment of competition, any given position will degrade over time as our opponents maneuver against it. Because of this, we must see clearly how our current position enables us to move forward. Strategy teaches us to continually look for opportunities to advance our position. Sun Tzu argued clearly that not all positions are equal in this regard. Some positions give us a great deal of freedom; others give us no freedom at all. Some positions are easy to defend; others are open to attack. The six characteristics covered here are the basis for understanding the problems posed by certain positions in terms of future advancement.

Lesson 195: The Unobstructed Position

What is the disadvantage of an unobstructed position?

A.   You have to choose a direction.

B.   The enemy can attack you easily.

C.   The position is easy to block.

D.   There are no disadvantages.

> *You can attack from some positions easily.*
> *Others can attack you easily as well.*
> *We call these unobstructed positions.*
> *These positions are open.*
> *On them, be the first to occupy a high, sunny area.*
> *Put yourself where you can defend your supply routes.*
> *Then you will have an advantage.*

THE ART OF WAR 10:1.7-13

Answer: B. The enemy can attack you easily.

The topic of the above stanza is the *open* or *unobstructed* position. Any position that makes it easy for us to change our position is also an easy position to attack. Remember, an attack is not necessarily conflict. It means specifically the ability of an opponent to move into our territory. Absence of barriers works both ways. If we can move into our opponents' territory easily, our opponents can move into our territory easily as well. In modern business terms, an unobstructed position is open to attack because it offers no barriers to entry. Any political position that both opposing candidates can claim is an open position.

In terms of future movement, open positions are good because they allow us to move in any direction. Claiming open positions is beneficial, but we have to manage them well. We must get to these positions first and successfully stake a visible claim on their "high, sunny areas." We must also continually make sure that we can defend our support —"supply routes"—in these areas so that opponents cannot poach on our open position.

Positions are defined by the number of obstacles they contain. The *unobstructed* position is one extreme, with no obstacles. The *barricaded* position (discussed later) is the opposite extreme, with many obstacles.

Lesson 196: The Entangling Position

There are some positions you can't move back to once you have moved away. How do you use these positions?

A.   Never leave them.

B.   You can't use them; avoid them.

C.   Leave them as soon as possible.

D.   Leave them only when you are sure to win.

> *You can attack from some positions easily.*
> *Disaster arises when you try to return to them.*
> *These are entangling positions.*
> *These field positions are one-sided.*
> *Wait until your enemy is unprepared.*
> *You can then attack from these positions and win.*
> *Avoid a well-prepared enemy.*
> *You will try to attack and lose.*
> *Since you can't return, you will meet disaster.*
> *These field positions offer no advantage.*
>
> THE ART OF WAR 10:1.14-23

Answer: D. Leave them only when you are sure to win.

We normally think of entangling positions as those we cannot get out of. Sun Tzu's definition is more thought provoking. He defines them as positions that we cannot get back into once we move out of them. These positions are like one-way streets. We can leave them, but when we do, we leave them forever. These are dangerous positions in Sun Tzu's estimate because they force us to make certain that our advance out of them is successful. As we know from earlier lessons such as lesson 48, failure is likely.

We would never choose entangling positions. We get caught in them because we don't look far enough ahead. Socially entangling positions are more common than physically entangling positions. Moving out of these positions destroys our credibility. Politicians often discover this when they try to change their position on an issue. They can change their minds once, but then they cannot go back to their previous position without being labelled as untrustworthy. We must make sure that our new position is successful because moving to it in effect undermines the old position.

Lesson 197: The Supporting Position

What do you do if a position supports you so well that you simply can't move out of it?

A.   Never leave it.

B.   Search for an exit.

C.   Leave it as soon as possible.

D.   Leave it only when you are sure to win.

> *I cannot leave some positions without losing an advantage.*
> *If the enemy leaves this ground, he also loses an advantage.*
> *We call these supporting field positions.*
> *These positions strengthen you.*
> *The enemy may try to entice me away.*
> *Still, I will hold my position.*
> *You must entice the enemy to leave.*
> *You then strike him as he is leaving.*
> *These field positions offer an advantage.*
>
> THE ART OF WAR 10:1.24-32

Answer: A. Never leave it.

Remember when Coca-Cola tried to bring out New Coke? The company was in a supporting position and tried to move away from it. It soon discovered that it is impossible to move from these positions. Both supporting and entangling positions are defined by Sun Tzu as dangerous because they make advancing more difficult. In the case of supporting positions, we can extend or expand them, but we cannot give them up.

Supporting positions are different from entangling positions because we can move back to them. Coke was able to move back into its traditional strong position as "the real thing" after New Coke failed.

If we find ourselves in a supporting position, we must build that position up rather than trying to advance by moving onward. Supporting positions trap us, but in a beneficial way. They are not an endpoint in our progress but an anchor point. If our opponents are in a supporting position, we must patiently wait for them to make the mistake of trying to move from it. If we can encourage them in this mistake, so much the better. If they move, we should be prepared to take over their old position as quickly as possible.

Lesson 198: The Constricted Field Position

When you find yourself in a niche of very limited size, what should you do?

A.   Get out of it quickly.

B.   Get 100 percent of its business.

C.   Take whatever business comes easily.

D.   Avoid getting pigeonholed.

> *Some field positions are constricted.*
> *I try to get to these positions before the enemy does.*
> *You must fill these areas and await the enemy.*
> *Sometimes, the enemy will reach them first.*
> *If he fills them, do not follow him.*
> *However, if he fails to fill them, you can go after him.*
>
> THE ART OF WAR 10:1.33-38

Answer: B. Get 100 percent of its business.

There are many types of constricted positions, but small market niches are good examples. A common mistake small businesses make is focusing on markets that are too large for their size. Many companies avoid completely filling small niches because they are afraid of being "pigeonholed" in those markets. Being pigeonholed and firmly established in a small niche is less of a problem than being overwhelmed in a large arena. Small, constricted positions are the ideal building blocks of a large organization. For example, the Democratic Party is built largely by securing virtually 100 percent of certain core groups such as African Americans and environmentalists.

In positioning, we are always looking for a dominant position. It is easier to dominate small niches than it is to dominate large open ones. If we are fortunate enough to discover a small niche that we can dominate, we should immediately try to satisfy all the demand in that niche before anyone else discovers it. These niches are extremely easy to defend once we fill them completely. This is why we should never try to take away such a niche from a competitor if it has filled the niche completely. Distance is one of the three basic dimensions for evaluating position. *Constricted* positions are the positive extreme, consisting of the most limited space. *Spread-out* positions (lesson 200) are the negative extreme, consisting of too much space.

Lesson 199: The Barricaded Position

When an area is naturally difficult to get into, how should you react to it?

A. Get into it first.
B. Wait for others to develop it.
C. Wait until the costs of entry have been reduced.
D. Avoid it entirely.

> *Some field positions give you a barricade.*
> *I get to these positions before the enemy does.*
> *You occupy their southern, sunny heights and wait for the enemy.*
> *Sometimes the enemy occupies these areas first.*
> *If so, entice him away.*
> *Never go after him.*

THE ART OF WAR 10:1.39-44

Answer: A. Get into it first.

In lesson 195, we discussed the opportunities in areas with few barriers to entry. Here we look at the opposite situation: the opportunities presented by the existence of barriers to entry. It is easy to say that we should look for positions where barriers to entry protect us so that we can easily defend ourselves against our opponents. In real life, however, getting into a barricaded position is difficult.

Areas that provide barriers to entry are, by definition, difficult to enter. When we first encounter them, we are not struck by how easily they are defended. Instead, we see the difficulty and cost of placing ourselves in these positions. Strategy is opportunistic, and in many situations we should follow the path of least resistance. However, there is also an advantage to be gained by surmounting difficulties. To be of any value at all, organizations must solve problems. The more difficult the problems that a person or organization can solve, the more difficult it is for opponents to attack. If a position is difficult to achieve when it is empty, it is much more difficult to attain when someone else already controls it.

We said earlier that positions are defined by the number of obstacles they contain. *Unobstructed* positions and *barricaded* positions are the two extremes. Both types of positions have their positive sides: the first because we can enter easily; the latter because the competition cannot enter easily.

Lesson 200: The Spread-Out Position

When you are as large as your competitors but involved in many more widely separated competitive arenas, what should you do?

A.   Look for more areas to get involved in.

B.   Recognize that you are weaker than the competition.

C.   Use the diversity in your business as a strength.

D.   Abandon many of your businesses.

> *Some field positions are too spread out.*
> *Your force may seem equal to the enemy.*
> *Still you will lose if you provoke a battle.*
> *If you fight, you will not have any advantage.*

THE ART OF WAR 10:1.45-48

Answer: B. Recognize that you are weaker than the competition.

Remember that, strategically, unity, not size, is the key to strength. When we evaluate how strong an organization is, the first question we should ask is how unified its focus is. Larger organizations tend to become more diversified, but this is not a strength. Companies that can grow large and yet remain focused on a clear, core goal are much stronger.

Growth in many different areas is not an inherently bad thing if those areas are tied together. The problems arise when the areas are diverse and distant from one another, geographically and philosophically. We cannot fool ourselves about our strength in each of these areas compared to that of our opponents. In a competitive battle against a more focused and unified opponent, we are at a serious disadvantage. In a spread-out position, we cannot defend all the space we occupy. There are too many holes in our organization, too many different ways to flank us. If more focused opponents come after us, we must move out of their way.

As organizations grow, their need for focus creates competitive problems. Strategy calls for us to advance our position. Unless we are willing to give up old areas as we cultivate new ones, strategy becomes a growth philosophy. Strategy teaches that we should try to keep our areas of growth as closely related as possible. The more closely related the areas we occupy, the less an organization's growth disrupts its focus.

Lesson 201: Evaluating a Position

Does every position you develop fall into one of the six types of field positions?

A. Every position falls into one of these six types.

B. Every position is a combination of types.

C. These six types are generalities, and each position is unique.

D. You must be able to categorize a position to understand it.

> *These are the six types of field positions.*
> *Each battleground has its own rules.*
> *As a commander, you must know where to go.*
> *You must examine each position closely.*
>
> THE ART OF WAR 10:1.49-52

Answer: C. These six types are generalities, and each position is unique.

Each position is unique. Field positions can be categorized by their number of obstacles, danger of movement, and distance. The six positions that Sun Tzu describes—*unobstructed, barricaded, entangling, supporting, constricted,* and *spread out*—are the extremes. These extremes allow us to gauge other positions. How many barriers does a position offer? How spread out or constricted is it? Can we leave it, and, if we do, can we return?

It helps if we think of this as a three-dimensional map in the form of a cube of opportunity space. The three dimensions—obstacles, dangers of movement, and distance—make up the six faces of the cube. Opposing sides represent opposing concepts: *barricaded/unobstructed, supporting/entangling,* and *constricted/spread out.* Every field position (and every proposal or planned project that develops a position) can be evaluated on this three-dimensional map.

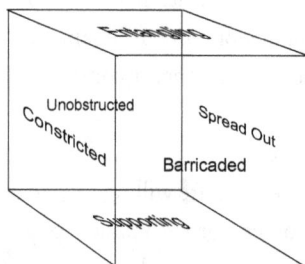

Positions that are near the intersection of *barricaded, supporting,* and *constricted* are the easiest to defend, but they are also the hardest to move out of. Positions near the intersection of *entangling, unobstructed,* and *spread out* are the easiest to attack and the easiest to move into and out of.

Lesson 202: Problems with Field Position

Where does failure in dealing with different types of field positions first appear?

A.   In your philosophy.
B.   In your leadership.
C.   In your organization.
D.   In the trends.

> *Some armies can be outmaneuvered.*
> *Some armies are too lax.*
> *Some armies fall down.*
> *Some armies fall apart.*
> *Some armies are disorganized.*
> *Some armies must retreat.*

THE ART OF WAR 10:2.1-6

Answer: C. In your organization.

For people reading *The Art of War* in English translation, many of the interconnections in the text are largely hidden. These interconnections are explained in detail in our book *The Art of War Plus Its Amazing Secrets*. These six problems with armies or organizations represent one of those connections, which is why the discussion appears in this chapter on field position.

The six extreme conditions in field position that are the central topic of this chapter show up as organizational failure. The strength of an organization comes from the weakness or openness of the ground. Conversely, the weakness of the organization arises based on the strong characteristics of the ground. Those who are poorly trained in strategic analysis are likely to overlook possible uses of the ground they hold, but most find some way to use some aspect of their position. The weakness of an organization can be hidden on many types of ground, but that weakness reveals itself when the organization finds itself in specific, extreme conditions.

Sun Tzu describes six categories of organizational collapse. The types of organizational problems are revealed by the six categories of field positions that begin the chapter. These organizational weaknesses exist on all types of ground. They may be disguised in most situations, but it is inevitable that we will encounter a field position that exposes these weaknesses.

Lesson 203: Source of Organizational Weakness

What is the source of the six possible weaknesses in your organization?

A. Your philosophy.

B. Your leader.

C. Your people.

D. Your position.

> *Know all six of these weaknesses.*
> *They lead to losses on both good and bad ground.*
> *They all arise from the army's commander.*

THE ART OF WAR 10:2.7-9

Answer: B. Your leader.

We describe the six weaknesses as organizational flaws because they describe various forms of breakdowns that appear in the organization, but as we learn more about these problems, we see that they all clearly reflect the failure of a leader to correctly manage his or her organization.

The important distinction made here is that these weaknesses do not arise from our field position, that is, our situation. A given type of field position may expose an organizational problem, and some weaknesses can only arise in certain positions, but this does not mean that the position itself caused the problem. Organizations are created by leaders. Leaders must take responsibility for their organizations' weaknesses.

Organizations frequently blame their internal weaknesses on conditions in their environment. Sun Tzu's point here is that these excuses are never valid. An organizational problem exists independent of the organization's situation. Organizations can develop problems on good ground or on bad— that is, in good positions or in bad positions—but these internal weaknesses do not come from external causes. They come from the leader's decisions.

If we are having problems, it is natural to blame the outside situation. However, only two field positions—the *entangling* position and the *spread-out* position—are negative. Two are positive—the *supporting* and the *barricaded*. And two others—the *constricted* and the *unobstructed*—are neutral. We can have problems in any of these positions if we don't have our organization working correctly. Defects in an organization are fairly simple, at the root.

Lesson 204: Being Outmaneuvered

When an opponent of equal size outflanks you, what is your flaw as a leader?

A.   Not knowing how to handle unobstructed positions.

B.   Not knowing how to handle entangling positions.

C.   Not knowing how to handle spread-out positions.

D.   Not knowing how to handle constricted positions.

> *One general can command a force equal to the enemy.*
> *Still his enemy outflanks him.*
> *This means that his army can be outmaneuvered.*
>
> THE ART OF WAR 10:2.10-12

Answer: A. Not knowing how to handle unobstructed positions.

In an *unobstructed* position, we have a great deal of freedom to move. Unfortunately, our opponents also have a great deal of freedom to move. In open terrain, the group that makes progress most quickly wins, but how do we progress so quickly? We must know the territory and keep a careful watch on what the opposition is doing.

There are a variety of ways to be outmaneuvered in any competitive arena from business to politics, but perhaps the best way to think about this issue is to ask how we allocate our limited resources. In open situations, we can go a number of different directions. We can put our resources in any number of different areas. Do we put our limited resources into research? Do we put resources into organization? Do we put them into public awareness? Such decisions about allocation determine our future capabilities. If we make the wrong decision about how to make the best progress in an open situation, we can find ourselves quickly falling behind the competition.

In an unobstructed position, we cannot afford to fall behind our opponents in any area. We have to match our opponents in research. We have to match our opponents in organization. We must match our opponents in public awareness. This is what Sun Tzu calls shadowing, keeping close to our opponents. This keeps us positioned to take advantage of their mistakes.

Eventually, our opponents will make a mistake that will create an opening for us. Only if we are certain that our opponents are making such a mistake can we separate ourselves from them. We use the opportunity to outmaneuver them.

Lesson 205: Organizational Laxity

What does it mean to be "too lax" in Sun Tzu's system of competition?

A.   Lacking energy.

B.   Lacking management.

C.   Lacking strength.

D.   Lacking support.

> *Another can have strong soldiers, but weak officers.*
> *This means that his army will be too lax.*
>
> THE ART OF WAR 10:2.13-14

Answer: B. Lacking management.

Laxity is associated with *supporting* field positions. Only when an organization is supported by its advantageous position can a lax organization develop. Organizations with weak management, that is, poor decision-makers, normally do not grow to become competitive. Only in supporting positions can these types of organizations do well enough to grow without strong management. However, these organizations are inherently limited because of their inability to expand their position.

The strength of a lax organization is the initiative, dedication, and ability of its supporters. However, each individual supporter is concerned only with his or her immediate responsibility. These organizations run into difficulty when decisions have to be made that affect more than one area of responsibility, that is, when the organization has to act as a cohesive whole.

Since lax organizations do best in supporting positions, they are the most at risk in entangling positions. Unlike supporting positions, entangling positions should be left only when we are certain we can win a new position. Without strong management, the lax organization can never be certain of winning a new position. Unity is the source of strength, and without the vision that comes from leadership, these organizations lack focus. The vision to see a viable new position and the responsibility for defining the roles in that position require management. These are typically the types of changes fought by lax organizations. These organizations are very uncomfortable with change. The only solution to the problem of a lax organization is to develop strong managers from among the strong employees.

Lesson 206: Organizational Downfall

When the average worker or supporter in your organization is unqualified and undedicated, what is the effect of adding more management?

A.   Better organization.

B.   Better motivation.

C.   Faster hiring.

D.   Worse performance.

> *Another has strong officers but weak soldiers.*
> *This means that his army will fall down.*
>
> THE ART OF WAR 10:2.15-16

Answer: D. Worse performance.

Overmanaged organizations are associated with *entangling* ground. The risk in entangling ground is that if we attempt more than we can accomplish, we cannot return to our original position. Entangling ground is a one-way trip to destruction if we are not careful in matching our attacks—that is, our movements into new territory—to the capabilities of our people. When our organization will fall down, entangling positions are a deadly trap. Unlike supporting positions, entangling positions cannot support us over the long term. We must move in order to survive.

What makes a worker or supporter weak and incapable of movement? Strategically, weakness is a lack of focus or unity, the twin concepts arising from a shared philosophy. We learned in lesson 189 that when our human resources are stretched too thin, we must do less and refocus on hiring and training new people. Sun Tzu teaches that people within an organization can be weak for two possible reasons. We are either hiring the wrong people or we are failing to train them correctly. In either case, we cannot expect them to carry the organization forward when it must move.

One of the worst things we can do when our workforce is weak is add more management, especially more layers of management. Strong managers make changes and push people harder. When people's abilities are already stretched too thin, the result is the organization's downfall. Organizations with too much management tackle more than they can accomplish. Such organizations are neither effective or efficient.

Lesson 207: The Spread-Out Organization

When an organization spreads itself over a wide area or wide variety of tasks, what is the biggest danger to the organization?

A.   Its lack of priorities.

B.   Its speed of communication.

C.   The focus of its managers.

D.   The movement of its forces.

> *Another has subcommanders that are angry and defiant.*
> *They attack the enemy and fight their own battles.*
> *As a commander, he cannot know the battlefield.*
> *This means that his army will fall apart.*
>
> THE ART OF WAR 10:2.17-20

Answer: C. The focus of its managers.

Sun Tzu describes these subcommanders as "angry and defiant," but a broader description would be overly concerned with personal goals. In classical strategy, emotions are personal, a luxury that we cannot afford in making strategic decisions. An organization has problems whenever its managers become more concerned with their personal goals than with the well-being of the organization as a whole. These organizations pull themselves apart.

Sun Tzu teaches that an organization's philosophy, its shared sense of mission, is what holds the organization together. This philosophy or mission must be the rallying point of the organization. Each manager must serve the shared goals of the organization rather than his or her own personal interests. Once managers start pursuing their own private goals, the organization's focus is lost. It doesn't matter if the managers involved are primarily concerned with their personal careers or their personal vision of what the organization's goals should be. If they aren't rallying around the shared vision of the organization, they can create devastating problems.

The problem of different managers going different directions is associated with field positions that are too *spread out*. Physical separation isn't the only possible form of distance within an organization. More important is the psychological distance between decision-makers who should all share the same goals. Every manager in the organization must see that his or her self-interest is best served by working together.

Lesson 208: Disorganization

Other than managers who focus on their personal issues, what problem causes disorganization?

A.   Poor training.

B.   Unclear orders.

C.   Few opportunities.

D.   Lack of honesty.

Another general is weak and easygoing.
He fails to make his orders clear.
His officers and men lack direction,
This shows in his military formations.
This means that his army will be disorganized.

THE ART OF WAR 10:2.21-25

Answer: B. Unclear orders.

Managers with their own goals can pull an organization apart, but it is the leader's job to make the people within the organization work well together. This means clearly defining everyone's goals and areas of responsibility. An organization requires that its people be trained, but the basis of training, as Sun Tzu has told us before, is clear direction. If a leader fails to make his or her specific desires clear, people will not know how to work together despite their best intentions.

As leaders, we must feel certain about what needs to be done in every situation. This doesn't mean that we won't get better ideas tomorrow, but for today we must be totally committed to what we feel is the right course. We must provide the focus around which our managers can prioritize their individual responsibilities. We can give our managers a lot of responsibility, but we must demand that they understand and share the organization's goals and focus. Everyone must work in the same direction.

Sun Tzu associates disorganization with *constricted* positions. Physical closeness requires well-defined responsibilities; otherwise, people get in each other's way. While a constricted position is not necessarily a bad thing, a constricted organization certainly is. This constriction comes from a leader who fails to lead. This constriction is as damaging in its own way as the spreading out caused by managers following personal priorities.

Lesson 209: Choosing the Wrong Battles

Why do some leaders always seem to find themselves fighting the wrong battles?

A. Their dreams are too large.
B. Their organizations are too small.
C. They fail to understand the territory.
D. They fail to predict their opponents.

> *Another general fails to predict the enemy.*
> *He pits his small forces against larger ones.*
> *He puts his weak forces against stronger ones.*
> *He fails to pick his fights correctly.*
> *This means that his army must retreat.*

THE ART OF WAR 10:2.26-30

Answer: D. They fail to predict their opponents.

This stanza brings us full circle through the six problems of organizations and the management weaknesses that create them. We started with leaders who are outmaneuvered because they are unable to make good choices about keeping up with their opponents. Here we have leaders who pick the wrong places and times to meet their opponents. Both types of leaders have a problem seeing the opponent's capabilities. Being outmaneuvered is associated with *unobstructed* positions. Picking the wrong battle is associated with *barricaded,* or the most obstructed, positions.

Barricades obstruct the competition from coming after us, which allows us to survive a battle when our opponents have more resources than we do. The point here is that no matter how well protected we are, given a big enough imbalance in forces, we are doomed if we try to meet a superior force. Barricaded positions are inherently strong, but no matter how strong our position is, we cannot survive if we pick the wrong battles.

In lesson 83, Sun Tzu gave us the success formula that allows us to calculate the factors of distance and time that enable us to focus more resources in an area than our opponents. Here, he is pointing out that some leaders fail to master the use of that formula. The result is that we underestimate our opponents, putting ourselves in a position where we must withdraw. Giving up a strong, barricaded position is a serious defeat.

Lesson 210: Understanding Organizational Problems

What is the primary way that understanding organizational problems helps you succeed?

A.   By helping you avoid these problems in your own organization.

B.   By helping you know the types of positions to take.

C.   By helping you understand your opponents' weaknesses.

D.   By helping you pick the right opponents.

> *You must know all about these six weaknesses.*
> *You must understand the philosophies that lead to defeat.*
> *When a general arrives, you can know what he will do.*
> *You must study each one carefully.*
>
> THE ART OF WAR 10:2.31-34

Answer: C. By helping you understand your opponents' weaknesses.

Sun Tzu continually relates each piece of his system to the larger whole. He ends this section by explaining that we must learn to predict our opponents by understanding the personal weaknesses that create organizational weaknesses. We can take advantage of these organizational weaknesses when we meet these opponents. From knowledge comes vision. By knowing our opponents, we can see the opportunities that they may offer us.

Two organizational flaws—being outmaneuvered and picking the wrong battles—come specifically from poor decision-making by leaders. These flaws are associated with positions that differ in their levels of obstacles. From an unobstructed or barricaded position, we can make mistakes about the real obstacle, our opponents.

Two other flaws are a mismatch of people and management. "Too lax" organizations offer too little management, while "falling down" organizations have too much management. These two opposite weaknesses tread the fine line between a supporting position and an entangling position.

The two final organizational flaws relate to strong middle management and weak central leadership. When middle management is too strong, organizations fall apart. When central management is too weak, disorganization results. Spread-out field positions tend to create problems with strong middle management while constricted positions tend to exacerbate the problems with top management.

Lesson 211: Choosing a Field Position

What should be one of your primary considerations in choosing your field position?

A.   The consensus of the organization.

B.   The costs of the position.

C.   How it affects your organization.

D.   Your ability as a leader.

> *You must control your field position.*
> *It will always strengthen your army.*
>
> THE ART OF WAR 10:3.1-2

Answer: C. How it affects your organization.

When we are considering moving to a new field position, we are proposing a change. In doing this, we take control of the future and shape it. Field positioning requires decision-making. Our decisions take us to our future positions, which in turn either strengthen or weaken us.

We must control our choice of ground. We cannot allow ourselves to be forced into certain positions by our opponents. In Sun Tzu's classical definition of strategy, advancing our position correctly over time determines our success. It is the most important thing we can control in our environment.

When analyzing our possible field positions, we must never lose sight of the central purpose of positioning: strengthening our organization. Sun Tzu means strengthening in the sense of increasing our internal cohesion. We need to pick field positions that minimize our weaknesses. This is why we must understand how organizational weakness is tied to field positions. Some positions can reveal certain weaknesses in our organization. Spread-out positions create problems with independent managers who can tear the organization apart. Other field positions make certain weaknesses fatal. Lack of organization in a constricted position is deadly. We must know the position that we are in and watch out for these weaknesses.

We have been talking here about many issues that determine the desirability of a given field position, but we don't want to lose sight of the basic premise of competition: we must make victory pay. Each position must gain us something. Sun Tzu makes this point clear.

Lesson 212: Predicting Opponents' Movements

What should you examine to predict where and when your opponents will put themselves at a disadvantage?

A.   The history of their past performance.

B.   The size of their current resources.

C.   The characteristics of their available choices.

D.   The philosophy of their mission.

> *You must predict the enemy to overpower him and win.*
> *You must analyze the obstacles, dangers, and distances.*
> *This is the best way to command.*
>
> THE ART OF WAR 10:3.3-5

Answer: C. The characteristics of their available choices.

We can control our own future by carefully selecting our position. And we must assume that our competitors are doing the same thing. Certainly, knowing their history, resources, and goals helps us predict their moves, but we must learn to look at their opportunities from their viewpoint to predict how they are likely to move. We must know their leaders and organizations to predict when those moves will be to our advantage.

This is like mastering the game of chess. Before we move, we must consider our opponent's likely responses. In considering our move, we must carefully examine the various scenarios. We cannot directly control where our opponents move, but because of our analysis we should instantly recognize when they make a mistake that puts them at a disadvantage.

Sun Tzu describes the six extremes of position by the three dimensions that define them. These three-dimensional planes are described here as obstacles, dangers, and distances. Obstacles describes the *unobstructed/barricaded* dimension. Dangers describes the *supporting/entangling* dimension. Distances describes the *spread-out/constricted* dimension. We must also understand our opponent's personal and organizational flaws and how those flaws—weaknesses or openings—create opportunities in a given field position.

As leaders, we must know beforehand all of the possibilities. Our vision must recognize what our opponents are likely to do and where those actions might create opportunities for us.

Lesson 213: The Failure of Analysis

When you fail to properly analyze your field position before you commit to meeting a challenge, what is the most likely outcome?

A.   Wasted effort.
B.   Organizational confusion.
C.   Learning about our opponents.
D.   Limited future possibilities.

Understand your field position before you meet opponents.
Then you will win.
You can fail to understand your field position and still meet opponents.
Then you will lose.

THE ART OF WAR 10:3.6-9

Answer: A. Wasted effort.

Certainly organizational confusion, limited future possibilities, and even learning about our opponents are also possible, but the most certain result is that we will waste limited resources on an effort that cannot succeed. Remember, Sun Tzu doesn't define success as beating an opponent. He defines success as making victory pay. Wasting effort in a confrontation, even if we happen to win the battle, leads eventually to defeat.

We must see each decision-making step as critical to our long-term success. All resources are limited in running a competitive organization. We only get to play the game as long as we have the resources we need to continue. Organizations that waste resources on doomed efforts are soon out of the game. Decisions about what proposals to offer, what projects to undertake, and what changes to make are critical in this process of continually advancing our position. These changes are all part of the strategic process that moves our organization forward one step at a time.

Here, Sun Tzu doesn't necessarily mean that meeting an opponent is a direct confrontation with the competition. As we said in lesson 14, "battle," "attack," and "fight" have specific meanings in the text. Here the term used is "battle," meeting an opponent. We can afford to meet an opponent or a challenge only when our plans are the most likely to produce positive results, that is, to produce profit, to increase the resources and power of the organization.

Lesson 214: Pressure from Supporters

What should you do if your supporters, investors, customers, or other partners insist that you undertake a losing proposition?

A.   Ignore them.

B.   Find a compromise.

C.   Realize that they are your bosses.

D.   Make a limited investment.

> *You must provoke battle when you will certainly win.*
> *It doesn't matter what you are ordered.*
> *The government may order you not to fight.*
> *Despite that, you must always fight when you will win.*
>
> *Sometimes provoking a battle will lead to a loss.*
> *The government may order you to fight.*
> *Despite that, you must avoid battle when you will lose.*
>
> THE ART OF WAR 10:3.10-16

Answer: A. Ignore them.

In Sun Tzu's time, there was always political pressure to fight a given
enemy, to take a certain position, or to capture a certain prize. In our time,
there is little difference. People within organizations want to win specific
battles for reasons of ego or prestige that have nothing to do with the success
of the organization or the success of the campaign over the long run.

Organizations all develop their own internal goals. Each person or group
within an organization has its own internal goals. Some battles further those
private goals even when they don't help the organization as a whole. Individuals become personally invested in certain courses of action for a variety of
reasons. Some want to engage in certain battles to build their prestige or win
a name for themselves within their organization. Others prefer other battles
simply because fighting them would make their job easier.

Sun Tzu teaches that we must always resist these internal pressures for
external action. We must disregard company politics when we choose where
and when to invest our limited resources. We cannot meet every challenge
successfully. We must pick and choose our battles based solely upon whether
or not they will bring us success in the long term.

Lesson 215: Desire for Success

When should you establish a position solely to win credibility and improve people's opinion of your organization?

A.   When you can afford the investment.

B.   When the position is highly visible.

C.   When your people need encouragement.

D.   Never.

> *You must advance without desiring praise.*
> *You must retreat without fearing shame.*
> *The only correct move is to preserve your troops.*
> *This is how you serve your country.*
> *This is how you reward your nation.*

THE ART OF WAR 10:3.17-21

Answer: D. Never.

We must never fall into the trap of acting because we are concerned about people's opinions. In our modern era, it is easy to justify these actions on the basis of publicity, but the recognition and praise of the press never make a lasting difference in competition. Think of the dozens and perhaps hundreds of dot-coms that were praised to the heavens during the Internet boom, only to go out of business. Think of how many politicians endorsed Howard Dean as a candidate for the Democratic presidential nomination before his first defeat in the 2004 Iowa caucuses.

No serious competitor can afford to focus on praise or criticism or even popular opinion. We certainly should never plan what positions we will go after on the basis of general consensus. If an idea is popular or popularized in the media, many people will be attracted to it. A crowded arena is never the recipe for success. Pragmatically, these highly publicized areas are not good bets.

The position of a leader—a political leader in the polls or a market segment leader in business or an athlete who leads in statistics—is particularly susceptible to praise and criticism. A leader's position is a focal point. Leaders can easily fool themselves into thinking that it is good for their organization if they make themselves into celebrities, but they are wrong. Our focus must always be on doing what is profitable.

Lesson 216: The Role of Leadership

When you think about your role of leading others in your organization, how should you feel?

A.   Honored.

B.   Humbled.

C.   Confident.

D.   Concerned.

> *Think of your soldiers as little children.*
> *You can make them follow you into a deep river.*
> *Treat them as your beloved children.*
> *You can lead them all to their deaths.*

THE ART OF WAR 10:4.1-4

Answer: D. Concerned.

Sun Tzu is offering three important ideas in this stanza.

First, he is telling us that we must care about the people who work with us. We must love them. We must be concerned about what happens to them. If we really care about how our decisions affect them, they will know it and respond in kind.

Second, he is telling us that we must take the lead. We must expect our supporters to follow our lead. Competitive organizations do not survive as democracies. Leaders must know better than anyone else what needs to be done. If we do not have this understanding or confidence in our ability, we shouldn't be leading. We are guides. People must know to trust us. Strategically, organizations with strong leadership are more united and powerful than those with uncertain leadership.

Finally, Sun Tzu is telling us that our responsibility is a serious one. When others accept us as their leaders, they are literally putting their future in our hands. In war they trust their leaders with their physical life, but in other competitive arenas they trust their leaders with their livelihood and their success in life. We must accept the fact that our bad decisions can ruin the lives of others. If we are not concerned about their future when we make decisions about new positions, we will be taking risks that we should not be taking.

Lesson 217: Caring for Your People

If you truly care about your supporters, how should you treat them?

A.   Consider their feelings.

B.   Force them to do what is right.

C.   Give them everything that you can.

D.   Treat them as equals.

> *Some leaders are generous, but cannot use their men.*
> *They love their men, but cannot command them.*
> *Their men are unruly and disorganized.*
> *These leaders create spoiled children.*
> *Their soldiers are useless.*
>
> THE ART OF WAR 10:4.5-9

Answer: B. Force them to do what is right.

Sun Tzu's analogy comparing people within an organization to little children works extremely well on a number of levels, but, of course, our supporters and those who are working with us are not children. They are usually capable adults. Some may be more capable than we are. But if we lead the organization, they don't have our job. As an organization's leaders, our strategic perspective is unique. We have the responsibility of seeing what needs to be done and providing everyone with a clear framework within which they can work. If we aren't certain what needs to be done, we shouldn't be leading.

This doesn't mean that we can't respect the people with whom we work. We can and should. Many and often most will take as much responsibility for getting the work done as we give them. But we must make them responsible. They must know that if they fail in their responsibility, there will be consequences. Respect and authority are not given without this type of responsibility.

This means that we must have the courage and strength to discipline people when they fail in their responsibility. Firing people is one of the most difficult aspects of any manager's job, but if we fail to fire people who have proven unworthy of our trust, we destroy our credibility within the organization.

Lesson 218: The Winning Knowledge

What must you know in order to win most of the time in a competitive environment?

A.   That the enemy is vulnerable to attack.

B.   That your people are ready to attack.

C.   How to position yourself on the field of battle.

D.   All of the above.

> *You may know what your soldiers will do in an attack.*
> *You may not know if the enemy is vulnerable to attack.*
> *You will then win only half the time.*
> *You may know that the enemy is vulnerable to attack.*
> *You may not know if your men are capable of attacking him.*
> *You will still win only half the time.*
> *You may know that the enemy is vulnerable to attack.*
> *You may know that your men are ready to attack.*
> *You may not know how to position yourself in the field for battle.*
> *You will still win only half the time.*

THE ART OF WAR 10:5.1-10

Answer: D. All of the above.

This lesson summarizes many ideas in this chapter.

First, we must know how to predict our enemies. To do this, we must understand the weaknesses of their organization and see their options from their point of view.

Next, we must know how to manage our own people. We must avoid organizational weaknesses, take command of our people, and make sure that the battles we fight strengthen the organization.

Finally, we must understand the importance of field position. We must learn to see our next step by analyzing it according to the dimensions of Sun Tzu's system.

Strategy is based on the proposition that knowledge is the source of all power. Knowledge leads to vision, which gives us our ability to predict the future. Knowledge of our organization allows us to predict how our people will behave. Knowledge of our opponents allows us to predict their behavior. Knowledge of our relative positions allows us to predict who will succeed if we challenge one another.

Lesson 219: Mastering Field Position

How do you know if you have mastered Sun Tzu's lessons regarding field position?

A.   You see more new opportunities.

B.   You are more aware of your weaknesses.

C.   You are always confident of what must be done.

D.   You are more careful about avoiding failure.

You must know how to make war.
You can then act without confusion.
You can attempt anything.

                                        THE ART OF WAR 10:5.11-13

Answer: C. You are always confident of what must be done.

Confidence in predicting the future in a competitive situation is hard to describe to those who haven't experienced it. Most people make decisions through a cloud of confusion. How can we know the future? More information seldom clarifies our situation. More information just confuses the issue even more. The framework of classical strategy gives us confidence in our decisions.

Sun Tzu gives us a simple, direct method for evaluating each new proposal, project, and campaign. We can see immediately the relative strengths of the various types of actions that we must choose from. We realize that the competition faces the same types of decisions. Evaluating these decisions makes it clear which are the most likely to be successful.

This does not mean that we expect every new campaign to work exactly as we planned. This will almost certainly not be the case. Sun Tzu teaches us that most attacks fail. All we can do is make decisions that have a higher probability of success. These are always the right decisions. Over time, making a high percentage of correct decisions assures us of victory.

When we are confident of our decision-making skills, we know that we can tackle any challenge. The rules of competition do not change. The ground, the time, and the competitors we face may change, but as long as we understand the basic rules by which success is won, we can be successful at any endeavor.

Lesson 220: Knowing Yourself and Your Opponents

What does knowing your organization and your opponents' organizations accomplish?

A.   It reduces the costs of competition.

B.   It makes victory likely.

C.   It makes victory profitable.

D.   It reduces your chances of failure.

> *We say:*
> *Know the enemy and know yourself.*
> *Your victory will be painless.*
> *Know the weather and the field.*
> *Your victory will be complete.*

THE ART OF WAR 10:5.14-18

Answer: A. It reduces the costs of competition.

To find strategic success, we must concern ourselves with two separate issues. First and foremost, we must be concerned about keeping costs low. Then, we must be concerned with making victory pay.

We make victory painless by keeping costs low. This means that we understand how to avoid costly failures. This ability comes from understanding organizational strengths and weaknesses—specifically, how we compare with the competition. If we understand what we can do that the competition cannot do, we can compete without a large investment. This means that we must look for field positions that are not costly to develop and that have a high probability of success.

Simply preventing expensive loss is not enough. We must make victory pay. Income doesn't come from beating or outmaneuvering opponents. Income comes only from the ground, that is, from winning positions that generate income. The field positions that we choose must not only have a low risk of failure; they must have the potential to pay off. Wherever we work—business, politics, sports, or any other competitive arena—we know the payoff that we are looking for. We try various field positions at low cost to learn enough to win that payoff. Notice here that Sun Tzu describes field position as a combination of time and place, weather and the field. That is the secret to finding the payoff: being at the right place at the right time.

Chapter 11

九地

Types of Terrain

The literal translation of this chapter's title is "nine grounds," but "ground" in Chinese (*di*) also means our physical condition or situation. Here Sun Tzu is describing nine common strategic situations and how we must respond to them. We can also see these nine situations as different stages that a strategic project or campaign goes through as it develops. These stages are part of the natural evolution of any competitive campaign. They occur as a project develops over time. Though all do not occur in every strategic process, these situations are common and should be familiar to anyone who lives or works in a competitive environment.

In each of these situations or stages, strategy dictates a specific response. We sometimes describe these situations as "controlling" because they determine what our appropriate response should be. The purpose of understanding these situations is to enable us to make quick decisions about our proper course of action. Sun Tzu's strategic system is analytical and deliberate. Positioning is a systematic process that works over time, but success often requires instant reactions. This need for instant reflexes is made clear in lesson 243, which is in many ways at the center of this chapter. Understanding the nine common situations detailed here helps us make the right decision in situations in which we need to act quickly.

After listing the nine basic situations and the right response to them, Sun Tzu explores them more deeply through the course of this chapter. Many of these detailed discussions address the management of people, especially in the context of winning the support of followers when our situations grow ever more challenging as they do during the course of a campaign.

Lesson 221: Nine Situations

When evaluating the development of a project or campaign, what aspect defines the essential elements of your situation?

A.   Your advance into new territory.
B.   Your condition in comparison with that of the competition.
C.   Your situation on the ground.
D.   All of the above.

> *Use the art of war.*
> *Know when the terrain will scatter you.*
> *Know when the terrain will be easy.*
> *Know when the terrain will be disputed.*
> *Know when the terrain is open.*
> *Know when the terrain is intersecting.*
> *Know when the terrain is dangerous.*
> *Know when the terrain is bad.*
> *Know when the terrain is confined.*
> *Know when the terrain is deadly.*
>
> THE ART OF WAR 11:1.1-10

Answer: D. All of the above.

Here Sun Tzu gives us nine basic competitive situations in which we can find ourselves. Unlike the field positions discussed in the previous chapter, these situations do not describe qualities of the ground itself. Instead, they describe how a strategic campaign develops over time. These situations combine the stage of our advance, our relationship with our opponents, and the conditions of the ground. Some of these situations—such as the *easy* and *dangerous* situations—are defined primarily by how far along we are in our advance. Others—such as *open* or *bad* situations—are defined primarily by conditions on the ground. Still others—such as *disputed* or *deadly* situations—are defined primarily by our relationship with others.

Before we can react appropriately to our situation, we must first correctly identify it. Since every situation is complex, we often need to boil down our conditions to their essential elements. This is Sun Tzu's purpose in the next section of this chapter. He devotes a stanza to each of these nine situations, which define the stages of an advance.

Lesson 222: Scattering Terrain

What is the biggest challenge to the unity of your organization?

A.   Meeting an opponent.

B.   Advancing into new territory.

C.   Defending your own territory.

D.   Being besieged by an opponent.

> *Warring parties must sometimes fight inside their own territory.*
> *This is scattering terrain.*

THE ART OF WAR 11:1.11-12

Answer: C. Defending your own territory.

"Scattering," according to Sun Tzu, means losing unity and focus—a breakdown of an organization's cohesion. This is most likely to happen when we are forced to defend our own territory as it is invaded by an opponent. This breakdown is why strategy dictates that we should always take the battle to our opponents rather than be forced to defend our own territory.

There is a difference between defending our strong points and defending our territory. Scattering means leaving the place where we have developed our strength and attacking opponents at places of their choosing within the boundaries of ground we own. This is always a serious mistake because our support tends to melt away as we are forced to chase opponents in our own ground who are undermining our sources of income.

Though the parallel is not immediately apparent, market fragmentation is an example of a scattering situation. We can use the beer market as an example. When light beer came along, instead of defending their brands' strengths, the major beer manufacturers all brought out their own versions of light beer, confusing their customers about which version of their brand to buy. The lack of focus on brand added impetus to light beer sales, but companies known for light beer picked up more market share. After the success of light beer, "ice" beer, "dry" beer, and so on were introduced, further fragmenting the market.

Scattering or fragmentation within our territory has a number of ramifications. When organizations fight battles inside their borders, they tend to lose members and supporters, and people choose sides. Fighting inside our own territory fragments our position and our organization as well.

Lesson 223: Easy Terrain

What is the easiest time, in terms of competitive pressure, for any organization, project, or campaign?

A.   When you first start.

B.   After you have tested your concept.

C.   After you have invested time and energy.

D.   After you have begun generating revenue.

> *When you enter hostile territory, your penetration is shallow.*
> *This is easy terrain.*

THE ART OF WAR 11:1.13-14

Answer: A. When you first start.

We should think of the beginning of a project or campaign as the honeymoon period. Three things make beginnings easy: our psychological attitude, our stock of resources, and the lack of competitive response. At the beginning of any new enterprise, enthusiasm is high and success seems most certain. We are well supplied, or we wouldn't have the time or energy to even consider a new project. We encounter the fewest problems from active competitors because we do not yet appear on anyone's competitive radar.

This *easy* terrain is very different from the *unobstructed* ground described in the previous chapter, though the two are confused in most translations of *The Art of War*. There may or may not be obstacles at the beginning of a new venture, but these obstacles do not stop us since we wouldn't start the advance unless we had discovered a way—real or imaginary—around them.

In the beginning, people have a great deal of energy to put into a new project. When we are looking forward to a new project, we are at our most creative. We have a fresh perspective that makes it easy to come up with inventive ideas.

This is also the time when we have the most physical resources. We have invested very little. We have not made any serious mistakes that destroyed our resources. Our strength for this particular project is at its maximum.

Finally, our progress hasn't yet created any resistance. As we move into other people's territory, they don't notice at first. As they do, it takes time for opponents to recognize the challenge and formulate their response.

Lesson 224: Disputed Terrain

When everyone knows that a new area is very rich but no one organization yet controls it, what do you know for certain?

A.   The first to get to this area will dominate it.

B.   This area will make a number of organizations successful.

C.   Those who put the most investment into this area will win it.

D.   This area will be the source of costly battles.

> *Some terrain gives me an advantageous position.*
> *But it gives others an advantageous position as well.*
> *This will be disputed terrain.*

THE ART OF WAR 11:1.15-17

Answer: D. This area will be the source of costly battles.

This idea echoes many of Sun Tzu's lessons on emptiness and fullness, weakness and strength. We don't want to go where everyone else is going and pursue opportunities that many others are pursuing because opportunities are few in these crowded situations. Strategy is a game of numbers. If a prize is popular, it will be fought over. Conflict is costly, and if a prize is fought over, it will be much less profitable than it appears.

Most people are naturally attracted to opportunities others are pursuing. We should be attracted to areas that everyone else overlooks. The advantages that we are looking for are those that everyone else misses. As a matter of fact, the advantages that we are looking for should look like problems to everyone else. This is nonintuitive. In a way, it says that if something is clearly very good, in competitive terms it is actually very bad.

Notice that in this *disputed* terrain our behavior doesn't change the situation. We can get to these areas first, but since we cannot control them—"fill them completely" is how Sun Tzu puts this—we cannot get any long-term benefit from them. Putting more and more resources into battling for these areas will not work either. The problem is that *everyone* will tend to invest more and more resources into these areas.

The problem with disputed areas is that the cost of fighting for them makes it impossible to profit from them. We might make temporary use of them, but we should not get into costly battles over them.

Lesson 225: Open Terrain

Are there some situations in which both you and others can make progress without being partners?

A.   No, for you to win, others must lose.

B.   No, to create a win-win situation you must work with others.

C.   Yes, but your progress in these situations is difficult.

D.   Yes, and your progress in these situations is easy.

> *I can use some terrain to advance easily.*
> *Others can advance along with us.*
> *This is open terrain.*

THE ART OF WAR 11:1.18-20

Answer: D. Yes, and your progress in these situations is easy.

In lesson 223, we discussed how *easy* is different than *unobstructed*. Here we make a similar distinction between *open* and *unobstructed*. In doing so, we also must understand that, according to strategy, easy progress in a campaign is not the same as success, that is, reaching our goals.

Open terrain is not unobstructed ground. It is a situation in which more than one competitor can make easy progress without conflict with others and without having to overcome challenges of the ground. It is in some respects the opposite of disputed terrain, which brings people into conflict with one another. This situation is not defined by its riches but by its conduciveness to movement and change.

Trying to make progress alongside potential competitors and opponents has its special challenges. Progress is easy, but to think strategically we must always think about how our position is changing over time, especially relative to the positions of others. In open situations, our current position degrades quickly because everyone is advancing. If we don't move forward as quickly as everyone else, we are really falling behind.

In open terrain, the contest is a race. We aren't fighting over territory. We are fighting to stay ahead of others. These situations not only encourage advancement, they demand it. We have to take full advantage of the openness of these territories to make as much progress as we can. To succeed in these situations, we must keep ahead of or at least stay with everyone else.

Lesson 226: Intersecting Terrain

When a competitive arena is naturally easy for many people to get into, what should your strategy be?

A.   You should avoid that area entirely.

B.   You should enter that area only after others have gotten into battles.

C.   You should enter the area first but welcome others as allies.

D.   You should enter the area first but defend it from others.

> *Everyone shares access to a given area.*
> *The first one there can gather a larger group than anyone else.*
> *This is intersecting terrain.*

THE ART OF WAR 11:1.21-23

Answer: C. You should enter the area first but welcome others as allies.

On *intersecting* terrain, we find ourselves in a situation in which it is in our best interests to join with others. We cannot keep people out of these areas, but unlike disputed terrain, the area is not valuable enough to fight over. Its primary value is that it brings people together. Different parties in these intersecting situations share common interests. Those who get to these areas first and build the largest alliances are the most successful. Intersecting terrain is a crossroads that brings together different types of organizations that can work together to reach their own individual goals.

In our time, there are many areas that require different types of organizations to work together in order to develop an opportunity. The technological era has taught many businesses the power of intersecting terrain. Originally, every tech company tried to develop its own proprietary products, whether they were for video recording or computers. But as technology has grown more complicated, companies have come to understand that they cannot develop all the opportunities on their own.

People in high tech now realize that they cannot develop new markets by themselves. The result is exactly what Sun Tzu describes. Instead of trying to own a new technical arena, each company wants to get into that arena first and make itself the center of a coalition that develops standards for that industry. The organization that is able to develop the broadest support for its new standard is the organization that is going to be successful, even though it is working with its potential competitors.

Lesson 227: Dangerous Terrain

When you have invested heavily in a campaign without a clear opportunity for success, what will happen?

A.   You will lose your investment.

B.   Your source of supply will be threatened.

C.   You will be forced to withdraw to regroup.

D.   You will be forced into a fight.

> *You can penetrate deeply into hostile territory.*
> *Then many hostile cities are behind you.*
> *This is dangerous terrain.*
>
> THE ART OF WAR 11:1.24-26

Answer: B. Your source of supply will be threatened.

When we invest heavily in a development project or political campaign, we must be very concerned about our resources being cut off. All investment is limited. Our project may have been viewed favorably at first, but as time passes without it producing results, support from others will evaporate. Good ideas gradually become pariahs if they don't pay off once we are heavily committed to them. Even if our plans didn't call for these ideas to pay off at this particular point in time, others will grow impatient and turn against further support. This is one of the reasons that Sun Tzu promotes short, limited campaigns.

When we have heavily invested in a course of action and have yet to show results, our political opponents will start sniping at us. Those opponents were there all along, but in earlier stages we didn't have to worry about them; now, however, we do because they will begin to threaten our sources of supply.

We can see this pattern in both international politics and business. When a president heavily invests in a costly action—for example, that invasion in Iraq—the program doesn't have to fail for its political opponents to start threatening it. The same is true of investors in new businesses. After investments are made and before the enterprise is profitable, the critics of the project will start challenging it. In both cases, opponents will try to cut off further funds to strangle the project.

Lesson 228: Bad Terrain

What should you expect in every competitive campaign that you undertake?

A.   Problems will eventually arise.

B.   New opportunities will appear.

C.   Competitors will make mistakes.

D.   Supporters will always waver.

> *There are mountain forests.*
> *There are rugged hills.*
> *There are marshes.*
> *Everyone confronts these obstacles on a campaign.*
> *They make bad terrain.*

THE ART OF WAR 11:1.27-31

Answer: A. Problems will eventually arise.

Each competitive campaign is unique, but each will suffer setbacks and encounter problems. These setbacks usually do not occur initially. Sun Tzu believes that beginnings are often the easiest times, for the reasons discussed in lesson 223. However, as a campaign progresses, especially as it nears success, we are certain to encounter *bad* terrain, difficult challenges that we must meet and overcome.

Sun Tzu realizes that difficulties in making progress are simply unavoidable. A project progresses easily at the start, but it is only a matter of time before problems arise. This is almost a mathematical certainty because in moving forward, we move into more and more areas, any of which can create problems. Progress can also be defined as eventually getting ourselves into trouble. The same might be said of living in general.

Sun Tzu does not see difficulties as simply bad. The Chinese term he uses is closer in meaning to "ruined" or "destroyed" situations, but his view of these situations is complicated. Problems slow us down. They pose risks, but they also offer opportunities. Surviving bad terrain is a source of strength. Getting through these stages of competition makes us tougher.

Strategy teaches us to expect and prepare to meet obstacles. We cannot see them when we start, but they are always there. Our goal from the beginning must be to surmount them.

Lesson 229: Confined Terrain

In the competitive process, when are you most vulnerable to competitive attack?

A.   When good opportunities require taking large risks.

B.   When others discover how valuable your position is.

C.   When you must rely on limited resources during a transition.

D.   When you have just had a large success.

> *In some areas, the passage is narrow.*
> *You are closed in as you enter and exit them.*
> *In this type of area, a few people can attack our much larger force.*
> *This is confined terrain.*

THE ART OF WAR 11:1.32-35

Answer: C. When you must rely on limited resources during a transition.

At first glance, the *confined* terrain sounds a lot like the *constricted* field position from lesson 198. They are completely different concepts. This situation is a transition period that we must pass through. It isn't a position that we seek to establish; it is a temporary stage. We can think of confined terrain as a bridge over which we must pass to get to where we need to go. During these transitions, we cannot convert or move all our resources at once. Instead, we rely on relatively few people or resources at a time, and this makes us vulnerable.

We are vulnerable to competitive attacks in the limiting situation of confined terrain. When we are crossing a bridge, our options are limited. We can only go forward or backward, a few people at a time. Whenever we must pass through a narrow window of opportunity, we can be easily attacked.

Think of the confined stage as any important transition point for an organization. For example, when we are moving to a new technology, only a few people initially understand our new methods. During this period, we are dependent on this small group. When we move to a new job, we know only a few people whom we must rely upon for advice. This dependency makes us vulnerable to any opponent's attack. We must pass through these transitions quickly and secretly before our competitors become aware of our vulnerability. The more quickly we can make these transitions, the less vulnerable we are.

Lesson 230: Deadly Terrain

When your survival is directly threatened if you don't act immediately, what should you do?

A. Fight.
B. Withdraw.
C. Surrender.
D. Compromise.

> *You can sometimes survive only if you fight quickly.*
> *You will die if you delay.*
> *This is deadly terrain.*

THE ART OF WAR 11:1.36-38

Answer: A. Fight.

While Sun Tzu teaches that conflict is expensive and ideally avoided, he also teaches that there are situations in which we cannot avoid meeting a competitive challenge, and, in *deadly* situations, we must act quickly. Deadly terrain defines situations in which we have run out of options and time is working against us. Our resources are running out. Our opponents are growing stronger. When we are in this type of situation we will have no future at all unless we prove ourselves against our opponents.

When we are on deadly terrain, we must fight. "Fight" in the original is the character *zhan*, which means battle, meeting a challenge or an opponent. In this context, it also means using every means available, working to our utmost. We challenge our opponents. We use direct confrontation. We pull out all the stops and, for the moment, forget about tomorrow. We must use all of our remaining strength and resources to win the day.

If we aren't comfortable using this extreme action, we must wonder whether or not we are really in a deadly situation. We may have problems, but if we aren't willing to fight with everything we have, our problems may not be as serious as they might seem.

Sun Tzu does not see these desperate situations as negatives. Necessity is the mother of invention. Desperate action at the right time is one of the keys to our success. When we are in this situation, we work as hard as we can. We can only succeed in facing difficult tasks by working with total focus.

Lesson 231: Situational Response

Once you identify which of the nine basic situations best defines your current situation, what must you do?

A.   Know the alternative ways to respond to that situation.

B.   Find a creative response to your situation.

C.   Move to a new situation as soon as possible.

D.   Respond in the one way that the situation demands.

> *To be successful, you control scattering terrain by not fighting.*
> *Control easy terrain by not stopping.*
> *Control disputed terrain by not attacking.*
> *Control open terrain by staying with the enemy's forces.*
> *Control intersecting terrain by uniting with your allies.*
> *Control dangerous terrain by plundering.*
> *Control bad terrain by keeping on the move.*
> *Control confined terrain by using surprise.*
> *Control deadly terrain by fighting.*
>
> THE ART OF WAR 11:1.39-46

Answer: D. Respond in the one way that the situation demands.

We need to identify which of the nine basic strategic situations best describes our current situation because that situation defines our best course of action. Though Sun Tzu teaches creativity and adaptation, strategically, we must behave consistently with the demands of our situation. In these specific situations, only one dominant course of action is appropriate. We are *not* free to act in any way we choose. We can take control of the situation by responding appropriately.

This principle leads to a simple list of rules. We don't attack competitors on our own territory. We make as much progress as possible at the beginning of a project when the going is easy. We avoid disputed territory that leads to fights. In open situations, we keep up with the competition. When the territory is too large for us alone, we find allies and build associations. When we are heavily invested in a project, we must find a way for it to generate revenue. We keep going when we encounter problems. We move through transitions without letting competitors know our vulnerability. When we have exhausted all options, we put everything into the fight.

Lesson 232: Windows of Opportunity

When you are looking for a window of opportunity, what conditions should you look for?

A.   Conditions that fragment the competition.

B.   Conditions in which money is plentiful.

C.   Conditions that demand all of your resources.

D.   Conditions in which others have failed.

> *Go to an area that helps you in waging war.*
> *Use it to cut off the enemy's contact between his front and back lines.*
> *Prevent his small parties from relying on his larger force.*
> *Stop his strong divisions from rescuing his weak ones.*
> *Prevent his officers from getting his men together.*
> *Chase his soldiers apart to stop them from amassing.*
> *Harass them to prevent their ranks from forming.*

THE ART OF WAR 11:2.1-7

Answer: A. Conditions that fragment the competition.

In this new section, Sun Tzu addresses the early-stage conditions of *scattering, easy, disputed,* and *open* situations, expressing the larger idea that we must take the battle to our opponent. Here, Sun Tzu explains that we avoid scattering situations, fighting in our own territory, by embracing easy situations and targeting opponents' openings. We put ourselves on easy terrain by putting our opponents on scattering terrain. Since fighting within our own territory divides us, we must look for opportunities to fight in our opponents' territory because that will divide them and make them weaker.

How do we find opportunities or openings to invade our opponents' territories? We look for the separations that divide our enemy and move into those openings. Dividing opponents means attacking their unity. An attack on unity means identifying openings in our opponents' positions or areas of responsibility that we can move into without facing them directly. An attack on unity is an attack on strength. It prevents an opponent from amassing enough power to attack us in our own territory, which would divide us and put *us* on scattering terrain. These overlooked opportunities within an opponent's territory move us onto easy ground.

Lesson 233: Engaging in Battle

When you see an opening in the position of your competition, what must you assure yourself of before you move into it?

A.   That your people support you.

B.   That your superiors agree

C.   That winning will benefit you.

D.   That battling will not hurt you.

> *When joining battle gives you an advantage, you must do it.*
> *When it isn't to your benefit, you must avoid it.*
>
> THE ART OF WAR 11:2.8-9

Answer: C. That winning will benefit you.

We are still discussing the need to avoid fighting on *scattering* terrain in our own territory. Here the idea is combined with the prescription for avoiding *disputed* territory. Again, Sun Tzu teaches us to avoid problem situations by seeking the opposite condition.

To defend our territory, we must take the battle to our opponents, but we must first find an advantage. In Chinese, the concept of advantage is *li*. It means both having an edge and getting the benefit of something. In this context, it means that we look for both types of advantage before we commit our resources to meeting an enemy. First, we look for an edge that will allow us to win the contest, but we also look for the benefit that we will get from battle. The first type of advantage tells us why our efforts will succeed. This is the advantage that we seek in openings left by the competition. The second type of advantage forces us to consider what we will win if we are successful. Victory must pay. Seeing an opening isn't reason enough. Knowing that we will win isn't enough reason to invest the effort. Our victory must gain us something that is worth more than this effort.

To avoid scattering terrain, we must look for areas outside our territory in which to battle. However, an area that everyone is willing to battle over—*disputed* terrain—cannot pay. Success in the long term is determined more by the battles we don't fight than by the ones we do fight. We must avoid marginal battles that consume our resources but return too little benefit from winning.

Lesson 234: Defending Our Territory

If you discover that a large, skilled competitor is planning to invade your territory, what should you do?

A.   Retreat and build your defense.

B.   Quickly invade that competitor's territory elsewhere.

C.   Quickly attack that competitor's forces.

D.   Propose an alliance.

> *A daring soldier may ask:*
> *"A large, organized enemy army and its general are coming.*
> *What do I do to prepare for them?"*
> *Tell him:*
> *"First seize an area that the enemy must have.*
> *Then he will pay attention to you.*
> *Mastering speed is the essence of war.*
> *Take advantage of a large enemy's inability to keep up.*
> *Use a philosophy of avoiding difficult situations.*
> *Attack the area where he doesn't expect you."*
>
> THE ART OF WAR 11:2.10-19

Answer: B. Quickly invade that competitor's territory elsewhere.

Ending the section on *scattering* terrain and avoiding battle in our own territory, we now hear Sun Tzu's prescription for dealing with *open* situations. When we move into open area, we have to keep ahead of our opponents. Large organizations have no advantage in these situations, no matter how well run they are. As Sun Tzu says in lesson 61, "Small forces are not powerful. However, large forces cannot catch them."

Large organizations cannot compete with small organizations in open situations because the basis of competition is speed. Open situations are won by organizations that know how to change and evolve. Large organizations are systematic, disciplined, and predictable. In an open situation, small organizations can always keep a step ahead of them. This is why organizations researching new technologies are always relatively small.

Strategically, size is never the issue. It is matching our size to the situations so that we have an advantage over our opponents.

Lesson 235: Bringing People Together

When you want to create strength through unity, how do you bring people together?

A.   By invasion.

B.   By inspiration.

C.   By surprise.

D.   By invention.

> *You must use the philosophy of an invader.*
> *Invade deeply and then concentrate your forces.*
> *This controls your men without oppressing them.*
>
> THE ART OF WAR 11:3.1-3

Answer: A. By invasion.

In this new section, the topic changes to invasion, specifically deep invasions that represent a middle stage of a campaign, *intersecting* and *serious* terrain. The focus here is specifically on the needs of intersecting situations, in which we must join with allies in order to succeed. In lesson 226, Sun Tzu said that the key to controlling intersecting situations is uniting with allies. In lesson 8, he teaches that the key to unity is a shared philosophy, but in dealing with allies, Sun Tzu goes further. He says that we specifically need the philosophy of an invader. What is the philosophy of an invader?

The shared danger of deeply invading a hostile area turns individuals into a team and separate groups into a working whole. The philosophy of an invader is the enthusiasm for discovery, the desire to expand, the need to explore new regions. This philosophy is the brotherhood of shared danger, the sense of being isolated together, surrounded by enemies, and trusting only in each other. We will never bond with any allies unless we feel that we are all at risk, all in an alien land, which no one can control.

In intersecting terrain, we must share risk and uncertainty in order for potential competitors to work together. Associations never evolve among competitors who are not at risk. Alliances never work when the parties involved are merely trying to maintain their positions in their territory. The only alliances that create the strength of unity are those in which the individuals involved are moving into new areas.

Lesson 236: Finding Resources

When you must invest heavily in a new competitive area, how do you make sure that you have enough resources?

A.   Find wealthy supporters.

B.   Conserve your resources.

C.   Borrow money from other cash streams.

D.   Get revenue from the new area itself.

> *Get your supplies from the riches of the territory.*
> *It is sufficient to supply your whole army.*
>
> THE ART OF WAR 11:3.4-5

Answer: D. Get revenue from the new area itself.

When we have penetrated deeply into a new competitive area or heavily invested in a risky project, we must find ways to make that exploration pay for itself. Sun Tzu calls this *dangerous* terrain because we are far from our established markets and we cannot trust our "supply routes" over long distances or long periods of time. No matter how dedicated we think our investors are, when we get deep into a new area without profits, they will lose faith.

The solution to this problem is finding a way for the new area to pay for its own development. These initial sources of revenue do not have to be the same as those for our long-term plan, but they have to be large enough to support the development of the area. Sun Tzu called this "plundering," winning short-term resources by any means out of necessity. We might also describe it as taking any easy money wherever we find it, even though that revenue source is not sustainable in the long term.

This is another part of the philosophy of an invader. Sun Tzu teaches us to make forays into new areas. These are small forays in terms of their cost because we must find a way for these forays to quickly pay for themselves. If they cannot pay for themselves, they will have to be abandoned. The people involved must know that they must find their own revenue sources or fail. They must feel completely dependent on their new venture and be forced to survive on their own. This is why dangerous situations are not really as dangerous as they seem. The potential income is there. If people must find it, they will.

Lesson 237: Facing Difficulties

When your organization struggles against the inevitable problems in a campaign, what do you do?

A.   Push your people forward.

B.   Avoid overtaxing your people.

C.   Find a new route.

D.   Change your goals.

> *Take care of your men and do not overtax them.*
> *Your esprit de corps increases your momentum.*
> *Keep your army moving and plan for surprises.*
> *Make it difficult for the enemy to count your forces.*
> *Position your men where there is no place to run.*
> *They will then face death without fleeing.*
> *They will find a way to survive.*
> *Your officers and men will fight to their utmost.*

THE ART OF WAR 11:3.6-13

Answer: B. Avoid overtaxing your people.

The topic here changes to the final stages of a campaign. As *scattering* controls our thinking about early stages and *danger* controls our thinking about middle stages, *deadly* situations control our thinking about the three final stages. In this stanza the specific prescription is for dealing with *bad* and *confined* terrain in this larger context.

First, when we are moving through bad situations, facing difficult problems, we have to make sure that we keep moving, but at the same time, we cannot push our people too hard. Problems are frustrating. We can overcome them, but solving them often takes time. We cannot be impatient with our people's progress without damaging their enthusiasm for the organization.

When we must make a dangerous transition through confined terrain, when we rely on only a few people, we have to make sure our competition doesn't know our plans. This is also part of maintaining our esprit de corps. This spirit increases our momentum, which is fed by surprise—that is, by innovation. Both bad and confined terrain can be deadly terrain. Because of this, we want to make sure that no one gives up.

Lesson 238: Ending Worry

What emotional state frees people from worrying about the real difficulties of their situation?

A.   Ignorance.

B.   Commitment.

C.   Courage.

D.   Training.

> *Military officers who are committed lose their fear.*
> *When they have nowhere to run, they must stand firm.*
> *Deep in enemy territory, they are captives.*
> *Since they cannot escape, they will fight.*
>
> THE ART OF WAR 11:3.14-17

Answer: B. Commitment.

Commitment is an interesting concept, especially in the late, difficult stages of a campaign. When we are committed, we have gone past the point where a decision needs to be made. When we are committed, we no longer have a decision to make; we no longer have a choice. This lack of choice clarifies the situation.

Courage is required before we reach deadly terrain. It takes courage to make a difficult decision. This is where fear comes in. Courage must overcome fear, but fear doesn't fade until we have made the commitment. Once we are committed, we can focus on the situation.

We want people's commitment. We want them to get the decision behind them. To do this, we have to put people in positions where the choice is clear. We must either be successful or fail completely. In these types of black-and-white situations, people know where they stand. We have to make it clear that their situation is black and white and that they have no fallback position.

Removing choice means putting people on deadly terrain, that is, in a do-or-die situation. We fight when we have no other alternative. Deadly terrain is closely associated with all dangerous situations in which we are deeply invested on hostile ground.

Lesson 239: The Key to Trust

When can you trust your supporters to make the right decisions for your organization without being supervised?

A.   When they are at personal risk.

B.   When they are thoroughly trained.

C.   When they have esprit de corps.

D.   When they have been rewarded well.

> *Commit your men completely.*
> *Without being posted, they will be on guard.*
> *Without being asked, they will get what is needed.*
> *Without being forced, they will be dedicated.*
> *Without being given orders, they can be trusted.*
>
> THE ART OF WAR 11:3.18-22

Answer: A. When they are at personal risk.

The essence of commitment is feeling that we have something to lose and something to gain. The risk must be real. This is why the best way to get people involved in our cause is to get them to invest something, no matter how minor, in it. Once people are invested, they become committed. When people have been or will be rewarded no matter what the outcome, they are not committed to success. Risk is the foundation of success. This is why entrepreneurs are so successful in comparison to hired managers. Entrepreneurs are risking their own money, whereas professional managers know that they can go on to their next job no matter what the outcome.

If our people are as committed as we are, we no longer have to manage them in the traditional sense. They will watch out for the well-being of the organization because they are protecting their own well-being. Once they understand the connection between the organization's success and their own, they will do whatever they can to make the organization successful. This is, of course, the power of ownership. In our era, this most often takes the form of stock options. A sense of risk is not as easy to create in our era. People are too quick to move to another company when conditions get difficult. This is why we must hire people who might find it difficult to find jobs elsewhere. We want misfits who find a home in our organization.

Lesson 240: Committed Leadership

What characteristic do you want as a leader to help your people understand how strongly committed you are?

A.   Charisma.

B.   Decisiveness.

C.   Caring.

D.   Trustworthiness.

> *Stop them from guessing by removing all their doubts.*
> *Stop them from dying by giving them no place to run.*
>
> THE ART OF WAR 11:3.23-24

Answer: B. Decisiveness.

In lesson 27, we learned that to be leaders, we must be strict or disciplined. We must be caring and trustworthy as well, but the way we take care of people is by making our positions clear and making it equally clear how committed we are to our positions. Uncertainty is disastrous to an organization. If people never know what the direction is, they are always wavering and are never committed. It is much better to "remove all their doubts" so that they know exactly what they are committed to.

People have a tendency to doubt and second-guess their leaders. They never think that they are getting the straight story or the whole story. They always suspect that management is hiding problems from them. They secretly think that the stated needs and goals are inflated. They are always wondering what the real goals and problems are.

We stop people from guessing by being straightforward with them. We gain nothing by sugarcoating a bad situation. Quite the opposite. We can often get more commitment by emphasizing the risks. If we want people to believe us, we cannot mislead them. We can be optimistic about our chances of success, but this doesn't mean that we should minimize the difficulties.

We keep people from failing by eliminating uncertainty. We stop them from failing by challenging them. We stop them from failing by focusing their abilities on the task at hand. They must never think that what they are doing isn't important and critical to success.

Lesson 241: The Source of Dedication

What trait will keep your supporters dedicated to their tasks?

A.   Desire for recognition.

B.   Self-interest.

C.   Spirit of brotherhood.

D.   Devotion to duty.

> *Your officers may not be rich.*
> *Nevertheless, they still desire plunder.*
> *They may die young.*
> *Nevertheless, they still want to live forever.*

THE ART OF WAR 11:3.25-28

Answer: B. Self-interest.

Strategy demands that we be realistic about what motivates people. Every one of us is motivated by some form of self-interest. To understand the self-interest of others, we must learn to see the world from others' point of view. What appeals to our self-interest isn't necessarily the same as what appeals to the self-interest of others. Adolf Hitler and Mother Teresa had very different lives, but Mother Teresa recognized that she was acting selfishly while Hitler claimed to be working for others. Motivating people begins and ends with our understanding their individual sense of self-interest.

Sun Tzu identifies two primary areas of self-interest: wealth and health. Interestingly enough, he presents them in this order. People will often put their desire for wealth ahead of concern for their health.

This passage also implies another important element of self-interest: the future. People are surprisingly concerned with the long-term implications of their decisions. They will often pass over better pay in the short term for a much bigger reward in the long term. People don't want to just get by. They want to find a path to real success. When we build an organization, we have to build in a pathway to success for the people who join us.

People are looking for a way to fulfill their dreams. People work with others to find a shared pathway to mutual success. All companies should be built with the self-interest of their employees in mind. We do not want people who are looking for an easy time. We want people who want to make their hard work pay off.

Lesson 242: Handling Complaints

When your supporters and especially the leaders among your supporters complain about what they must do, how should you respond?

A.   Listen to their complaints and sympathize.

B.   Agree to address their concerns in the future.

C.   Don't discuss their complaints, but rethink your decisions.

D.   Put them in a position where they have no choice.

> *You must order the time of attack.*
> *Officers and men may sit and weep until their lapels are wet.*
> *When they stand up, tears may stream down their cheeks.*
> *Put them in a position where they cannot run.*
> *They will show the greatest courage under fire.*

THE ART OF WAR 11:3.29-33

Answer: D. Put them in a position where they have no choice.

If we want to lead, we have to make tough decisions. Once our decisions are made, we and those who follow us must know for certain that the course is set. When we leave ourselves and those who follow us no choice, we can act directly, without second-guessing ourselves.

We will always complain. Those affected by our decisions will always complain as well. When it comes to strategic competition, the world is full of complainers, naysayers, and second-guessers. Even if others agree with our decisions, they will play devil's advocate out of habit, challenging our decisions. We should expect complaints. They are a fact of life. We can sympathize and even agree with the complaints of others, but we can never let these complaints affect our decisions once they are made.

The most critical role that a leader plays is the role of the decision-maker. The world of competition is uncertain. Many of our decisions are going to be wrong, but making decisions is vital. Organizations that never decide cannot compete successfully. One of the handicaps of the Japanese *ringi* system is its slow method of seeking internal agreement before the organization can act. Organizations in today's world have to respond quickly to rapid changes in the environment. This means that the leaders of competitive businesses must be trained in making quick and correct decisions.

Lesson 243: Appropriate Response

What is the purpose of identifying your current situation and undertaking the appropriate response?

A.   To make the best possible move.

B.   To enable you to react quickly.

C.   To make the best use of your strength.

D.   To enable you to spot your opponent's weaknesses.

> *Make good use of war.*
> *This demands instant reflexes.*
> *You must develop these instant reflexes.*
> *Act like an ordinary mountain snake.*
> *If people strike your head then stop them with your tail.*
> *If they strike your tail then stop them with your head.*
> *If they strike your middle then use both your head and tail.*

THE ART OF WAR 11:4.1-7

Answer: B. To enable you to react quickly.

The strategy taught by Sun Tzu's system is largely analytical. It requires that we balance a number of factors together to arrive at the appropriate conclusion. It combines the disciplines of mathematics and human psychology. The previous chapter on analyzing our field position is an excellent example of strategy's systematic nature. Though many aspects of Sun Tzu's system are methodical and deliberate, the purpose of recognizing the nine situations discussed in this chapter is so that we can quickly pick the right response.

In competitive situations, the difference between success and failure is often in how quickly we can react. The purpose of this chapter is to describe the situations in which a quick decision is required. When we recognize that we are in one of these situations, we must react appropriately and instinctively like a snake. We don't really have a decision to make since our situation dictates our reaction. Our situation determines when we must fight, keep moving, keep vital secrets, and so on.

When some of our resources or plans are blocked by conditions, we always have other resources with which we can respond appropriately. Once we know how to respond, we cannot let the fact that we have been challenged deter us from making the appropriate response with what we have.

Lesson 244: Instant Reflexes

When is the organization's ability to respond quickly to a situation more important than good analysis and planning?

A.   Always.

B.   Usually.

C.   Sometimes.

D.   Never.

> *A daring soldier asks:*
> *"Can any army imitate these instant reflexes?"*
> *We answer:*
> *"It can."*

THE ART OF WAR 11:4.8-11

Answer: A. Always.

Strategy is not the art of planning, although we commonly use the word in that sense. Strategy is the ability to make the right decisions quickly. When the situation is clear-cut, our reactions should be instantaneous.

How can we be certain that these nine situations and their responses will work for our organizations today, especially since each situation is unique? If these concepts aren't exactly right, won't we create more problems for ourselves than we solve by instant reaction instead of careful judgment?

Sun Tzu's concepts were crafted from deep insight and long experience. He saw that the response didn't have to be perfectly correct to be right. Even if a better, more nuanced reaction is possible, it takes too much time to identify that move, and a tentative approach creates its own problems. We are more successful if we react quickly and with certainty. This chapter isn't only about having the right answer. It is also about speed and creating confidence.

The nine situations listed here require quick decision-making. Under these specific conditions, we don't need to debate our basic course of action. We can know and trust what will usually work. Speed is its own reward. Even if we make mistakes, speed allows us to uncover them quickly and change our course. We must have a preference for action if we are to be successful in business. Organizations that hesitate and debate create uncertainty among their people. People are simply more effective when the direction is clear and our decisions certain.

Lesson 245: Working Together

If you want people to work together more smoothly when everything is going well, what should you do?

A.   Give them discussion time.

B.   Give them more control over their environment.

C.   Let them choose their coworkers.

D.   Create a crisis.

> *To command and get the most of proud people, you must study adversity.*
> *People work together when they are in the same boat during a storm.*
> *In this situation, one rescues the other just as the right hand helps the left.*
>
> THE ART OF WAR 11:4.12-14

Answer: D. Create a crisis.

Strong organizations are not built from lucky breaks and good fortune. They are forged from overcoming adversity. We need not fear difficult challenges if we first prepare ourselves and our supporters when times are good.

The larger context here is developing our organization's natural reflexes. Difficult times, that is, *bad* situations, arise naturally, but we can prepare before adversity is thrust upon us. As leaders, we can manufacture internal challenges to draw our people together. A boss can choose to be the bad guy who creates internal challenges to prepare for external threats. Too many leaders are too concerned about being liked. The military learned twenty-five hundred years ago that tough leadership draws people together and gives them a shared sense of accomplishment.

People need to be challenged. They want to succeed in situations that are difficult. They want to prove themselves. Strategically, we must run our organizations to encourage people to meet the challenges and enjoy a sense of accomplishment. Of course, we must give them the ability to succeed. Challenging people isn't the same as constantly criticizing them. Challenging people requires that we set high but attainable standards and recognize our supporters for meeting them.

Of course, when our situation provides the challenges, we don't want to continue to pressure our people. If we train them correctly during good times, they will know how to respond.

Lesson 246: Sharing Standards

How do you get all of your people to share in the organization's high standards?

A.   Peer pressure.

B.   Monetary rewards.

C.   Management discipline.

D.   Strict controls.

> *Use adversity correctly.*
> *Tether your horses and bury your wagon's wheels.*
> *Still, you can't depend on this alone.*
> *An organized force is braver than lone individuals.*
> *This is the art of organization.*
> *Put the tough and weak together.*
> *You must also use the terrain.*

THE ART OF WAR 11:4.15-21

Answer: A. Peer pressure.

This is another practice that is used extremely well by our military academies. The topic is still preparing people to respond instantly to challenges. People join and stay with organizations because of their hope for eventual reward, but on a day-to-day basis their behavior is governed more by peer pressure than by management pressure.

Sun Tzu teaches that the first key to peer pressure is making sure that everyone shares in the success and failure of the organization. We use our best people to serve as visible examples for everyone else. This means that we don't want our weakest and most poorly motivated people working in groups together. Bad people can also reinforce one another within an organization. We do not want to create pockets of dissatisfaction. Instead we want new or weaker people working with our best-trained and best-motivated people. These are the people we want spreading values within the organization.

In modern management, we address quality problems by improving measurement and visibility. These measurement systems are valuable and necessary, but not everything can be measured. People set the real standards within the organization. This is why organizations, like individuals, develop a certain character, or lack of it.

Lesson 247: Using Unity

When your organization is united behind you, what must you prevent your people from doing?

A.   Never let them overextend themselves.

B.   Never let them become too aggressive.

C.   Never let them lose focus.

D.   Never let them give up.

> *Make good use of war.*
> *Unite your men as one.*
> *Never let them give up.*

THE ART OF WAR 11:4.22-24

Answer: D. Never let them give up.

In preparing our people to face difficult challenges, we use unity to ensure persistence. Sun Tzu teaches that unity and focus come from our core philosophy, our shared goals. They also come from everyone understanding the situation that we are in and responding appropriately. We don't want any of our efforts to be wasted. When our situation dictates a particular response, we must persist in that response no matter how difficult the situations becomes.

According to the principles of strategy, unity gives an organization its strength. An organization that is united has a clear focus. When we get our people working together, we enable them to use all their capabilities. But this doesn't mean that everything that we attempt will be successful initially. The type of strength that comes from unity is critical to success, but success also requires time.

Unity means that the organization has a single focus at any given point in time. Persistence means that we are capable of maintaining that focus over a long period of time. Unity is good. Unity and persistence together are unstoppable.

One of the ways that we instill persistence in an organization is to put people into situations in which they simply cannot quit. In other words, when we must make progress, we keep the organization on dangerous ground. The situation itself should make it difficult if not impossible for our people to give up.

Lesson 248: A Leader's Demeanor

If you want to be a successful leader, how should you appear to your subordinates?

A.   Relaxed and approachable.

B.   Confident and remote.

C.   Strict but friendly.

D.   Mysterious and unknowable.

The commander must be a military professional.
This requires confidence and detachment.
You must maintain dignity and order.
You must control what your men see and hear.
They must follow you without knowing your plans.

THE ART OF WAR 11:5.1-5

Answer: B. Confident and remote.

This stanza begins a new section on leadership. When we lead, we must accept that the role separates us from the people with whom we work. Many people are not comfortable with this separation, but it is necessary. We want our people to have confidence in us. Being a friend requires that we be open and honest, even about our doubts. We cannot share our doubts and insecurities. This will only make the people we lead insecure. We also cannot confide our plans and secrets in others, which will also isolate us. As the old saying says, familiarity breeds contempt. If we want to lead people, we cannot be too familiar with them.

For this reason, Sun Tzu teaches us as leaders to have a formal, dignified relationship with our employees. As leaders, we represent the organization as a whole. We should expect people to treat us with a certain amount of respect, just as we would insist that they treat their fellow employees with respect. People should never be completely comfortable when we are around. They should be on their best behavior. Over time, this best behavior becomes a standard for the organization itself.

As leaders of the organization, it is our responsibility to interpret what happens in a way that puts everyone's efforts in the best light. People should see the organization and its potential through a filter that we create for them.

Lesson 249: People's Expectations

What should your followers expect from you in terms of how you define their roles within your organization?

A.   People should expect stable roles.

B.   They should expect well-defined roles.

C.   They should expect to choose their roles.

D.   They should expect their roles to change at any time.

> *You can reinvent your men's roles.*
> *You can change your plans.*
> *You can use your men without their understanding.*
>
> THE ART OF WAR 11:5.6-8

Answer: D. They should expect their roles to change at any time.

Continuing the topic of leadership, we must explain to our followers that they are bigger than the role they play at any given time within the organization. The topic of this chapter is how our situation changes over time. We should train everyone to recognize that they have only one real job: making the organization successful in every situation. This means that all roles are temporary. Roles can and must change as the situation changes and the challenges that the organization faces change.

One of the biggest defects of the U.S. labor movement in decades past was its unfortunate focus on rigid roles for employees. The union's goal was to prevent people from being abused by their employers and to solidify the employment contract, but the effect was to freeze organizational structure. The inevitable result was that highly unionized businesses could compete only in highly unionized industries. The unionized part of the workforce began to shrink as these industries faded in the face of change. The government became the one and only growth sector for union employment, but this has not created a more efficient government.

People who work for us must understand that our goal is continued success—success for everyone in the organization. We will use whatever skills we develop in the best possible way to achieve that success. This means that the organization and people's roles within it will always be susceptible to change. People should expect their roles to shift and evolve as the needs of the organization change.

Lesson 250: Repeating Success

When you have found success with your methods in the past, when do you change those methods?

A.   When your business runs into trouble.

B.   When competitors find success with different methods.

C.   When customers demand something different.

D.   Whenever you get the chance.

> *You must shift your campgrounds.*
> *You must take detours from the ordinary routes.*
> *You must use your men without giving them your strategy.*
>
> THE ART OF WAR 11:5.9-11

Answer: D. Whenever you get the chance.

The topic here is leadership in adjusting to changing situations. Strategy always requires innovation to create momentum. This was the topic of chapter 5. Here, Sun Tzu reinforces that idea in the context of getting the most out of our people in challenging situations.

People generally don't like change. In most organizations, people are threatened by change. They work, consciously or subconsciously, to subvert changes to the organization, trying to protect their existing methods and responsibilities. How do we address this natural tendency?

We must train our followers to accept that change is a requirement for survival in a fast-changing environment. Today, every aspect of our civilization changes with technological advancement. The only way we can stay competitive is by changing continuously. We change methods as a matter of habit. We continuously experiment and encourage our people to experiment.

Certainly, one advantage of continuous change is that our opponents cannot predict what we will do, but Sun Tzu takes this idea even further. Even our own people shouldn't think that they can predict us. If they can predict our strategy, our opponents can predict us as well. Our followers don't want to feel like they know as much as their leaders. They want their leaders to be ahead of them, to have more insight and vision than they have. If we don't have greater vision than our people, why should they follow us?

Encouraging change is the primary job of a leader.

Lesson 251: Discovering Opportunities for Success

Which of these nine situations gives you as a leader the best chance to discover an opportunity to succeed?

A.   The *dangerous* situation.
B.   The *open* situation.
C.   The *easy* situation.
D.   The *deadly* situation.

> *A commander provides what his army needs now.*
> *You must be willing to climb high and then kick away your ladder.*
> *You must be able to lead your men deeply into different surrounding territory.*
> *And yet, you can discover the opportunity to win.*
>
> THE ART OF WAR 11:5.12-15

Answer: A. The *dangerous* situation.

Dangerous situations are the deep penetrations into an opponent's territory that Sun Tzu describes here. Does this statement contradict Sun Tzu's other strategic concepts? In the early chapters, Sun Tzu teaches us that small, quick attacks are the best. They put us at less risk, and, should we fail, we only lose what we can afford. Here, however, he says that to find opportunity, we must take risks. We must get deeply involved—move to dangerous ground—to see the opportunity that we need.

Both concepts are equally true and not necessarily contradictory. We do want to limit the cost of our explorations or experiments in new areas. We want to pick small, doable projects. We want to tackle small projects, small improvements in our organization, and small, quick campaigns.

However, at the same time, we must use the philosophy of an invader. We must go deep into opponents' territory to unite and focus the organization. These thrusts need not take a long time or involve large forces. We can travel quickly if we move through empty areas. We must commit to these campaigns completely. We can't dabble and expect success. We will not see the opportunity in a given area unless we are completely committed to it.

The group of people involved in these small expeditions must be totally dependent upon their success. These projects need not put the company at risk, but the individuals involved should feel as though they personally are at risk. This commitment is what creates success.

Lesson 252: The Use of Pressure

How should your people feel when you ask them to meet the challenge of the current situation?

A.   They should never feel pressured.
B.   They should always feel pressured.
C.   They should sometimes feel pressured.
D.   They should feel relieved of pressure.

> *You must drive men like a flock of sheep.*
> *You must drive them to march.*
> *You must drive them to attack.*
> *You must never let them know where you are headed.*
> *You must unite them into a great army.*
> *You must then drive them against all opposition.*
> *This is the job of a true commander.*

THE ART OF WAR 11:5.16-22

Answer: B. They should always feel pressured.

This lesson echoes the core ideas of lesson 247 but in more detail. As leaders, we must recreate within our internal organization the real pressures of the competitive environment that we operate in. Most organizations isolate people from these pressures. People don't even know that their organization is in a difficult situation until they are laid off.

This is not to say that we should overtax people. Sun Tzu says clearly in lesson 189 and in lesson 237 that we get less out of people when we overwork them. There is a difference between overtaxing people—that is, asking them to do more than can be done—and keeping them facing the challenges of the moment. When the resources get stretched too thin, it is the responsibility of the leader to pause the campaign and add more people.

The ideal working environment is one of steady pressure that keeps everyone working up to his or her potential. In this environment, the pressure becomes part of the job. New people should have to adjust to this challenging environment, but existing people become completely acclimated. Working hard should be part of the corporate culture, uniting the organization. Organizations that keep people doing their best work reap the best rewards for everyone.

Lesson 253: Organizational Limitations

What makes it difficult for many organizations to deal with difficult situations and discover new opportunities in them?

A.   They are unwilling to invest.

B.   They are unwilling to work hard.

C.   They are unwilling to change.

D.   They are unwilling to take the time.

> *You must adapt to the different terrain.*
> *You must adapt to find an advantage.*
> *You must manage your people's affections.*
> *You must study all these skills.*

THE ART OF WAR 11:5.23-26

Answer: C. They are unwilling to change.

The topic of this chapter is how to deal with the nine different situations in which we can find ourselves. Most people, unfortunately, cannot clearly see the situation they are in and categorize it, much less adapt to it. Strategy is valuable because it teaches us to identify shifts in our situation, changes in the ground. The problem for most people is that they want to believe that their situation is stable when strategically change is the major factor of life.

According to Sun Tzu, we have to learn to continuously look at our strategic situation with fresh eyes. We have to temporarily forget our past judgments, everything that we've thought and learned and known about our situation. We have to block out our preconceptions. In this state of mind, we have to reevaluate our situation. Are we on easy ground or dangerous ground? Are we fighting battles in our own territory or are we venturing deep into the enemy's territory looking for an opportunity?

We have to be willing to throw out our plans at a moment's notice if we see an opportunity. Moreover, we have to be looking for the type of opportunity that would make it a good idea for us to throw out all our plans. We can always make new plans. We cannot make new opportunities. They are gifts that the market gives us.

Through all of this, we have to keep our people with us. We have to keep them working hard and totally involved with the business.

Lesson 254: The Philosophy of an Invader

What does Sun Tzu mean when he says that you must have the philosophy of an invader?

A.   You must be an outsider.

B.   You must grab what you can as fast as you can.

C.   You must like other people's opportunities better than your own.

D.   You must be deeply committed.

> *Always use the philosophy of invasion.*
> *Deep invasions concentrate your forces.*
> *Shallow invasions scatter your forces.*
> *When you leave your country and cross the border, you must take control.*
> *This is always critical ground.*
> *You can sometimes move in any direction.*
> *This is always intersecting ground.*
> *You can penetrate deeply into a territory.*
> *This is always dangerous ground.*
> *You penetrate only a little way.*
> *This is always easy ground.*
> *Your retreat is closed and the path ahead tight.*
> *This is always confined ground.*
> *There is sometimes no place to run.*
> *This is always deadly ground.*

THE ART OF WAR 11:6.1-15

Answer: D. You must be deeply committed.

Being an invader means being willing to go somewhere new and get totally involved. We are willing to invest our entire lives and future on that new area to find success there. We must be willing to live off the land, not only for now, but for always.

This is a challenging mind-set, but it aptly summarizes the many different lessons of this chapter. It is the mind-set of the overachiever and the entrepreneur. For most people, it is a dangerous and frightening course of action, with real risks. We can only afford to follow this course because strategy teaches us how to control the risks involved. It is the path that leads most certainly and safely to success. It makes it easier to identify opportunities and adjust to those opportunities when we identify them.

Lesson 255: The Techniques of Terrain

How many different techniques must you master to address the types of situations that Sun Tzu covers in this chapter?

A. Eight.
B. Nine.
C. Ten.
D. Twelve.

> *To use scattering terrain correctly, we must inspire our men's devotion.*
> *On easy terrain, we must keep in close communication.*
> *On disputed terrain, we should try to hamper the enemy's progress.*
> *On open terrain, we must carefully defend our chosen position.*
> *On intersecting terrain, we must solidify our alliances.*
> *On dangerous terrain, we must ensure our food supplies.*
> *On bad terrain, we must keep advancing along the road.*
> *On confined terrain, we must stop information leaks from our headquarters.*
> *On deadly terrain, we must show what we can do by killing the enemy.*
>
> THE ART OF WAR 11:6.16-24

Answer: B. Nine.

This should be, at this stage, an easy question. Each of the nine different situations that we face requires mastering the appropriate response.

The most interesting aspect of this stanza is comparing it to the similar one in lesson 231 to understand exactly what is required in each of these situations. Together, the two stanzas provide a bigger picture of what Sun Tzu is telling us. For example, when we are on *confined* terrain, going through a difficult transition, he first tells us to "use surprise," that is, keep it a secret. Here, we are told how to do that: we must block the flow of information from our headquarters. When we are on *scattering* ground—that is, being tempted to fight a battle in our own territory—we must avoid fighting. Instead, to avoid scattering, we must unite our people by inspiring their devotion. Wherever such contradictions seem to exist in Sun Tzu's work, they can always be resolved by studying the bigger ideas that Sun Tzu is communicating instead of the specific words he uses in a given stanza. This is one reason why it is frustrating when people quote stanzas of Sun Tzu out of context.

Lesson 256: Using Deadly Ground

When will people try their hardest?

A.   When they see chance of gain.

B.   When they fear their superiors.

C.   When they cannot avoid it.

D.   When you inspire them.

> *Make your men feel like an army.*
> *Surround them and they will defend themselves.*
> *If they cannot avoid it, they will fight.*
> *If they are under pressure, they will obey.*
>
> THE ART OF WAR 11:6.25-28

Answer: C. When they cannot avoid it.

In this stanza, Sun Tzu extends earlier points he made in lessons 251 through 253 about putting our supporters under pressure. If people are trained under pressure, they will respond well to the pressure of threatening situations, in this case, the pressure of *deadly* ground. When trained people are put into a do-or-die situation, they find a way to get the job done. The inevitable deadly situation is the final test of an organization. If an organization doesn't respond to these deadly challenges it will not survive at all.

In the first line of this stanza, Sun Tzu points out that pressure, like any form of adversity, unites people. It makes them feel like an army, a brotherhood. When they face a common foe, the issues that divide and separate them fall away, and they see their role more clearly.

This sense of belonging, of course, arises from their mutual self-interest. When people are threatened and have no opportunity to run from danger, they must defend themselves. Of course, if they can run when threatened, many people will try to flee. This is why we always leave an outlet for our opponents but never leave a similar out, or excuse, for our own people or for ourselves.

Pressure also makes people more willing to obey orders. When people are doing well and feel secure, they have the luxury of questioning authority. However, when they are under pressure they no longer feel that they have that luxury. They want and need a clear-cut role in a crisis.

Lesson 257: Ignorance of Competitive Plans

If you don't know what your competitors are planning, what should you never do?

A.   Directly confront them.

B.   Enter into their territory.

C.   Build alliances against them.

D.   Make progress against them.

> *Do the right thing when you don't know your different enemies' plans.*
> *Don't attempt to meet them.*

THE ART OF WAR 11:7.1-2

Answer: A. Directly confront them.

In this new section, the focus changes to the need for information. This is an important larger theme in Sun Tzu's work. Here, he relates the need for information specifically to understanding the nine situations or terrains that are the central focus of the chapter.

Knowing the nine situations and how to respond to them creates both a problem and an opportunity. This stanza addresses both. The problem is that without information, we cannot know exactly what our situation is. If we don't know our exact situation, we cannot meet the challenge correctly. However, knowing the nine situations is also an opportunity. If we know our opponents' situation, we can also predict their best response. In other words, we can know their plans—or what their plans should be.

The only one of the nine situations that demands meeting the enemy is a do-or-die situation. The message here is that we cannot meet our opponents unless we know what their plans are, what their situation is. This means we must make sure that we know about our opponents' situation before we get ourselves into a do-or-die situation.

Do-or-die situations usually come at the end of a campaign, after we have passed through many of the other situations. If we are not constantly accumulating information about our competitors' plans, we will not be in any condition to face them in a do-or-die situation at the end of the process. This is not to say that a confrontation must end every competitive campaign. However, it often can, so we must get the needed information.

Lesson 258: Unknown Areas

When you campaign in an area where you have little experience, what should you do?

A.   Hire an experienced person.

B.   Explore on your own.

C.   Talk to your allies.

D.   Hire a consulting organization.

> *You don't know the local mountains, forests, hills, and marshes?*
> *Then you cannot march the army.*
> *You don't have local guides?*
> *You won't get any of the benefits of the terrain.*

THE ART OF WAR 11:7.3-6

Answer: A. Hire an experienced person.

To understand our situation, we need information. "Getting the benefits of the terrain" can also be translated as "getting an advantage from the situation." In acquiring information, there is no substitute for the relevant knowledge of people rather than vast amounts of data in machines. If we don't have direct experience ourselves with a given situation, we need to buy it from someone who does. Sun Tzu states in lesson 287 that too little money is spent on getting the right information. This is especially true when we are moving into new areas.

For most of us, our impulse is to explore the territory on our own. We think that we can save money and get information for free. Our ego tells us we don't need help from others. Unfortunately, most people, including our allies, have ulterior motives in giving us information. We must expect that their information is slanted toward their own self-interest. We cannot know how to evaluate information if we don't know the territory.

We must also be wary of consulting organizations. These organizations sell advice. They are not necessarily experienced with the terrain that we are interested in, but it is in their own best interest to magnify their knowledge. Consulting organizations are experts at feigning experience. They cast themselves as impartial observers, but observing is not the same as experiencing. Their opinions and biases are not formed in or by the territory we are interested in.

Lesson 259: Information Gathering

In dealing with different situations, should you focus information gathering on the enemy, the territory, or your own people?

A.   The enemy.

B.   The territory.

C.   Your people.

D.   You shouldn't focus your information gathering.

> *There are many factors in war.*
> *You may lack knowledge of any one of them.*
> *If so, it is wrong to take a nation into war.*
>
> THE ART OF WAR 11:7.7-9

Answer: D. You shouldn't focus your information gathering.

In this chapter, we learn to think about a competitive process that passes through many common stages and many different situations. Each of these situations demands a different type of knowledge. To see the process through, we must have all the different types of knowledge and skill the nine situations demand. These situations are defined by the ground, our position on it, and our opponents' position on it as well.

This means that we must master a range of knowledge in order to be successful. We should not be leading an organization unless we have developed knowledge in every area. Competition is a complex process. It requires a complex understanding of situations in order to master competition.

Undertaking new projects or conquering new territories is an especially risky process. Our first concern must be the well-being of our existing organization and business. We have to be extremely careful when undertaking new projects because of the risks to the organization.

We cannot always know when we lack information. It may sound strange, but it is certainly true that we sometimes do not know what we do not know. Knowledge is never perfect. To act, we must have information on the three main factors that contribute to success—the territory, the competition, and our own people. If we know we are missing information in these areas, we must not go forward.

Lesson 260: Knowledge of the Target

When you are planning to target an opponent, what must you know about his or her situation?

A.   The size of his or her forces.

B.   His or her character weaknesses.

C.   The divisions in his or her organization.

D.   The readiness of his or her people.

> *You must be able to dominate a nation at war.*
> *Divide a big nation before they are able to gather a large force.*
> *Increase your enemy's fear.*
> *Prevent his forces from getting together and organizing.*
>
> THE ART OF WAR 11:7.10-13

Answer: C. The divisions in his or her organization.

This message goes back to lesson 232, where we first began discussing the use of strategy in dealing with early-stage situations. We don't want to fight in our own territory. To move into an opponent's territory, we need to find an opening. The size of the opponent is relatively unimportant. Knowing the weaknesses of the leader is useful in predicting what an opponent will do, but it doesn't tell us where to target our efforts. We are usually more concerned about the readiness of our own people than we are about the readiness of our opponents. Since we plan on attacking where their force is the weakest, their readiness is less of an issue.

Openings can be found in many different places, depending on what viewpoint we use to analyze our opposition. In business, an opponent's weakness may be in holes in the product line. In politics, it may be in rivalries between the groups an opponent is targeting. In both cases, the opening may be in our rival's geographical coverage. Its weakness can also be in the way the organization groups supporters together, neglecting one group or another. The weakness might be in communication, leaving certain supporters hungry for attention that they cannot get.

When we first target an opponent, we have to know where these holes are. All competitive organizations have these holes. It is simply a matter of locating them. Our first priority should be to figure out how to isolate a small area of the opponent's position to attack.

Lesson 261: Competing for Alliances

When do you want to compete with your opponent for alliances to amass a larger force?

A.   Whenever you have the opportunity.

B.   When the price isn't too high.

C.   Whenever you are on *intersecting* terrain.

D.   You should never compete for alliances.

> *Do the right thing and don't try to compete for outside alliances.*
> *You won't have to fight for authority.*
> *Trust only yourself and your own resources.*
> *This increases the enemy's uncertainty.*
> *You can force one of his allies to pull out.*
> *His whole nation can fall.*

THE ART OF WAR 11:7.14-19

Answer: D. You should never compete for alliances.

The key word here is "compete." We never want to compete with the competition for alliances. We can compete for territory, supporters, income, communication, and any other resource, but we don't want to compete for alliances. The exact prescription for intersecting ground is to get to it first so we can build our alliances without competition. If we don't get into this situation first, we cannot play "me too" in building associations.

Alliances are not really the strength that most people think they are. Strength comes from unity. Alliances are seldom united enough to be strong. They give people a false sense of strength when there is really no strength at all. In an alliance, each member will work for its own self-interest, regardless of the agreements among them. Alliances destroy the one element Sun Tzu requires for a true competitive unit: a clear leader.

There are other problems with alliances. Alliances create a battle for authority. If we are not the founding members of an association, we have even less authority. As the founding members of an alliance, we have a greater degree of control over that association. In these situations, we have to take the lead in controlling our relationships if alliances are to succeed. If we don't control the alliance, it controls us.

Lesson 262: On Your Own

What is the main benefit of competing as a single organization rather than as part of an alliance?

A.   A strong leader.
B.   A good philosophy.
C.   A clear goal.
D.   Control of the money.

> *Distribute plunder without worrying about agreements.*
> *Halt without the government's command.*
> *Attack with the whole strength of your army.*
> *Use your army as if it were a single man.*

THE ART OF WAR 11:7.20-23

Answer: D. Control of the money.

Certainly good leadership, philosophy, and goals are all worthy ideas, but they are not guaranteed by competing alone. What is guaranteed is that there will be no question about how the benefits of success are divided. The goal of strategy is to make victory pay. By working alone, we have a much better chance of getting control of the money. As this stanza points out, there are other advantages as well, including our ability to act on our own and our superior unity, but it is control of the money that makes these other capabilities possible.

From a business standpoint, this flow of money makes the customer-vendor relationship far superior to any voluntary alliance. In customer-vendor relationships, customers control the money. For example, in technology markets, it is frequently necessary to bring together hardware, software, and services from different companies to provide a complete solution. Companies try to ally themselves to provide this complete product, but it always works better if one company acts as a primary contractor, buying products from the other companies and selling them to the end user. The primary contractor has control of the money and the responsibility for the final product.

When we stop wasting time trying to create voluntary alliances and focus on the "money flow" relationship, we take control of our future. We know what has to be done and that we are responsible for doing it.

Lesson 263: The Necessary Advantage

When you pursue an opportunity in which you have an advantage, especially one with some risk, which of the following should you do?

A.   You should not try it if you might fail.

B.   You should discuss it with your people.

C.   You should let everyone know the dangers.

D.   You should try even if you might fail.

> *Attack with skill.*
> *Do not discuss it.*
> *Attack when you have an advantage.*
> *Do not talk about the dangers.*
> *When you can launch your army into deadly ground, even if it stumbles, it can still survive.*
> *You can be weakened in a deadly battle and yet be stronger afterward.*

THE ART OF WAR 11:7.24-29

Answer: D. You should try even if you might fail.

The topic is still knowledge. Strategy teaches us the skill of attack, the skill of invading new territories. If we are skilled, we will know when the time is right for an attack. We see a clear advantage. We know both a reason why we should win and a benefit if we win. We balance our chances and calculate that the risk is worth the gain. When we know the time is right, we must move. Our knowledge of the situation dictates what we must do.

We should not talk about the dangers before we move. We talk about the benefits. We want to create enthusiasm for the move. The beginning is an easy time. We should keep people moving. We want to get our supporters deeply involved before they recognize the risks. We don't want them to worry about the difficulties and risks until they have no choice but to succeed.

We can fail, but this cannot dissuade us from moving forward. No matter how good we are or how big our advantage, competition is always uncertain. This is why Sun Tzu included uncontrollable changes among his five key factors in strategic analysis. Even a reasonable risk is a risk. If we are smart, we calculate the size of risk we can take and still recover. We never bet it all on a single throw of the dice. We can lose battles but still win the war.

Lesson 264: Surviving Difficulties

When you run into trouble, how do you make sure that you can still survive?

A.   You make sure that you are large enough to survive.

B.   You adapt yourself to the needs of the situation.

C.   You move far away from your opponents.

D.   You must find a new opponent to attack.

> *Even a large force can fall into misfortune.*
> *If you fall behind, however, you can still turn defeat into victory.*
> *You must use the skills of war.*
> *To survive, you must adapt yourself to your enemy's purpose.*
> *You must stay with him no matter where he goes.*
> *It may take a thousand miles to kill the general.*
> *If you correctly understand him, you can find the skill to do it.*
>
> THE ART OF WAR 11:7.30-36

Answer: B. You adapt yourself to the needs of the situation.

There is an old saying that winners lose more often than losers. Winners lose more often because they are willing to take a chance. They win more often simply because they are persistent.

No matter how successful, large, or well known we become, we can always make a misstep and fall victim to the unpredictable shifts in the competitive climate.

Our opponents can and will make brilliant moves that we do not foresee. Someone else's vision can turn our situation on its head, redefining the terms of success. This kind of shift redefines the battleground, creating *open* situations. When this happens, we must copy our opponents' new methods. We must keep up with them. We must be persistent. We must be patient. If we keep up with them, eventually we will find an opportunity to turn the market around again and defeat them.

High tech is a great example of misfortune and recovery because markets change so fast. Microsoft has been the master of the strategy of copying emerging market leaders. It copied Apple and its graphical interface. It copied Netscape in the browser wars. Other companies have always had market leadership, but Microsoft follows strategically and always maintains its leadership through persistence.

Lesson 265: The New Competitive Threat

What should you do first when a friendly relationship suddenly turns into a competitive contest?

A.   Cut off communication.

B.   Try to mend the relationship through diplomacy.

C.   Attack your new competitor without waiting.

D.   Protect your mutual alliances.

> *Manage your government correctly at the start of a war.*
> *Close your borders and tear up passports.*
> *Block the passage of envoys.*
> *Encourage politicians at headquarters to stay out of it.*
> *You must use any means to put an end to politics.*
> *Your enemy's people will leave you an opening.*
> *You must instantly invade through it.*

THE ART OF WAR 11:8.1-7

Answer: A. Cut off communication.

It is common in every competitive arena for onetime partners to become opponents. Teammates can become opponents. People we buy from can become our opponents. People we sell to can become our opponents. This happens constantly in every competitive area as organizations look for ways to expand. In these situations, we may not have planned the competitive campaign, but it is thrust upon us. However, we can quickly respond, expecting the evolution of campaign situations explained in this chapter.

To meet an unexpected competitive challenge, the first thing we must do is cut off communication. We must quickly protect our information. Information is the key to response. If people want to compete with us, they want information about what we are doing. We want to stop them from learning about us, stealing our secrets, hiring our employees, and getting insight into our thinking. We don't try to keep the door open or repair the relationship. If we do, our opponents will steal us blind.

After defending ourselves in the information war, we don't attack immediately. We wait for our opponents to leave an opening. Openings are inevitable. When we see the opening, we cannot hesitate. We must take advantage of it immediately and attack our new opponents.

Lesson 266: The Defensive Attack

Once you invade a new opponent's territory, what do you have to do?

A.   Attack his or her stronghold.

B.   Seize something he or she needs.

C.   Take your first steps carefully.

D.   Plunder his or her border.

> *Immediately seize a place that they love.*
> *Do it quickly.*
> *Trample any border to pursue the enemy.*
> *Use your judgment about when to fight.*

THE ART OF WAR 11:8.8-11

Answer: B. Seize something he or she needs.

When war is thrust upon us, we must avoid an invasion of our territory. This means that we must attack first. Speed is the essence of warfare. So we must act quickly. In invading, we must avoid our opponent's strong points. Instead, we must find a sensitive weak point.

In the scenario of former partners or allies becoming enemies, we know their situation well enough to know what they love, that is, what is important to them. We must identify one of these areas as a weak point and go after it. We must win it away from our opponents even if it is expensive to do so. Controlling a place that they love gets their attention and diverts them from attacking us.

We cannot worry about niceties when we face this type of contest. We shouldn't worry about past agreements or contracts. Normally we must honor agreements scrupulously. Leadership is built on trust. In this situation, all bets are off. We must do whatever it takes to compete.

We must use our competitive skills to redefine the battleground. We want to force our competitors to fight in their own territory on the terms that we determine. In other words, we want to lure them into a *scattering* situation, fighting within their border. In this situation, they are tempted to fight on our terms. This gives us the advantage. This in turn gives us the opportunity to lure away their supporters, followers, and other allies. We use this opportunity to gather their people and those people's expertise. We make ourselves stronger while making our opponent weaker.

Lesson 267: Avoiding Traps

How do you keep new opponents from trapping you within their territory?

A.   By not invading too deeply.

B.   By amassing a force too large to fight.

C.   By moving faster than they can.

D.   By trapping them first.

> *Doing the right thing at the start of war is like approaching a woman.*
> *Your enemy's men must open the door.*
> *After that, you should act like a streaking rabbit.*
> *The enemy will be unable to catch you.*

THE ART OF WAR 11:8.12-15

Answer: C. By moving faster than they can.

This one stanza summarizes Sun Tzu's approach to strategy. He describes warfare as wooing a woman. It is an excellent analogy.

We first must wait for an opening. We must be invited into a competitive area. The need of the market must draw us in. We don't create the opening; our competition does. We can't push ourselves forward. If we do, we will be rebuffed. We must see the need. We must understand the opening.

After we see an opening, we must use it to invade as far and as fast as we can. In a romantic relationship, we would want to get deeply involved in our lover's life. We must get ourselves in so deeply that we are totally committed. If we don't, we will be frightened away by the first sign of adversity. If we commit ourselves, we can suffer a lot of rejection and still persist.

In Chinese culture, the rabbit has a number of qualities. Rabbits are tactful, diplomatic, and friendly. Their most important quality to Sun Tzu is that they keep out of conflict. They avoid great challenges and stressful situations. The purpose of invasion is not to fight battles; it is to change the situation and to discover opportunities.

We don't want to attack our opponents' forces directly. We want to capture something that they care about so that they come after us. We don't want to pursue them. Nor do we want them to catch us. Our purpose is to catch them off guard, undermine their confidence, and destroy their plans. If we are successful in doing that, the battle is already won without ever being fought.

Chapter 12

火攻

Attacking with Fire

Though we don't use fire today as a weapon in the modern world of competition, Sun Tzu's chapter on fire works as a metaphor for using any weapon, especially those that leverage the power of the larger environment.

Did Sun Tzu write this chapter as a metaphor? Probably not, but it is interesting to note that we use the word "fire" in English to describe the shooting of any type of weapon. The term, of course, arose in the era of cannons, but today we fire guns, missiles, and even spitballs. In many if not most languages, concepts related to fire are linked with the use of force.

However, fire is more than a weapon. It is a natural force. It leverages conditions in the environment to create disasters. Things are not going well when we are "fighting fires." It is easier to understand the strategic implications of this chapter if we think of "fire" as a problem that arises out of the environment. Though such problems can arise naturally, they can also be set intentionally. We can start fires for our opponents to fight, but we don't totally control these fires. The environment must provide us the fuel to support these fires for them to work.

We can set many types of fires in today's world. We can use the media as an environmental weapon, creating bad press. We can use the law as an environmental weapon, attacking our opponents in the courts—not by bringing the suit ourselves, but by encouraging others to do so.

This chapter is an essay on the use of these dangerous environmental weapons. It discusses where we can use them, that is, what we should target. It discusses what we have to do to make their use successful. It prepares us not only for using these weapons against our opponents but also for defending ourselves against these fire attacks.

Lesson 268: Categories of Targets

How many categories of targets for environmental weapons does Sun Tzu teach you to look for?

A. One.

B. Five.

C. Nine.

D. Unlimited.

> *There are five ways of attacking with fire.*
> *The first is burning troops.*
> *The second is burning supplies.*
> *The third is burning supply transport.*
> *The fourth is burning storehouses.*
> *The fifth is burning camps.*

THE ART OF WAR 12:1.1-6

Answer: B. Five.

Before we can use an environmental weapon, we must have a target. Sun Tzu identifies five. Like all of the lists of five in *The Art of War*, this list relates back to the five key factors in strategy. Troops are connected to philosophy (which is people-centric), supplies to heaven (because of their connection to time) transport to the ground (distance), storehouses to leadership (planning), and camps to methods (organization).

In this list, people are the first target of any weapon. We can target our opponents' supporters or followers. We can discredit their philosophy or win them away with our philosophy.

Next, we can target our opponents' supplies, that is, their long-term resources. We can also target their relationships with their suppliers.

Next, we can target our opponents' transportation system, that is, their distribution channels. In modern parlance, we can seek to disrupt our opponents' supply chain or sales channels.

Next, we can attack storehouses. We can understand these attacks better if we think of them as related to attacking assets our opponents have planned to build up, that is, their cash position or their storehouse of goodwill.

Finally, we can also target our competitors' locations or organizations. We target specific geographical areas or particular demographic categories.

Lesson 269: Preparing Environmental Attacks

After you identify a target for an environmental attack, what do you do next?

A.   Prepare materials.

B.   Wait for an opportunity.

C.   Consult with a specialist.

D.   Act immediately.

To make fire, you must have the resources.
To build a fire, you must prepare the raw materials.

THE ART OF WAR 12:1.7-8

Answer: A. Prepare materials.

All weapons that are fired require ammunition. All environmental weapons require fuel for the fire. If the weapon is the media, we need to supply damaging information. The ammunition is the inside story. If the weapon is money for a hostile takeover, we need the financial backing, the investors. If the weapon is a lawsuit, we need the lawyers, the witnesses, the evidence, and possibly even the complainants, if we aren't playing the role ourselves. If we don't have this ammunition, we can't use the weapon.

Fuel also requires preparation. It may exist in the environment, but we have to gather it and arrange it to "set" the fire. These weapons can work on their own naturally, but when we want to use them intentionally, we have to arrange the fuel. We have to carefully prepare and test materials that we plan to use. This means that we have to verify the damaging information. We have to guarantee the money for the takeover. We have to double-check our evidence for the lawsuit. We cannot be too careful in assuring that we have the exact ammunition that we need.

We prepare because we cannot afford mistakes. Attacks with environmental weapons are the most dangerous form of competition. We don't want to rush this form of attack. If we can find a good target, we must make sure that we have the right ammunition to attack it. We must make sure the ammunition will work. A failed "fire" attack is especially costly.

Lesson 270: Resources for Environmental Attacks

What other resource do you need besides ammunition for an environmental attack?

A.   Labor.

B.   Time.

C.   Money.

D.   Weight.

> *To attack with fire, you must be in the right season.*
> *To start a fire, you must have the time.*
>
> THE ART OF WAR 12:1.9-10

Answer: B. Time.

Strategically, Sun Tzu does not recommend direct confrontations unless they are unavoidable. Environmental attacks are direct attacks, but without the confrontation. They are impersonal because the fire does the fighting for us. Because we are not necessarily directly involved except in setting the fire, we might assume that these attacks are inexpensive. That is not the case. To make such attacks work, we must invest in the time to start them.

We must plan environmental attacks for occasions when we will have time to follow through. We can't attempt to start these attacks without committing the time to complete them. If our business has a slack season, we then might have the time to devote to developing this type of attack.

We must also recognize that it isn't quick and easy to start environmental attacks on our opposition. If we want to leak information to the press, we can't just tell one person and hope the news gets around. We have to work at it. If we want a third party to attack an opponent with a hostile takeover, we must spend the time to build the financial case for them to do so. Again, we cannot simply hope this happens naturally if we want to set the fire. In the case of lawsuits, even when the suit is brought by a "neutral" third party, setting them up is extremely time-consuming, both before and during the attack. Environmental attacks will simply fall apart unless we are willing to devote the time they require. We may not play a central role in these attacks once we start them, but starting them takes time away from other efforts.

Lesson 271: Using Environmental Weapons

What is the second key to using environmental weapons successfully?

A.   Picking the right time.
B.   Picking the right place.
C.   Picking the right issues.
D.   Picking the right angle.

> *Choose the right season.*
> *The weather must be very dry.*
>
> *Choose the right time.*
> *Pick a season when the grass is as high as the side of a cart.*
>
> *You can tell the proper days by the stars in the night sky.*
> *You want days when the wind rises in the morning.*
>
> **THE ART OF WAR 12:1.11-16**

Answer: A. Picking the right time.

In independent attacks, third parties must have their own motives and interests to attack our opponent. No such environmental weapon attacks our opponent just because we want it to. Most of these attacks are possible only in very specific situations. The key here is recognizing when the conditions are right for an environmental attack.

Going back to the five key factors in strategy, time is controlled by the factor of *climate* or *heaven*. This factor is closely associated with weather. The climate is, by nature, beyond our control. It works in cycles. We have to observe and predict it in order to use it correctly. In using environmental attacks, we are leveraging temporary conditions in the environment for our success. As such, fire attacks become a metaphor for Sun Tzu's strategy in general.

In other words, we need the right climate to use environmental weapons. A damaging story will only work if the press is looking for that type of news. In a hostile takeover, financial backing depends on the condition of the markets. In a lawsuit, the court must show itself receptive to the kind of claim the plaintiff is making against our opponent. Because these attacks depend on the environment, we must understand the trends of the time.

Lesson 272: The Source of Environmental Attacks

Who should you suspect will use environmental attacks against you?

A.   Those who are too frightened to attack you directly.

B.   Those who have experience with environmental attacks.

C.   Those who have pretended friendship in the past.

D.   Everyone.

> *Everyone attacks with fire.*
> *You must create five different situations with fire and be able to adjust to them.*

THE ART OF WAR 12:2.1-2

Answer: D. Everyone.

The point of this stanza is that we are potential targets as well as potential attackers. Because of this, we must always be aware of how the environment can support such attacks. Given the appropriate conditions, the use of environmental weapons is almost unavoidable. If we can use them, we should. If others can use them against us, they will. The conditions allow us to leverage the environment and the trends of the time against our rivals, but they also allow our opponents to leverage the environment against us.

We must be continually aware that we are potential targets of these attacks. Strategically, we always defend first. We only attack when we have an excess of resources. To defend what we have, we must continually be aware of the conditions in the environment that might lend themselves to an attack against us. What type of story is the press looking for? What conditions might make us a target for takeover? Who might bring a lawsuit against us and why? This attentiveness to the larger environment allows us to defend against possible attacks and to identify opportunities to target our opponents.

People don't even have to be our enemies to attack us with fire. Just like fires, environmental problems can occur by accident. These weapons are not only enabled by environmental conditions; they can be driven by them. We can also get drawn into environmental problems without planning on them. We must be constantly monitoring the situation. If a fire is going to break out, we want to use it, not be victimized by it.

Lesson 273: Following Up on Environmental Attacks

What is the ideal relationship between your activities and the action of an environmental weapon?

A.   The weapon and your actions should focus on the center.
B.   The weapon focuses on the periphery and you attack the periphery.
C.   The weapon focuses on the periphery and you attack the center.
D.   The weapon focuses on the center and you attack the periphery.

> *You start a fire inside the enemy's camp.*
> *Then attack the enemy's periphery.*
>
> THE ART OF WAR 12:2.3-4

Answer: D. The weapon focuses on the center and you attack the periphery.

This is the first of the five types of fire attacks. Though all fire attacks are primarily controlled by the key factor of heaven—that is, time—it shouldn't surprise anyone that these five categories also loosely follow the five key factors in strategic positioning. The first of those key factors is philosophy.

Environmental weapons should target the core of our opposition. Strategically, the core of an organization is its philosophy. If the environmental weapon is bad publicity, the publicity should focus on some central, inherent component of our opposition. If it is a takeover, the takeover should target the core business of our opposition. If the weapon is a lawsuit, the legal attack should focus on the most sensitive and valuable part of the opposition's organization.

Our regular competitive efforts can support these environmental attacks, but we should keep the two forms of attack separate. We want to keep some distance between the environmental attack and ourselves. The danger, of course, is that if we find ourselves positioned near the environmental target, we will become a victim of the environmental attack ourselves.

We can and should attack our opponents when they are distracted by environmental attacks, but we must keep ourselves out of harm's way. We should take full advantage of these opportunities in the marketplace, but we shouldn't join in on the environmental attack directly. Once we have started it, we want to keep ourselves out of it as much as possible.

Lesson 274: Responding to Environmental Attacks

What is the best way to respond to an environmental attack?

A.   By remaining calm.

B.   By attacking back.

C.   By running away.

D.   By running in circles.

> *You launch a fire attack, but the enemy remains calm.*
> *Wait and do not attack.*

THE ART OF WAR 12:2.5-6

Answer: A. By remaining calm.

The second key factor is climate, which represents time. Here the issue is how we use our time. The best defense against environmental attack is to remain calm. Problems in the larger environment always ease in time. The biggest mistake that people make in defending themselves against environmental attack is overreacting. In these situations, we are judged by our reactions. Given enough time, these attacks always blow over.

If we remain calm in the face of bad publicity, we defuse it. If we remain calm in the face of a hostile takeover or a lawsuit, we encourage negotiation. Remember that the heart of all competition is information. When we remain calm, we are not only better able to deal with a difficult situation; we are also sending out a message to our people, the environment, and our opposition that things are not as bad as they might seem. More people are damaged in these situations by their own reactions than by the incidents themselves.

If our opposition remains calm in the face of an environmental attack, we should wait and see what happens. We should withhold any direct competitive attack. In attacking during an environmental problem, we are taking advantage of the confusion that these attacks cause. If there is no confusion, there is no opportunity. If we wouldn't normally attack the opposition, we shouldn't do it now. The environment is fickle. It can easily turn on us. If we attack our opponents when they are in some difficulty but handling it well, we invite the disapproval of others.

Lesson 275: An Opponent's Difficulties

When do you use your opponents' environmental difficulties against them in your normal course of competition?

A.   Always.

B.   Never.

C.   When it provides a path.

D.   When nothing else works.

> *The fire reaches its height.*
> *Follow its path if you can.*
> *If you can't follow it, stay where you are.*
>
> THE ART OF WAR 12:2.7-9

Answer: C. When it provides a path.

The third key strategic factor is the ground. Here, we use the effect of the environmental weapon to create a path on the ground for us to follow. To do this successfully, we must first wait until an opponent's problem reaches its peak before we can see what our opportunity is. We have to see how the problem builds or if it simply fades away. As stated in the last lesson, acting too early in these situations can be a mistake. As he so often does, Sun Tzu advises patience to see how the situation finally develops. While we wait, we study the ground to see if the fire will create an opening for us.

Even when the situation does get serious, it is a mistake to always think that we can directly use the path of an environmental attack for our own attack. Some people think that the best way to leverage the difficulties of their opponents is to spread the word about their problems. This doesn't always work out to their advantage. This type of malicious gossip can arouse sympathy for an opponent, especially when it comes from someone everyone knows is a direct competitor.

But sometimes the difficulties of our opponents are directly related to our competitive position. If there is a clear connection between their problems and our competitive message, we can use the difficulty as evidence to support our position. The problem itself must "provide the path" for us to attack. We cannot use our opponents' problems against them unless the connection is clear. If such a connection exists, we cannot ignore it.

Lesson 276: The Focus of Attack

If you can't start an environmental attack focused at the heart of an opponent's business, can you still use such an attack?

A.   Peripheral attacks work only if they happen quickly.

B.   Peripheral attacks work only if time is devoted to them.

C.   Peripheral attacks work only in a minor way.

D.   Peripheral attacks never work.

> *Spreading fires on the outside of camp can kill.*
> *You can't always get fire inside the enemy's camp.*
> *Take your time in spreading it.*

THE ART OF WAR 12:2.10-12

Answer: B. Peripheral attacks work only if time is devoted to them.

The fourth key factor in strategy is leadership, and this type of attack requires the most planning. A peripheral environmental attack is one that is focused on minor issues, minor people, or less important parts of the organization. These attacks clearly are not as damaging as core attacks. They may do some damage, but they don't cause the panic that creates a major opportunity. However, given enough planning, they can be effective.

Because of the planning required, these peripheral attacks are more time-consuming to start than more direct environmental attacks. If we are trying to create bad press, the media is not very interested in stories about peripheral characters or minor issues. A takeover of a minor subdivision isn't terribly interesting to the financial community. A lawsuit that doesn't offer a big reward is unlikely to find immediate acceptance. If we want these minor attacks to succeed, we must work harder at them. The opportunity may be there, but we have to invest more in order to get people interested.

However, the fact that peripheral attacks are more time-consuming than direct attacks doesn't mean that they are not worthwhile. They can still be damaging to opponents and still worth the effort. As always, we must take what the environment gives us. If the opportunity is there to do damage to the opposition, we should take advantage of it. We should just know ahead of time that peripheral attacks are more difficult than more direct attacks.

Lesson 277: Supporting Environmental Attacks

Which of the following factors best supports an environmental attack?

A.   Ignorance.

B.   Mystery.

C.   Visibility.

D.   Intelligence.

> *Set the fire when the wind is at your back.*
> *Don't attack into the wind.*
> *Daytime winds last a long time.*
> *Night winds fade quickly.*

THE ART OF WAR 12:2.13-16

Answer: C. Visibility.

In the last type of attack, we address the fifth key factor in strategy, methods. By their nature, environmental attacks must be supported by the trends of the time, the "wind" of the environment. Suing cigarette manufacturers was a losing proposition for fifty years because people felt that the individual decision to smoke was the relevant factor. Today, people are much more ready to find fault with large organizations. These changing trends are an aspect of the element of heaven, one of the five elements introduced in the first chapter. As we said earlier, both the ground and heaven must support environmental attacks. The ground provides the fuel and heaven provides the appropriate "air" that gives the attack life.

Why is visibility important in this process? What methods should we use? Clearly, the more visible a trend is, the more powerful it is. In human society, people follow one another. They group together. If a lawsuit gets good visibility, more people will join in. If one hostile takeover receives publicity, it inspires more hostile takeovers. Visibility gives life to a trend. The greater the visibility, the longer that trend will last. Environmental attacks depend upon human enthusiasm. Visibility brings in the crowd, and the bigger the crowd, the greater the enthusiasm. We want to take advantage of the most visible trends. We also want our environmental attacks to generate maximum visibility.

Lesson 278: Protection from Environmental Attacks

How can you protect yourself from environmental attacks?

A. By keeping your plans a secret.

B. By controlling the environment.

C. By educating your people.

D. You cannot protect yourself.

> *Every army must know how to deal with the five attacks by fire.*
> *Use many men to guard against them.*
>
> THE ART OF WAR 12:2.17-18

Answer: C. By educating your people.

Attacks from the environment have one thing in common with attacks from the opposition. Both attacks require an opening. We cannot be the target of bad press unless we have undertaken some questionable practices. We cannot be the target of a lawsuit unless we first create the basis for action. We cannot be the target of a takeover unless we give our shareholders a reason to want to sell out to the highest bidder. We must realize that we ourselves are the source of all environmental attacks against us.

As often as not, the openings that allow environmental attacks do not form because of the decisions of top management. These openings form because of thoughtless or overzealous employees. The problems created by poorly trained employees are as dangerous as those created by bad management decisions. The best protection we have against creating openings for environmental attack is to educate the people we work with. Everyone should know that today's environment is dangerous. We should teach our employees which activities are likely to create bad press or generate lawsuits against us.

We must also teach people to be on the lookout for those who are trying to foment these types of problems. We have to identify the potential trouble-makers with whom we come in contact. Fires can start accidentally, but more often people start them. If we can identify competitors who are trying to create fires for us, we can usually put the fires out before they get started.

Lesson 279: Environmental Attacks versus Change

Why is using an environmental attack better than simply leveraging the trends in climate against your competition?

A.   It is less expensive.

B.   It is more forceful.

C.   It takes away the opponent's resources.

D.   It gives you additional assets.

> *When you use fire to assist your attacks, you are clever.*
> *Water can add force to an attack.*
> *You can also use water to disrupt an enemy.*
> *It doesn't, however, take his resources.*

THE ART OF WAR 12:3.1-4

Answer: C. It takes away the opponent's resources.

As environmental forces under the control of heaven—that is, the climate—fire and water are closely related. Water is the most common metaphor in *The Art of War*. In Sun Tzu's strategic system, water represents change or trends, the force of the shifting environment. From a business perspective, water represents shifts in the marketplace. From a political perspective, it represents changes in popular opinion. Like the winds that drive fire, environmental change has a direction. An environmental shift is similar to an environmental attack. Both represent the hostile effects of the environment.

While we can and should always be looking to leverage changes in the marketplace against our opposition, we generally want to stay away from shifting environments. Sun Tzu teaches us that shifting environments are dangerous. If we can maneuver our opposition into changing markets, we can improve our position, especially if we can get our opponents fighting us against the currents or trends of the time.

Leveraging the business environment to get one group or another to attack our opponents is more destructive than a shifting environment. Groups have their own interests. They too are trying to get something from our competitors. The press is always trying to take away people's reputations. Finding villains makes the media successful. Financial companies try to get assets at a discount. In battling these forces, our opponents will lose something.

Lesson 280: Victory in Competition

Strategically, how do you succeed in a competitive environment?

A.   By developing your resources.

B.   By inspiring your people.

C.   By advancing your position.

D.   By leveraging your efforts.

> *You win in battle by getting the opportunity to attack.*
> *It is dangerous if you fail to study how to accomplish this achievement.*
> *As commander, you cannot waste your opportunities.*

THE ART OF WAR 12:4.1-3

Answer: C. By advancing your position.

As is often the case, Sun Tzu finishes the chapter by reviewing the basic concepts of strategy, but now in the context of environmental attack. In Sun Tzu's text, attacking doesn't mean just hurting our enemies; it means advancing our position. How do these destructive environmental attacks relate to advancing our position?

The skill needed for environmental attack is seeing the opportunity to use an attack to advance our position. Though fire attacks are focused on our opponents, these attacks must provide us with an opportunity to advance our position as well as hurt our opponent. In Sun Tzu's system, we don't create the opportunity to win; we see the opportunity. This is especially true environmental attacks. We cannot create the proper environmental conditions to support these attacks, nor can we create the conditions that leverage this type of attack for our personal advance.

We must attune ourselves to see these opportunities when they occur. The difficulty is that situations that lend themselves to bad press, legal action, and takeovers are rare and that they can often hurt us as much as they hurt our opponents. We can get out of the habit of looking for the right environmental conditions because we cannot use environmental attacks every day. We have to study and analyze our situation, remembering to look for valuable opportunities. Sun Tzu sees the environment as full of opportunity. What is truly rare is our ability to see the opportunity. When we do see the opportunity, we must act.

Lesson 281: Choosing Not to Attack

When should you refrain from working to start an environmental attack on
your opponents?

A.   When there is nothing to gain.

B.   When the situation is dangerous.

C.   When you have few resources.

D.   When your opponents are strong.

> *We say:*
> *A wise leader plans success.*
> *A good general studies it.*
> *If there is little to be gained, don't act.*
> *If there is little to win, do not use your men.*
> *If there is no danger, don't fight.*
>
> THE ART OF WAR 12:4.4-9

Answer: A. When there is nothing to gain.

In the last stanza, we began the discussion of how the use of fire allows
us to advance our position. Here, we continue that discussion more specifically. When we think we see an opportunity to start an environmental
attack, we have to analyze whether or not it is really an opportunity. In Sun
Tzu's system, opportunity doesn't consist simply of damaging our opponents
or even of winning a battle. Success requires that we win something valuable. Advancing our position means gaining something valuable. We aren't
looking simply to beat our opponents. We are looking to enrich ourselves.

An opportunity is defined by its ability to win something that we
consider valuable. In looking for the opportunity to start an environmental
attack, we must look to answer the questions: What is in it for us? How does
this attack fit into our larger goals? We must not simply hurt the enemy; we
must gain something valuable in the process.

We must not be tempted by false opportunities that allow us to attack
the competition but gain nothing in return. Since any attack costs resources,
we are wasting effort and time. We must see a way to gain from the situation.
Even though an environmental attack leverages the resources of the environment, time and effort are not free. We cannot create such attacks without
diverting resources from elsewhere.

Lesson 282: Offensive Behavior

If your opponents' behavior angers you, how should you respond?

A.   By teaching them a lesson.

B.   By waiting until your anger passes.

C.   By acting when there is a benefit.

D.   By taking away what they love.

> *As leader, you cannot let your anger interfere with the success of your forces.*
> *As commander, you cannot fight simply because you are enraged.*
> *Join the battle only when it is in your advantage to act.*
> *If there is no advantage in joining a battle, stay put.*
>
> THE ART OF WAR 12:4.10-13

Answer: C. By acting when there is a benefit.

This continues the discussion of the need to focus on what we win rather than on hurting opponents. The point here is that we must act or not act depending only on whether we are rewarded or not. Many things that our opponents do may anger us. We can easily see bad behavior as a justification for an environmental attack, but that doesn't mean we should attack. We also cannot let anger blind us to opportunity or paralyze us into inaction. When we are angry, we must do what we always must do: act when it is in our best interests to act.

Sun Tzu tells us that we must get beyond our feelings. In the course of competition, we will certainly have personal conflicts that affect us emotionally. We will often find our opponents dishonest, despicable, and generally loathsome. This is the natural mind-set that competitors develop toward each other. This viewpoint can easily blind us to the true qualities of our competitors. We cannot judge our opportunity for an environmental attack unless we can learn to see our competitors objectively.

People often want to attack their opponents simply because of their anger. We cannot fall into this trap. There is only one basis for attacking an opponent. We must get something out of it. It must generate a material reward. Any reward that isn't tangible is simply emotional gratification.

Strategy is the art of thinking longer term. It is the process of looking for opportunities. It combines the study of mathematics and psychology so that we have a framework for action based on something other than emotion.

Lesson 283: Perception of Failure

What is the difference between your perception of failure and the reality of failure?

A.   There is no difference.

B.   Perception changes.

C.   You fear only real failure.

D.   You feel only real failure.

> *Anger can change back into happiness.*
> *Rage can change back into joy.*
> *A nation once destroyed cannot be brought back to life.*
> *Dead men do not return to the living.*
>
> THE ART OF WAR 12:4.14-17

Answer: B. Perception changes.

Sun Tzu teaches us not to trust emotions because emotions change so easily, and emotions change our perspective just as easily. Today's bitter enemies can become tomorrow's partners. Alliances shift continuously. We should always realize that the emotions of today could vanish tomorrow. The world perceived through a cloud of emotion is very different from the world perceived through strategic analysis.

The conditions in the physical world that make fire attacks possible are purely physical. Our opinion doesn't change them. The social conditions that make environmental attacks possible in our modern world are largely emotional. The motivation for environmental attacks is also largely emotional. If we work to start attacks, we must realize that the basis for them is a temporary state of mind.

When we are clearly focused on advancing our position, we realize that hurting an enemy isn't justification enough for using an environmental attack. Today's enemy may well be tomorrow's ally. An attack that hurts the enemy but doesn't advance us is strategically shortsighted.

If we destroy potential allies because we are temporarily at odds with them, we can actually weaken our position long term by using these fire attacks. The use of such destructive forces may give us a temporary advantage, but it can also damage our reputation longer term.

Lesson 284: The Goal of Strategy

What is the final goal of strategy?

A. Survival.

B. Wealth.

C. Fame.

D. Victory.

> *This fact must make a wise leader cautious.*
> *A good general is on guard.*

> *Your philosophy must be to keep the nation peaceful and the army intact.*
>
> THE ART OF WAR 12:4.18-20

Answer: A. Survival.

Sun Tzu's treatise on strategy has more in common with Darwin's *Origin of Species* than it does with most other texts on military matters. In many ways, it is a survival handbook. Victory is simply a necessary step toward material gain, and material gain is just a necessary step toward survival. As Sun Tzu says in the first stanza of his work, the art of war is the basis for life and death, survival and destruction.

In the last five stanzas of this chapter, Sun Tzu brings us back to the basics of strategy, applying them specifically to our use of environmental attacks. We must only use such attacks when there is a clear opportunity. We should only use these attacks when we can make them pay. Our purpose is never to destroy our opponents; it is to build something for ourselves. Competition should be constructive. In the end, our only purpose is to preserve our organization and ourselves.

The greatest danger of competition is that we get caught up in the competitive battle and forget the purpose for which we are fighting. We are always fighting only for our survival. We should hate the idea of destruction. The purpose of competition is to put productive power in the hands of those who can use it best. If we can succeed without battling others, that is even better. This is important to remember in considering such a damaging form of attack.

Chapter 13

用 間

Using Spies

Throughout his work, Sun Tzu makes it clear that information and knowledge are critical to strategy. In lesson 34, he explains that succeeding in competition requires "deception," that is, the ability to control information. Long before the present information age, Sun Tzu taught that information was the key to success. Long before people spoke of "military intelligence" or "business intelligence" or "political intelligence" as being contradictions in terms, Sun Tzu laid out the methods that we must use to acquire good competitive information.

In this chapter, the discussion of the value of information starts with understanding the costs of competition. All competition is economic. As they say in the movies, failure is not an option. The way we reduce our costs is to leverage information, eliminating the need to invest in people and materials because we are putting just enough resources exactly where they are needed.

Sun Tzu then explains the five strategic types of information that we need to acquire. He frames this discussion in terms of "spies," but the actual Chinese term used, *gaan*, means a "space between," that is, a go-between or conduit of information rather than a fictional spy like James Bond. His concepts are easily understood in terms of information sources. He defines the five types of information and then describes how we acquire them.

The discussion teaches us how we must use and manage our information sources. The chapter ends by exhorting us to study history to get the most important lessons about information management. By "studying history" Sun Tzu also means looking at the trends and statistics, that is, following how situations develop over time.

Lesson 285: Competitive Information

What aspect of competition should dominate your thinking about information?

A.   The competition itself.

B.   The environment.

C.   The opportunity.

D.   The cost.

> *Altogether, building an army requires thousands of men.*
> *They invade and march thousands of miles.*
> *Whole families are destroyed.*
> *Other families must be heavily taxed.*
> *Every day, thousands of dollars must be spent.*
>
> THE ART OF WAR 13:1.1-5

Answer: D. The cost.

All competition is, at its core, economic. Sun Tzu first makes this point in chapter 2, where he defines success not just as winning but as making victory pay. The problem with competition is that it is expensive. We have to invest money one way or another to make money. Our search for knowledge must start with the certainty that by engaging in competition, we are going to spend more than we expect.

We put a lot of effort into our plans, but because we work in a competitive environment, there is never any certainty that this effort will be productive. In business, we can be certain that we will produce a certain product at a certain cost, but we cannot be certain that a competitor won't produce a better product at a lower price. In politics, we can produce advertisements and position papers, but those don't necessarily translate into votes.

If a better alternative is available, our "product" is actually a waste. We actually destroyed the resources we used instead of putting them to productive use. Our goal is to produce wealth and create value, but if our competition satisfies the market need, we are creating waste. Our efforts actually become destructive. The central issue in information management in competition is making sure that we are not wasting our investment. We want to know that our efforts are effective, not wasted.

Lesson 286: The Failure of Planning

Why can't you know that you will produce value simply by executing your plans?

A.   Because you fail to spend enough time planning.

B.   Because most plans are too detailed.

C.   Because events always overtake your plans.

D.   Because people keep shifting their focus.

> *Internal and external events force people to move.*
> *They are unable to work while on the road.*
> *They are unable to find and hold a useful job.*
> *This affects seventy percent of thousands of families.*

THE ART OF WAR 13:1.6-9

Answer: C. Because events always overtake your plans.

Do we plan for success or plan for failure? Is failure itself a failure of planning? Sun Tzu believes in planning, but he believes that all plans are inherently limited. Strategy is more a systematic process of exploring opportunities rather than a traditional planning tool. Problems and failure are inevitable with or without plans. This is why chapter 8, on adaptability, makes the point that we must always be willing to put aside our plans to adjust to current events. We can do many different things to improve our planning—especially improving our vision so that we can foresee the contest's events—but there are always events that no one foresees.

We can plan what we want, but it is certain that events will occur that no one foresees. Sometimes these events result from the actions of our competitors who are actively working against us. More often, these events arise simply from living in a fast-changing environment. This is even truer today than it was in Sun Tzu's time.

The problem with unexpected events is that they are bound to disrupt our efforts. Competitors' efforts can turn our efforts into waste, but chance events can also create waste. For example, we can spend months putting together a business agreement, only to have our whole project fall apart in a minute because a key price suddenly changes, or interest rates climb, or, more definitively, the person with whom we are dealing suddenly dies. Our effort is wasted because of unforeseen events.

Lesson 287: Strategic Expectations

If a competitive situation is stable for years, what should you expect tomorrow?

A.   That it will change dramatically.

B.   That it will never change dramatically.

C.   That it will change little by little.

D.   That life is full of surprises.

> *You can watch and guard for years.*
> *Then a single battle can determine victory in a day.*
> *Despite this, bureaucrats hold onto their salary money too dearly.*
> *They remain ignorant of the enemy's condition.*
> *The result is cruel.*

THE ART OF WAR 13:1.10-14

Answer: D. That life is full of surprises.

A stable situation may remain stable for a long period of time or it may change dramatically in a moment. The past does not dictate the future. Some changes are gradual. Some changes are very quick. Sometimes we can see change coming. Sometimes we cannot. Sun Tzu puts "change" in the realm of heaven, which means simply that it is beyond our control.

This does not mean, however, that there is nothing we can do about change. If we spend the needed time, effort, and money, we have a good chance of seeing changes before they come to us.

This stanza equates money with information and information with military resources. In other words, we can leverage our investment by investing indirectly in information rather than directly in competitive resources. Good information can replace men, money, and materials used in competition. If we know where the competition is going to attack, we don't have to protect all the other places that aren't threatened. If we know where the competition is weak, we can focus our resources in that one area instead of wasting resources probing for weaknesses.

The unpredictable nature of the competitive arena makes information more valuable than money.

Lesson 288: Success in Competition

If you can't get good competitive information, how do you succeed in competition?

A. You can't.

B. By having enough money to invest in men and materials.

C. By being patient.

D. By focusing your efforts on the areas you know.

> *They are not leaders of men.*
> *They are not servants of the state.*
> *They are not masters of victory.*
>
> THE ART OF WAR 13:1.15-17

Answer: A. You can't.

The "they" referred to in this stanza are the bureaucrats that do not spend enough money on information. One of the four skills required of a leader is knowledge. Knowledge is the foundation of vision. Vision is required for action. Action is needed to win a position. Without knowledge—that is, the right competitive information—we cannot compete.

We should focus our efforts on areas that we know, but we must also continually invest in learning more about these areas. No matter how well we know or think we know a given area, there is always much that we don't know. We must not only be curious; we must be anxious to fill in the blanks.

Throughout these lessons, we describe Sun Tzu's methods as based on information. In the first chapter, he says that war is deception—that is, the ability to control information. Throughout the text, we are warned against divulging information about what we plan because the competition can use it against us. We are told again and again that we must know the ground, know our enemy, and know ourselves. In controlling information, we want to mislead the competition without being misled ourselves.

The purpose of strategy is not simply winning. It is making winning pay. This is how we "serve the state," in Sun Tzu's terms. If we do not leverage the value of information—that is, find an economical way to achieve our ends—we cannot be successful.

Lesson 289: Best Source of Information

What is the best source of information about the future?

A.   Computers.

B.   Analysis.

C.   People.

D.   Experience.

> *You need a creative leader and a worthy commander.*
> *You must move your troops to the right places to beat others.*
> *You must accomplish your attack and escape unharmed.*
> *This requires foreknowledge.*
> *You can obtain foreknowledge.*
> *You can't get it from demons or spirits.*
> *You can't see it from professional experience.*
> *You can't check it with analysis.*
> *You can only get it from other people.*
> *You must always know the enemy's situation.*

THE ART OF WAR 13:1.18-27

Answer: C. People.

Strategy teaches us that knowledge and information are the foundation of vision. We don't want to know what has happened in the past. We want to know what is going to happen in the future. People create the future by acting on their plans. A chocolate cake exists tomorrow because someone planned to bake it today. To know the future, we must know people's plans. How can we know those plans?

Sun Tzu tells us that we can't get this information from reading tea leaves or gazing at crystal balls. We can't get it from so-called experts or from analysis about what people *should* be planning to do. We can imagine an infinite number of scenarios, but they will tell us nothing about the future.

Today, it is also important to know that we cannot get the foreknowledge that we really need from computers or the Internet. It takes some person's time to find anything useful on the Internet. It is the work done by people that turns a mass of data into relevant information for decision-making. We learn about the future by finding out about what people plan. We can get this information only from people, by asking them.

Lesson 290: Types of Competitive Information

How many types of competitive information are there?

A.   One.

B.   Five.

C.   Seven.

D.   Nine.

> *You must use five types of spies.*
> *You need local spies.*
> *You need inside spies.*
> *You need double agents.*
> *You need doomed spies.*
> *You need surviving spies.*

THE ART OF WAR 13:2.1-6

Answer: B. Five.

Though we translated Sun Tzu's words as talking about different kinds of spies, as we have said, the Chinese word he used refers to channels of information. The five categories listed here refer to different types of information channels. It will come as no surprise that each of these five types of spies is directly related to one of the key strategic factors. This alone makes each of these categories of information critical.

In the modern world, we don't often think in terms of spies, but we do think about information sources. The information sources whom we are most interested in are those who know what the competition is thinking. In modern business, the competitive topography is complex. We need to find information sources that will tell us what customers and suppliers are thinking as well as sources that can tell us about our competitors.

In the next lessons, we will look at each of these five information categories and what they mean. For now, we need to know that information, like so much in Sun Tzu's system, is multidimensional. We need all five types of information to draw the complete strategic picture. If we are missing one of these categories of information, we have a dangerous hole in our picture of the market. By now, this multidimensional approach should be completely familiar. When we think about information, we need to think about several aspects of it at once.

Lesson 291: Leadership Resources

What is your most valuable resource as a leader?

A.   Your finances.

B.   Your sources of information.

C.   Your experience.

D.   Your vision.

> *You need all five types of spies.*
> *No one must discover your methods.*
> *You will then be able to put together a true picture.*
> *This is the commander's most valuable resource.*

THE ART OF WAR 13:2.7-10

Answer: B. Your sources of information.

It is not just experience that makes a true professional. It is his or her list of contacts. Over the years, we acquire experience and expertise, but more important than either of these are the contacts we make and the people we know. The old saying is that it is not what you know, but whom you know. Sun Tzu might say that it takes both, but certainly the value of people's contacts—and the portability of those contacts to new positions—is often overlooked.

Of course, Sun Tzu isn't saying that only our sources are critical. He is saying also that our ability to put together a complete picture from the information we get is a part of this valuable resource. All the contacts and information in the world won't do us any good unless we know how to put the information together into a complete picture. This is what Sun Tzu calls "knowing." Putting together a complete picture is one of the four leadership skills we covered again and again throughout *The Art of War*.

The complete picture contains elements from all five dimensions of information. The problem for many people is that they are too quick to imagine a picture without having all the facts. This is as bad as being unable to put together a picture once we do have all the facts. The value of strategy is that it provides a framework for organizing information into a whole.

Being a leader is about being a decision-maker. The decisions we make are only as good as the information we have and our ability to put those pieces of information together into a complete picture.

Lesson 292: Local Spies

In terms of the five key strategic factors, what do "local" spies tell you about?

A.   The ground.

B.   The climate.

C.   The leader.

D.   Methods.

> *You need local spies.*
> *Get them by hiring people from the countryside.*
>   THE ART OF WAR 13:2.11-12

Answer: A. The ground.

Local spies tell us about the local terrain, that is, the immediate competitive battleground. The purpose of this type of spy is to get information about the strategic factors of the ground. Sun Tzu refers to this type of information source in lesson 258 as a "local guide." He says that we need guides with experience in the local area to avoid the obstacles in that area.

In business, having local spies means that we have to know people in the markets that we are tackling. In politics, we have to know the people who know the voters in the various districts. We have to be able to get expertise from within these geographical areas. Sometimes we get this expertise from customers or prospects. However, we must always wonder about the honesty and objectivity of people when they work for someone else. Sun Tzu advises us to hire people who have experience in the market. We want to bring their expertise into our organization. We want to own that expertise. This is especially true when we are moving into a new market area.

This idea doesn't apply only to marketing. We need local knowledge whenever we venture into a new area with which we are unfamiliar. This is commonly the case with new technologies, new manufacturing systems, or new business methods. All of these can be considered new territories where we might need local guides. Whenever we move the organization to new methods in general, we want to hire people who are experienced with these methods to help guide us around the pitfalls.

Lesson 293: Inside Spies

Where do you get the best information about how a rival organization is run?

A.   From those who do work with it.

B.   From those who are part of it.

C.   From those who sell to it.

D.   From those who run it.

> *You need inside spies.*
> *Win them by subverting government officials.*
>
> THE ART OF WAR 13:2.13-14

Answer: B. From those who are part of it.

Here the goal is to get information about the thinking and the plans of the leader of a rival organization. Salespeople have always known that to sell to a large corporation, we need allies on the inside of the organization who can help us understand the decision-maker. We should work to develop contacts inside every organization with which we work, including our allies. It isn't even difficult to develop contacts inside direct competitors.

We can develop the inside information resources in a number of ways, but all of the methods are reduced to understanding the self-interests of our inside contacts. We want to reward them in a way that their organizations can't. This is what Sun Tzu means by "subverting" contacts. We can reward some by simply paying attention to them, especially in organizations where they feel ignored. We convert others by giving them hope of a future position within our organization. Others we can win simply by convincing them that we have the best interest of their organization at heart. This shouldn't be that difficult, especially when working with customers, since we really do want to help these people. These inside contacts are simply the first to recognize it.

Developing relationships with people inside the organizations that we do business with improves our communication with those organizations. Communication is absolutely necessary to our understanding of how these organizations think.

Lesson 294: Double Agents

What people within your organization do you need to pay special attention
to in order to control the flow of information within your company?

A.   Those who have external relationships.

B.   Those who work closely with management.

C.   Those who have specialized information.

D.   Those who are especially creative.

> *You need double agents.*
> *Discover enemy agents and convert them.*
>
> THE ART OF WAR 13:2.15-16

Answer: A. Those who have external relationships.

To understand our opponents, we need more than information about
their decision-making process. We need to get inside their methods, especially the methods that they use for collecting information. The people who
do this are the double agents that Sun Tzu is interested in. By the nature of
their jobs, people with outside contacts have the makings of double agents.
Even when these people work for us, there is always a question about whose
side they are on. When they work for our opponents, they are a resource to
be cultivated. Inside or outside of our organization, we treat them carefully.

Getting control of information channels that feed our opponents, supporters, and allies is extremely demanding. If we control our own people's
contacts, we limit their capabilities. We don't want to cut off communication
channels within our organization, but we need to control them. We want all
external contacts to create a certain picture of us to those they talk to. We
should not only know who these people are, but we should keep in constant
communication with them so that we understand what people are saying
about us and what questions are being asked.

Of course, for acquiring information, we want to cultivate double agents
inside other organizations. Our opponents, supporters, and allies also have
people with external contacts. We need to know who these people are, whom
they talk to, and how we can turn them into our own information channels.
We should especially develop contacts with those who talk to a wide variety
of people and organizations within our competitive arena.

Lesson 295: Doomed Spies

When do you intentionally damage your information channels?

A.   When you find that they have given you bad information.

B.   When you fail to keep your promises.

C.   When you find better sources of information.

D.   When you want to pass on bad information to others.

> *You need doomed spies.*
> *Deceive professionals into being captured.*
> *We let them know our orders.*
> *They then take those orders to our enemy.*
>
> THE ART OF WAR 13:2.17-20

Answer: D. When you want to pass on bad information to others.

"Doomed spies" are an alternative way to get information—or, more accurately, misinformation—out of our organization. These spies are used as messengers to spread our philosophy. When others pass on misinformation, they will be discredited once the truth is discovered. We don't normally want to discredit the double agents within our organization. This would destroy their utility. The only people who can carry misinformation are those with whom we are willing to destroy our relationships. This class usually includes certain types of "professionals"—reporters, lawyers, consultants, accountants, and other service people—with whom we have worked in the past but with whom we don't intend to work in the future.

We can use these professional channels to pass misinformation on to others that no one else should or could have access to. We do not want to mislead our followers or contacts in other companies about our plans. What they know about our plans is what they need to know to work with us. However, the special class of outside hired professionals could credibly have this type of inside information and, after we are done with them, don't need the straight story.

How can we be sure that this type of misinformation will get passed on? We can't, but when dealing with outside professionals, we should assume that it will be.

Lesson 296: Surviving Spies

Which type of information do you need most quickly?

A.   Information about your competitor's plans.

B.   Information about your competitive successes.

C.   Information about opposing decision-makers.

D.   Information about your competitive losses.

> *You need surviving spies.*
> *Someone must return with a report.*

THE ART OF WAR 13:2.21-22

Answer: D. Information about your competitive losses.

This channel of information addresses the important idea of time, that is, the key factor of climate. "Surviving" or "living" spies refers to those people who survive or live through a battle. It is very important that someone survive every enemy engagement so that the results of that engagement can get back to the headquarters. Even if the engagement is lost, the news is important enough that some people must survive to deliver it. It is important that these people get to us quickly, with the news as current as possible. It is timely information that tells us what the climate is.

The idea is to get information about a contest before anyone else does so we can control it ourselves. Even if we lose the battle and we know that others will discover it, we can control the information and spin it in a way that hurts us least. If we failed, we obviously miscalculated something and we need to adjust our calculations before we waste any more time and resources.

In many types of competition, it is usually easy to find out why we got a favorable decision, but it is usually very difficult to discover why we lost. The people involved are usually shy about giving us the pertinent information, even if they are our own people. In sales, prospects that decide to go with a competitor are shy about giving us the news. We might still think we are in a deal for weeks because we don't have a surviving spy who can bring us current information. We have to develop the types of relationships that allow fast communication, especially of negative information.

Lesson 297: Information Quality

How do you ensure that you will get good-quality information from your information sources?

A.   By developing the best-known sources.
B.   By keeping your relationships professional.
C.   By rewarding them generously.
D.   By publicizing your relationships.

> *Your job is to build a complete army.*
> *No relations are as intimate as those with spies.*
> *No rewards are too generous for spies.*
> *No work is as secret as that of spies.*
>
> THE ART OF WAR 13:3.1-4

Answer: C. By rewarding them generously.

Rewarding people—that is, appealing to their self-interest—is the correct way to work with others. Information is not free. It is extremely valuable. We should prize it and prize the relationships that bring information to us. Minimally, all relationships take time. Other relationships cost money. Both can be expensive, but they are well worth the investment.

More than simply paying for information, we have to take a personal interest in the people we use to control the flow of information. As Sun Tzu says, we must be "intimate" with them so we can know what rewards are meaningful to them. To some people, a free meal now and then is very important. To others, it is the ability to share their private goals and dreams. We cannot be standoffish or distant with those we wish to groom as information sources.

We must also keep these relationships private. We want to keep them as secret as possible. People value being on the inside of a "secret" relationship. They like feeling special. In cases in which these relationships are with persons in other organizations, sometimes it only makes sense to keep the relationships a secret. But even when it seems that no damage will be done by letting others know about a relationship, we should keep our information sources secret.

Lesson 298: Information Quality Evaluated

What type of information should you expect from your information sources?

A.   Clear, concise information.

B.   Information that others don't have.

C.   Detailed information.

D.   Anything you can get.

> *If you aren't clever and wise, you can't use spies.*
> *If you aren't fair and just, you can't use spies.*
> *If you can't see the small subtleties, you won't get the truth from spies.*
>
> THE ART OF WAR 13:3.5-7

Answer: D. Anything you can get.

Information management requires all the best characteristics of a leader: wisdom, intelligence, and fairness—but leaders seldom get information neatly packaged and easily understood. We have to develop a number of information sources because a lot of what we get won't be useful. We should value all our information sources, even if they aren't telling us what we need to know. We have to appreciate the relationships and the efforts that people make, regardless of the quality of information provided at any given time. In lesson 176, Sun Tzu points out that the dust itself can provide valuable information.

We are reminded by Sun Tzu to be patient and subtle in dealing with information. We must be willing to work at fitting the picture together. Even the dust can tell us a story if we pay attention to the small subtleties, the small patterns. We can't expect our information sources to do this for us. We need any kind of information we can get. It is our job to determine whether or not it is relevant.

When Sun Tzu says that we "won't get the truth from spies," he doesn't necessarily mean that they will lie to us. Lies are always possible, but mis-information without intentional deceit is more common. We have to pay attention to the subtleties because it is our job to determine the hidden truth in what is being said. Even a lie is useful if we can fit it into a larger picture that makes sense. Our ability to test information against our evolving under-standing of the situation is the skill we need to separate the information wheat from the chaff.

Lesson 299: Attention to Detail

Where do you need spies?

A.   In a handful of key areas.

B.   In the five areas defined by the types of spies.

C.   In every area.

D.   In areas where you meet your opponents.

> *Pay attention to small, trifling details!*
> *Spies are helpful in every area.*

THE ART OF WAR 13:3.8-9

Answer: C. In every area.

We are easily given to hubris. We think we know what the important areas are, but we are too often wrong. Although we cannot manage an infinite amount of information, we want as much information as we can acquire. We can never know what piece of information will be the key to finding success. The smallest details closely examined can tell surprising stories. The danger is not being open to every aspect of information, looking only for certain pieces of information while overlooking other important details.

Today's computers make it possible for us to capture and use more information than ever before in history. However, our computers cannot evaluate this information. We personally must pay attention to the small trifling details from which important patterns and vital new ideas can emerge.

Most leaders fail not because they are not intelligent or capable but because they let themselves become too myopic in their vision. When we limit ourselves to certain sources of information, we also limit our view of the world.

Great leaders always have a broad interest in what is happening in the world around them. They are interested not only in their own companies, but also in their industry. They are interested not only in their own industry, but in what is happening in the broader economy. They are curious not only about the business world, but about the larger world. They seek information in all these areas and they use that information in creating their vision of the future.

Lesson 300: Leaky Sources

How should you treat sources that give out critical information about your organization?

A. Cut them off.

B. Give them another chance.

C. Find a use for them.

D. Give them misinformation.

> *Spies are the first to hear information, so they must not spread it.*
> *Spies who give your location or talk to others must be killed along with those*
>   *to whom they have talked.*

THE ART OF WAR 13:3.10-12

Answer: A. Cut them off.

Of course, Sun Tzu's remedy is a little more radical, but it adds up to the same thing. The point is that we cannot take the distribution of critical information lightly. The purpose of developing a system of contacts is solely to control the flow of information. If we cannot trust an information channel to always work in our favor, we must cut it off. A sophisticated spy network may be able to manage people well enough to use these spies to deliver misinformation, but for most of us it is dangerous to stay too close to them.

Remember lesson 34 on deception. Success in competition depends upon our ability to control the flow of information. The goal is to influence everyone else's vision of the future to our benefit. This is no small task. It must be taken extremely seriously. Double agents who are working against us are more dangerous than the information that they provide is valuable.

In an earlier chapter, Sun Tzu goes so far as to say that we cannot let our own people know all of our plans, simply because we cannot trust them not to pass on this information. Our relationships with our information sources, both within our organization and outside of it, are even closer than those with our normal employees.

Information sources and channels must be completely trustworthy and confidential. They should not know our plans in detail, but they will know the type of information that we find vital. Their vital role in communication requires that we have complete control over them.

Lesson 301: Information Need

When is complete and detailed information most vital to your success?

A.   When you are hiring people.

B.   When you are moving to a new position.

C.   When you are planning your strategy.

D.   When you are looking for revenue.

> *You may want to attack an army's position.*
> *You may want to attack a certain fortification.*
> *You may want to kill people in a certain place.*
> *You must first know the guarding general.*
> *You must know his left and right flanks.*
> *You must know his hierarchy.*
> *You must know the way in.*
> *You must know where different people are stationed.*
> *We must demand this information from our spies.*
>
> THE ART OF WAR 13:4.1-9

Answer: B. When you are moving to a new position.

Sun Tzu's term for moving to a new position is "attacking." His philosophy is a philosophy of invasion, moving into new territories. Exploration of new positions is one of the most risky, costly, and dangerous parts of competition. This is especially true when we are moving into a position or marketplace currently controlled by competitors.

This stanza is a prescription for the type of information that we need before we move into a new area. We must know who currently controls that area. We must know the extent of their organization and how they are positioned. We must understand the internal organization of our competitors, prospects, and critical suppliers.

Most importantly, before we move into a new area, we must see an opening that gives us a natural advantage. We must see the weakness in the competition that leaves us an opening into the market. We may want to destroy certain people, but we do not want to face an opponent's main body of forces. We must be sure that the need is real before we make the investment to move our organization into the new arena.

Lesson 302: The Key Information Source

Of the five types of information sources, which are the most important?

A.   Local information sources.

B.   Inside information sources.

C.   Double agents.

D.   Those that bring you bad news quickly.

> *I want to know the enemy spies in order to convert new spies into my men.*
> *You find a source of information and bribe them.*
> *You must bring them in with you.*
> *You must obtain them as double agents and use them as your emissaries.*
>
> THE ART OF WAR 13:4.10-13

Answer: C. Double agents.

"Double agents" are people whose job it is to pass on information. They can work for us, for our opponents, or for neutral third parties. Those working for us are potential "enemy spies" for people outside our organization. Those working for others are potential information sources for our own organization. When we get control of these people, we get control of the information flow. We don't want people outside the organization to know that we are using these people as information channels.

Double agents serve two purposes at once. They give us information about what our opposition is interested in. They are also conduits of the desired information to those outside the organization. Their role as information channels to the outside makes these double agents extremely important in Sun Tzu's strategic system. Our goal in controlling these agents is to shape the larger environment's view of our organization and influence the decision-making of our opponents.

Careful communication is not possible unless the people involved understand that it is in their best interest to further the interests of our organization. We must make sure that they understand exactly how they will be rewarded for their efforts. These people are our true emissaries to the outside world.

Lesson 303: Using Double Agents

How should you use your internal double agents to do more than collect and pass out information?

A.   Use them to recruit other types of information sources.

B.   Use them to verify rumors that they have heard.

C.   Use them to pass on information about your successes.

D.   Use them to defend your organization in times of trouble.

> *Do this correctly and carefully.*
> *You can contact both local and inside spies and obtain their support.*
> *Do this correctly and carefully.*
> *You create doomed spies by deceiving professionals.*
> *You can use them to give false information.*
> *Do this correctly and carefully.*
> *You must have surviving spies capable of bringing you information at the right time.*

THE ART OF WAR 13:4.14-20

Answer: A. Use them to recruit other types of information sources.

To understand this stanza, we have to read it in the context of the previous stanza. Sun Tzu is saying that by correctly developing people who act as two-way information channels, we can use them to develop all other types of information sources as well.

Since these people are those in our organization with outside contacts, they are also the perfect people to find new information sources for us. In the last stanza, double agents are described as our emissaries, but we might also call them our missionaries. We should use them to convert other people to helping our organization, especially local and inside information sources.

This stanza also implies that all types of contacts can bring us new, different types of contacts. Each of these information sources plays a special role in building our information network. A complete information network must be assured of getting all five types of information and all the trifling details that create a complete picture.

Lesson 304: Information Economics

What should be your major economic consideration with regard to information?

A.   That you are spending too much.

B.   That you are spending too little.

C.   That you are saving too little.

D.   That you are misappropriating funds.

> These are the five different types of intelligence work.
> You must be certain to master them all.
> You must be certain to create double agents.
> You cannot afford to be too cheap in creating these double agents.
>
> THE ART OF WAR 13:4.21-24

Answer: B. That you are spending too little.

Investing in information is seldom a mistake. Sun Tzu anticipated information management budgets and the fact that they would always be too small to meet the real need.

Most people today spend all their money on internal information management. Billions are spent on software and systems to track and report on internal activity. Little if any money is spent on developing the type of external information network that Sun Tzu is concerned about. Individuals develop such networks, but organizations' systems do not track this information in any way. This is a major hole in today's focus on information management because this external information, coming from people in unplanned ways, is the key to understanding the competitive environment. Of course, the Internet has given us immediate access to a wide variety of external information that has never been available before.

We can think about information investment both in terms of dollars and in terms of time and effort. Developing an information network requires a great deal of time. One obvious tool for developing and maintaining an information network is the Internet. To develop networks, we start with the e-mail systems and phone systems already in place, but the information collected needs an access structure that no one yet provides. As e-mail, phones, and software become more integrated, communication channels will become more powerful than ever.

Lesson 305: The Key to Repeating Success

If you analyze people who have repeated successes, what characteristic sets them apart?

A.   Their vision.

B.   Their contacts.

C.   Their technical knowledge.

D.   Their courage.

> *This technique created the success of ancient emperors.*
> *This is how they held their dynasties.*
>
> *You must always be careful of your success.*
> *Learn from the past examples.*

THE ART OF WAR 13:5.1-4

Answer: B. Their contacts.

In this final section of the text, Sun Tzu returns to the lessons of history. He built his strategy based on what he saw working over time. Sun Tzu's work is largely mathematical. Whenever Sun Tzu refers to history, he focuses on the statistical likelihood of an event repeating itself. We can say that his view of history was somewhat statistical. Every case may not follow the rule, but over time we see a pattern take shape. He developed the rules of strategy not because they work every time, but because they work consistently more often than not.

In this case, Sun Tzu tells us that people who are successful are always those who have good channels of information. Successful people have always had highly developed information networks. Today, we have new examples of people who are able to repeat their success. If we read any modern success story, especially about someone who has repeated success in different companies and fields, we will see that the common connection between that person's successes was the people with whom he or she had contact.

The same is true for entrepreneurs who start one enterprise after another. They have developed good contacts that they can rely on and, more importantly, networks of people who trust them and are willing to work with them again and again.

Lesson 306: The People Needed

Which of your people should you use as double agents to develop information channels?

A.   Those with prior connections.

B.   Those whose jobs involve contact.

C.   Those who are your best and brightest.

D.   Those who are the most social.

> *Be a smart commander and good general.*
> *You do this by using your best and brightest people for spying.*
> *This is how you achieve the greatest success.*
> *This is how you meet the necessities of war.*
> *The whole army's position and ability to move depends on these spies.*

THE ART OF WAR 13:5.5-9

Answer: C. Those who are your best and brightest.

We can and should personally develop our own connections with information sources, but we also need our best people to work with us to build a true information network. We cannot act as our own double agents. Double agents have to be people in our organization that external people think will give them inside information. These outside contacts know that the management will protect the organization and manage external information. This is why they turn to other, nonmanagement people who work closely with those who make the key decisions.

Other people can say good things about us and our organization that we can say ourselves. However, because they are "unbiased," they are freer and viewed as more trustworthy than we are. To portray themselves as independent from the company, they have to be clever. The people they talk to have to feel that they are getting the inside scoop. This is what makes these double agents so valuable.

Everything else that we do as a competitive organization depends directly on our ability to use these people to get the needed information.

This is the idea that Sun Tzu chooses to end his work with. He focuses on the importance of people, the importance of their intelligence, and how it is the quality of our people and our information that determines our success.

Glossary of Key Strategic Concepts

This glossary is keyed to the most common English words used in the translation of *The Art of War*. Those terms only capture the strategic concepts generally. Though translated as English nouns, verbs, adverbs, or adjectives, the Chinese characters on which they are based are totally conceptual, not parts of speech. For example, the character for CONFLICT is translated as the noun "conflict," as the verb "fight," and as the adjective "disputed." Ancient written Chinese was a conceptual language, not a spoken one. More like mathematical terms, these concepts are primarily defined by the strict structure of their relationships with other concepts. The Chinese names shown in parentheses with the characters are primarily based on Pinyin, but we occasionally use Cantonese terms to make each term unique.

ADVANCE (JEUN 進): to move into new GROUND; to expand your POSITION; to move forward in a campaign; the opposite of FLEE.

ADVANTAGE, *benefit* (LI 利): an opportunity arising from having a better POSITION relative to an ENEMY; an opening left by an ENEMY; a STRENGTH that matches against an ENEMY'S WEAKNESS; where fullness meets emptiness; a desirable characteristic of a strategic POSITION.

AIM, *vision, foresee* (JIAN 見): FOCUS on a specific ADVANTAGE, opening, or opportunity; predicting movements of an ENEMY; a skill of a LEADER in observing CLIMATE.

ANALYSIS, *plan* (GAI 計): a comparison of relative POSITION; the examination of the five factors that define a strategic POSITION; a combination of KNOWLEDGE and VISION; the ability to see through DECEPTION.

ARMY: see WAR.

ATTACK, *invade* (GONG 攻): a movement to new GROUND; advancing a strategic POSITION; action against an ENEMY in the sense of moving into his GROUND; opposite of DEFEND; does not necessarily mean CONFLICT.

BAD, *ruined* (PI 圮): a condition of the GROUND that makes ADVANCE difficult; destroyed; terrain that is broken and difficult to traverse; one of the nine situations or types of terrain.

BARRICADED: see OBSTACLES.

BATTLE (ZHAN 戰): to challenge; to engage an ENEMY; generically, to meet a challenge; to choose a confrontation with an ENEMY at a specific time and place; to focus all your resources on a task; to establish superiority in a POSITION; to challenge an ENEMY to increase CHAOS; that which is CONTROLLED by SURPRISE; one of the four forms of ATTACK; the response to a DESPERATE SITUATION; character meaning was originally "big meeting," though later took on the meaning "big weapon"; not necessarily CONFLICT.

BRAVERY, *courage* (YONG 勇): the ability to face difficult choices; the character quality that deals with the changes of CLIMATE; courage of conviction; willingness to act on vision; one of the six characteristics of a leader.

BREAK, *broken, divided* (PO 破): to DIVIDE what is COMPLETE; the absence of a UNITING PHILOSOPHY; the opposite of UNITY.

CALCULATE, *count* (SHU 數): mathematical comparison of quantities and qualities; a measurement of DISTANCE or troop size.

CHANGE, *transform* (BIAN 變): transition from one CONDITION to another; the ability to adapt to different situations; a natural characteristic of CLIMATE.

CHAOS, *disorder* (JUAN 亂): CONDITIONS that cannot be FORESEEN; the natural state of confusion arising from BATTLE; one of six weaknesses of an organization; the opposite of CONTROL.

CLAIM, *position, form* (XING 形): to use the GROUND; a shape or specific condition of GROUND; the GROUND that you CONTROL; to use the benefits of the GROUND; the formations of troops; one of the four key skills in making progress.

CLIMATE, *heaven* (TIAN 天): the passage of time; the realm of uncontrollable CHANGE; divine providence; the weather; trends that CHANGE over time; generally, the future; what one must AIM at in the future; one of five key factors in ANALYSIS; the opposite of GROUND.

COMMAND (LING 令): to order or the act of ordering subordinates; the decisions of a LEADER; the creation of METHODS.

COMPETITION: see WAR.

COMPLETE: see UNITY.

CONDITION: see GROUND.

CONFINED, *surround* (WEI 圍): to encircle; a SITUATION or STAGE in which your options are limited; the proper tactic for dealing with an ENEMY that is ten times smaller; to seal off a smaller ENEMY; the characteristic of a STAGE in which a larger FORCE can be attacked by a smaller one; one of nine SITUATIONS or STAGES.

CONFLICT, *fight* (ZHENG 争): to contend; to dispute; direct confrontation of arms with an ENEMY; highly desirable GROUND that creates disputes; one of nine types of GROUND, terrain, or stages.

CONSTRICTED, *narrow* (AI 狹): a confined space or niche; one of six field positions; the limited extreme of the dimension distance; the opposite of SPREAD-OUT.

CONTROL, *govern* (CHI 治): to manage situations; to overcome disorder; the opposite of CHAOS.

DANGEROUS: see SERIOUS.

DANGERS, *adverse* (AK 阨): a condition that makes it difficult to ADVANCE; one of three dimensions used to evaluate advantages; the dimension with the extreme field POSITIONS of ENTANGLING and SUPPORTING.

DEATH, *desperate* (SI 死): to end or the end of life or efforts; an extreme situation in which the only option is BATTLE; one of nine STAGES or types of TERRAIN; one of five types of SPIES; opposite of SURVIVE.

DECEPTION, *bluffing, illusion* (GUI 詭): to control perceptions; to control information; to mislead an ENEMY; an attack on an opponent's AIM; the characteristic of war that confuses perceptions.

DEFEND (SHOU 守): to guard or to hold a GROUND; to remain in a POSITION; the opposite of ATTACK.

DETOUR (YU 迂): the indirect or unsuspected path to a POSITION; the more difficult path to ADVANTAGE; the route that is not DIRECT.

DIRECT, *straight* (JIK 直): a straight or obvious path to a goal; opposite of DETOUR.

DISTANCE, *distant* (YUAN 遠): the space separating GROUND; to be remote from the current location; to occupy POSITIONS that are not close to one another; one of six field positions; one of the three dimensions for evaluating opportunities; the emptiness of space.

DIVIDE, *separate* (FEN 分): to break apart a larger force; to separate from a larger group; the opposite of JOIN and FOCUS.

DOUBLE AGENT, *reverse* (FAN 反): to turn around in direction; to change a situation; to switch a person's allegiance; one of five types of spies.

EASY, *light* (QING 輕): to require little effort; a SITUATION that requires little effort; one of nine STAGES or types of terrain; opposite of SERIOUS.

EMOTION, *feeling* (XIN 心): an unthinking reaction to AIM, a necessary element to inspire MOVES; a component of esprit de corps; never a sufficient cause for ATTACK.

ENEMY, *competitor* (DIK 敵): one who makes the same CLAIM; one with a similar GOAL; one with whom comparisons of capabilities are made.

ENTANGLING, *hanging* (GUA 懸): a POSITION that cannot be returned to; any CONDITION that leaves no easy place to go; one of six field positions.

EVADE, *avoid* (BI 避): the tactic used by small competitors when facing large opponents.

FALL APART, *collapse* (BENG 崩): to fail to execute good decisions; to fail to use a CONSTRICTED POSITION; one of six weaknesses of an organization.

FALL DOWN, *sink* (HAAM 陷): to fail to make good decisions; to MOVE from a SUPPORTING POSITION; one of six weaknesses of organizations.

FEELINGS, *affection, love* (CHING 情): the bonds of relationship; the result of a shared PHILOSOPHY; requires management.

FIGHT, *struggle* (DOU 鬥): to engage in CONFLICT; to face difficulties.

FIRE (HUO 火): an environmental weapon; a universal analogy for all weapons.

FLEE, *retreat, northward* (BEI 北): to abandon a POSITION; to surrender GROUND; one of six weaknesses of an ARMY; opposite of ADVANCE.

FOCUS, *concentrate* (ZHUAN 專): to bring resources together at a given time; to UNITE forces for a purpose; an attribute of having a shared PHILOSOPHY; the opposite of *divide*.

FORCE (LEI 力): power in the simplest sense; a GROUP of people bound by UNITY and FOCUS; the relative balance of STRENGTH in opposition to WEAKNESS.

FORESEE: see AIM.

FULLNESS: see STRENGTH.

GENERAL: see LEADER.

GOAL: see PHILOSOPHY.

GROUND, *situation, stage* (DI 地): the earth; a specific place; a specific condition; the place one competes; the prize of competition; one of five key factors in competitive analysis; the opposite of CLIMATE.

GROUPS, *troops* (DUI 隊): a number of people united under a shared PHILOSOPHY; human resources of an organization; one of the five targets of fire attacks.

INSIDE, *internal* (NEI 内): within a TERRITORY or organization; an insider; one of five types of spies; opposite of OUTSIDE.

INTERSECTING, *highway* (QU 衢): a SITUATION or GROUND that allows you to JOIN; one of nine types of terrain.

JOIN (HAP 合): to unite; to make allies; to create a larger FORCE; opposite of DIVIDE.

KNOWLEDGE, *listening* (ZHI 知): to have information; the result of listening; the first step in advancing a POSITION; the basis of strategy.

LAX, *loosen* (SHII 弛): too easygoing; lacking discipline; one of six weaknesses of an army.

LEADER, *general, commander* (JIANG 將): the decision-maker in a competitive unit; one who LISTENS and AIMS; one who manages TROOPS; superior of officers and men; one of the five key factors in analysis; the conceptual opposite of SYSTEM, the established methods, which do not require decisions.

LEARN, *compare* (XIAO 效): to evaluate the relative qualities of ENEMIES.

LISTEN, *obey* (TING 聽): to gather KNOWLEDGE; part of ANALYSIS.

LISTENING: see KNOWLEDGE.

LOCAL, *countryside* (XIANG 鄉): the nearby GROUND; to have KNOWLEDGE of a specific GROUND; one of five types of SPIES.

MARSH (ZE 澤): GROUND where footing is unstable; one of the four types of GROUND; analogy for uncertain situations.

METHOD: see SYSTEM.

MISSION: see PHILOSOPHY.

MOMENTUM, *influence* (SHI 勢): the FORCE created by SURPRISE set up by STANDARDS; used with TIMING.

MOUNTAINS, *hill, peak* (SHAN 山): uneven GROUND; one of four types of GROUND; an analogy for all unequal SITUATIONS.

MOVE, *march, act* (HANG 行): action toward a position or goal.

NATION (GUO 國): the state; the productive part of an organization; the seat of political power; the entity that controls an ARMY or competitive part of the organization.

OBSTACLES, *barricaded* (XIAN 險): to have barriers; one of the three characteristics of the GROUND; one of six field positions; as a field position, opposite of UNOBSTRUCTED.

OPEN, *meeting, crossing* (JIAO 來): to share the same GROUND without conflict; to come together; a SITUATION that encourages a race; one of nine TERRAINS or STAGES.

OPPORTUNITY: see ADVANTAGE.

OUTMANEUVER (SOU 走): to go astray; to be FORCED into a WEAK POSITION; one of six weaknesses of an army.

OUTSIDE, *external* (WAI 外): not within a TERRITORY or ARMY; one who has a different perspective; one who offers an objective view; opposite of INTERNAL.

PHILOSOPHY, *mission, goals* (TAO 道): the shared GOALS that UNITE an ARMY; a system of thought; a shared viewpoint; literally "the way"; a way to work together; one of the five key factors in ANALYSIS.

PLATEAU (LIU 陸): a type of GROUND without defects; an analogy for any equal, solid, and certain SITUATION; the best place for competition; one of the four types of GROUND.

RESOURCES, *provisions* (LIANG 糧): necessary supplies, most commonly food; one of the five targets of fire attacks.

RESTRAINT: see TIMING.

REWARD, *treasure, money* (BAO 賞): profit; wealth; the necessary compensation for competition; a necessary ingredient for

VICTORY; VICTORY must pay.

SCATTER, *dissipating* (SAN 散): to disperse; to lose UNITY; the pursuit of separate GOALS as opposed to a central MISSION; a situation that causes a FORCE to scatter; one of nine conditions or types of terrain.

SERIOUS, *heavy* (CHONG 重): any task requiring effort and skill; a SITUATION where resources are running low when you are deeply committed to a campaign or heavily invested in a project; a situation where opposition within an organization mounts; one of nine STAGES or types of TERRAIN.

SIEGE (GONG CHENG 攻城): to move against entrenched positions; any movement against an ENEMY'S STRENGTH; literally "strike city"; one of the four forms of attack; the least desirable form of attack.

SITUATION: see GROUND.

SPEED, *hurry* (SAI 馳): to MOVE over GROUND quickly; the ability to ADVANCE POSITIONS in a minimum of time; needed to take advantage of a window of opportunity.

SPREAD-OUT, *wide* (GUANG 廣): a surplus of DISTANCE; one of the six GROUND POSITIONS; opposite of CONSTRICTED.

SPY, *conduit, go-between* (GAAN 間): a source of information; a channel of communication; literally, an "opening between."

STAGE: see GROUND.

STANDARD, *proper, correct* (JANG 正): the expected behavior; the standard approach; proven methods; the opposite of SURPRISE; together with SURPRISE creates MOMENTUM.

STOREHOUSE, *house* (KU 庫): a place where resources are stockpiled; one of the five targets for fire attacks.

STORES, *accumulate, savings* (JI 糧): resources that have been stored; any type of inventory; one of the five targets of fire attacks.

STRENGTH, *fullness, satisfaction* (SAT 實): wealth or abundance or resources; the state of being crowded; the opposite of XU, empty.

SUPPLY WAGONS, *transport* (ZI 輜): the movement of RESOURCES through DISTANCE; one of the five targets of fire attacks.

SUPPORT, *supporting* (ZHII 支): to prop up; to enhance; a GROUND POSITION that you cannot leave without losing STRENGTH; one of six field positions; the opposite extreme of ENTANGLING.

SURPRISE, *unusual, strange* (QI 奇): the unexpected; the innovative; the opposite of STANDARD; together with STANDARDS creates MOMENTUM.

SURROUND: see CONFINED.

SURVIVE, *live, birth* (SHAANG 生): the state of being created, started, or beginning; the state of living or surviving; a temporary condition of fullness; one of five types of spies; the opposite of DEATH.

SYSTEM, *method* (FA 法): a set of procedures; a group of techniques; steps to accomplish a GOAL; one of the five key factors in analysis; the realm of groups who must follow procedures; the opposite of the LEADER.

TERRITORY, *terrain*: see GROUND.

TIMING, *restraint* (JIE 節): to withhold action until the proper time; to release tension; a companion concept to MOMENTUM.

TROOPS: see GROUPS.

UNITY, *whole, oneness* (YI 一): the characteristic of a GROUP that shares a PHILOSOPHY; the lowest number; a GROUP that acts as a unit; the opposite of DIVIDED.

UNOBSTRUCTED, *expert* (TONG 通): without obstacles or barriers; GROUND that allows easy movement; open to new ideas; one of six field positions; opposite of OBSTRUCTED.

VICTORY, *win, winning* (SING 勝): success in an endeavor; getting a reward; serving your mission; an event that produces more than it consumes; to make a profit.

WAR, *competition, army* (BING 兵): a dynamic situation in which POSITIONS can be won or lost; a contest in which a REWARD can be won; the conditions under which the rules of strategy work.

WATER, *river* (SHUI 水): a fast-changing GROUND; fluid CONDITIONS; one of four types of GROUND; an analogy for change.

WEAKNESS, *emptiness, need* (XU 虛): the absence of people or resources; devoid of FORCE; the point of ATTACK for an ADVANTAGE; a characteristic of GROUND that enables SPEED; poor; the opposite of STRENGTH.

WIN, *winning*: see VICTORY.

WIND, *fashion, custom* (FENG 風): the pressure of environmental forces.

Index of *Art of War* Topics

This index identifies topics in the stanzas of *The Art of War*. The topics are keyed to the chapter, block, and line numbers used to identify each stanza of text shown in our three hundred and six lessons. Starting with chapter 1, stanzas can be found in their original order.

About the Author

This book's award-winning translator and primary author, Gary Gagliardi, is America's leading authority on Sun Tzu's *The Art of War*. A frequent guest on radio and television talk shows, Gary has written over wenty books on strategy. Ten of his books on Sun Tzu's methods have won award recognition in business, self-help, career, sports, philosophy, multicultural, and youth nonfiction categories.

Gary Gagliardi

Gary began studying Sun Tzu's philosophy over thirty years ago. His understanding of strategy was proven in the business world, where his software company became one of the Inc. 500 fastest-growing companies in America and won numerous business awards. After selling his software company, Gary began writing about and teaching Sun Tzu's strategic philosophy full time.

He has spoken all over the world on a variety of topics concerning competition, from modern technology to ancient history. His books have been translated into many languages, including Japanese, Thai, Korean, Russian, Indonesian, and Spanish.

Today he splits his time between Seattle and Las Vegas, living with his wife, Rebecca, and travels extensively for speaking engagements all over the world.

garyg@suntzus.com

@strategygary

Want to learn more about Sun Tzu's strategy?

SunTzuS.com
SCIENCE OF STRATEGY INSTITUTE
eBooks
Audio books
Audio seminars
Online training

Art of War and Strategy Books By Gary Gagliardi

Sun Tzu's Art of War Rule Book in Nine Volumes
Sun Tzu's The Art of War Plus The Art of Sales: Strategy for the Sales Warrior
9 Formulas for Business Success: the Science of Strategy
The Golden Key to Strategy: Everyday Strategy for Everyone
The Art of War Plus The Chinese Revealed
The Art of War Plus The Art of Management: Straegy for Management Warriors
Art of War for Warrior Marketing: Strategy for Conquering Markets
The Art of War Plus The Art of Politics: Strategy for Campaigns (with Shawn Frost)
Making Money By Speaking: The Spokesperson Strategy
The Warrior Class: 306 Lessons in Strategy
The Art of War for the Business Warrior: Strategy for Entrepreneurs
The Art of War Plus The Warrior's Apprentice: Strategy for Teens
The Art of War Plus Strategy for Sales Managers: Strategy for Sales Groups
The Ancient Bing-fa: Martial Arts Strategy
Strategy Against Terror: Ancient Wisdom for Today's War
The Art of War Plus The Art of Career Building: Strategy for Promotion
Sun Tzu's Art of War Plus Parenting Teens
The Art of War Plus Its Amazing Secrets: The Keys to Ancient Chinese Science
Art of War Plus Art of Love: Strategy for Romance